MANIFESTO OF A PASSIONATE MODERATE

MANIFESTO *of a*

PASSIONATE

MODERATE

Unfashionable Essays

SUSAN HAACK

THE UNIVERSITY OF CHICAGO PRESS

CHICAGO & LONDON

SUSAN HAACK is professor of philosophy and visiting professor of law at the University of Miami. She has been the national Phi Beta Kappa Romanell Professor of Philosophy (1997–98). Her publications include *Evidence and Inquiry: Towards Reconstruction in Epistemology; Philosophy of Logics;* and *Deviant Logic, Fuzzy Logic: Beyond the Formalism.*

The University of Chicago Press, Chicago 60637
The University of Chicago Press, Ltd., London
© 1998 by Susan Haack
All rights reserved. Published 1998
Printed in the United States of America
07 06 05 04 03 02 01 00 99 98   1 2 3 4 5

ISBN: 0-226-31136-8 (cloth)

Library of Congress Cataloging-in-Publication Data

Haack, Susan.
     Manifesto of a passionate moderate : unfashionable essays / Susan Haack.
        p.   cm.
     Includes bibliographical references and index.
     ISBN 0-226-31136-8 (cloth : alk. paper)
     1. Knowledge, Sociology of.   2. Knowledge, Theory of.   3. Science—Philosophy.   I. Title.
BD175.H28   1998
     121—dc21   98-22658
                                                                                                     CIP

⊗ The paper used in this publication meets the minimum requirements of the American National Standard for Information Sciences-Permanence of Paper for Printed Library Materials, ANSI Z39.48–1992.

The philosophy which is now in vogue . . . cherishes certain tenets . . . which tend to a deliberate and factitious despair, which . . . cuts the sinews and spurs of industry. . . . And all for . . . the miserable vainglory of having it believed that whatever has not yet been discovered and comprehended can never be discovered or comprehended hereafter. FRANCIS BACON

Contents

Preface, ix

Introduction, 1

O N E

Confessions of an Old-Fashioned Prig   7

T W O

"We Pragmatists . . .": Peirce and Rorty in Conversation   31

T H R E E

As for that phrase "studying in a literary spirit" . . .   48

F O U R

"Dry Truth and Real Knowledge": Epistemologies of Metaphor

and Metaphors of Epistemology   69

F I V E

Puzzling Out Science   90

S I X

Science as Social?—Yes and No 104

S E V E N

Knowledge and Propaganda: Reflections of an Old Feminist 123

E I G H T

Multiculturalism and Objectivity 137

N I N E

Reflections on Relativism: From Momentous Tautology

to Seductive Contradiction 149

T E N

The best man for the job may be a woman . . . and other alien

thoughts on affirmative action in the academy 167

E L E V E N

Preposterism and Its Consequences 188

Acknowledgments, 209

Index, 213

Preface

For an academic in the humanities today, there is a strong temptation to be an ostrich: to get on quietly with your own work and do your best to ignore the noisy battles around you. Unfortunately—or perhaps fortunately, depending how you look at it—this didn't work for me. Perhaps I don't have the ostrich temperament; in any case, some of the noisiest battles were over the legitimacy of the very questions I was trying to answer, about what makes evidence stronger or weaker, inquiry better or worse conducted. So I could scarcely ignore a great revolutionary chorus of voices announcing that disinterested inquiry is impossible, that all supposed "knowledge" is an expression of power, that the concepts of evidence, objectivity, truth, are ideological humbug.

The more I heard, the more disturbing the slogans. Some of the revolutionaries described themselves as neo-pragmatists; unsettling, to put it mildly, given how fruitful I had found the old pragmatists' reflections about the goal and conduct of inquiry. Some of these self-styled neo-pragmatists urged the ubiquity of metaphor and linguistic innovation as grounds for giving up evidence and argument and remaking philosophy as a genre of literature; unsettling, to put it mildly, given how useful I had found metaphors and neologisms myself. Other revolutionaries described themselves as feminists or multiculturalists; unsettling, to put it mildly, to hear that thinking about evidence and inquiry as I did revealed complicity with sexism or racism. Others maintained that admiration for the achievements of the natural sciences is foolish naïveté at best, reactionary conformism with the industrial-military complex at worst; unsettling, to put it mildly, to think that my understanding of the method of science might be so dangerously mistaken.

The more closely I listened, the sillier the revolutionaries' slogans sounded; but the hollower, also, some of the efforts to expose the silliness. Many seemed satisfied to dismiss the revolutionaries' extravagances as only the latest variations on familiar relativist themes long known to be self-defeating. But, noticing that not all the extravagances were relativist, and that not all forms of relativism are self-defeating, I didn't feel altogether reassured.

And so I began to puzzle over how metaphors can be cognitively useful, what is distinctive about scientific evidence and inquiry, how science differs from literature and philosophy from both, how pragmatism got transmuted from reformed, scientific philosophy into philosophy as "just a kind of writing," how the sexist stereotypes that old-fashioned feminists used to deplore came to be celebrated in new-fangled feminist ideas of "women's ways of knowing," . . . and so on.

Trying to get to grips with these questions, thinking about science, literature, pragmatism, feminism, the condition of the academy itself, I often found myself some way from the beaten philosophical track. So I hope the essays collected here—the results of that thinking—will be of interest not only to philosophers, but to everyone who believes, as I do, that it matters whether there is such a thing as truth, whether honest inquiry is possible or desirable, whether there is a real difference between knowledge and propaganda.

I have done my best to avoid fashionable jargon, unnecessary technicality, and that peculiar blandness with which much recent academic writing is afflicted. And, in the spirit of Russell's advice that "those who are solemn and pontifical are not to be fought by being even more solemn and pontifical," I have not only poked holes in bad arguments, but also occasionally allowed myself the pleasure of poking a little fun at particularly daft ideas and particularly grotesque intellectual pretensions. Perhaps it is unnecessary for me to say that, for all that, my purpose is entirely serious.

Perhaps it is also unnecessary for me to say that I call these essays "unfashionable" in anticipation of criticism both from those who think I haven't taken the revolutionaries seriously enough, and from those who think I have taken them too seriously. A few years back, a friend with whom I was discussing my ideas for one of the more irreverent of these essays asked me, "don't you have enough enemies already?" Of course I thought of the right answer only much later: better ostracism than ostrich-ism!

Introduction

Nobody seriously doubts the possibility, or the usefulness, of finding things out; that is something we all take for granted when we inquire about plane schedules, or the state of our bank accounts, or the best treatment for our child's illness, and so forth. Nobody seriously doubts, either, that sometimes, instead of really trying to find things out, people fudge, fake, and obfuscate to avoid discovering unpalatable truths; that is something we all take for granted when we ask who paid for this reassuring study, who stands to gain from an Official Inquiry minimizing that scandal, which party this expert witness works for, and so on.

Of late, however, radical feminists, multiculturalists, sociologists of knowledge, literary theorists, and (I am embarrassed to say) a good many philosophers as well—though they look into questions about their plane schedules, bank accounts, medical treatments, etc., just like the rest of us—profess to have seen through what the rest of us take for granted. It's all an illusion, they tell us: honest inquiry is really neither possible nor desirable. All that high-minded talk about disinterested inquiry, respect for evidence, finding out how things really are, is nothing but a smokescreen hiding the operations of power, politics, social negotiation, rhetoric. Those of us who are still taken in, they say, don't have a clear view of things; not to be quite so tactful about it, we are "old-fashioned prigs."

On the contrary: it is the devotees of the Higher Dismissiveness who don't have a clear view of things. Hence the title, and the agenda, of the first of these essays, "Confessions of an Old-Fashioned Prig": to articulate a clear view of what it means to care about the truth, what the difference is between genuine inquiry and the various kinds of pseudo-inquiry to which we sometimes succumb, why we value intellectual integrity, and what has gone wrong in the thinking of those who denigrate concern for truth.

Among those who take it upon themselves to unmask this supposed ideal, some describe themselves as "pragmatists." This is very strange; for among the most articulate, and even eloquent, of those who have seen that it really matters whether you genuinely want the truth, was C. S. Peirce, the founder of pragmatism.

But somehow classical pragmatism, in the form of Peirce's aspiration to renew philosophy by making it more scientific, has been transmuted into the vulgar pragmatism fashionable today, in the form of Stich's blithe assurances that "once we have a clear view of the matter," we will not see any value in having true beliefs, and Rorty's hopes of a post-philosophical culture in which "we pragmatists" give up the old-fashioned idea that truth is a goal of inquiry, and remake philosophy as a genre of literature, just a kind of writing.

This kind of talk, I find, brings out the playful side of an old-fashioned prig like myself. That is the mood of the second piece printed here, a "conversation" between Peirce and Rorty compiled from their own words, a philosophical boxing match in which Peirce gets his revenge on a self-styled neo-pragmatist who calls him a "whacked-out triadomaniac" whose only contribution to pragmatism was to give it its name.

But playfulness has its price; in the present instance, I found I had incurred an obligation to think seriously about the place of literary style in philosophy, and, more generally, about the relation of philosophy to literature. That is my purpose in "As for that phrase 'studying in a literary spirit' . . . " (essay 3), where I suggest an account of how philosophy differs from science and from literature—and show how the literary dilettantism of Rortyesque neo-pragmatism is crippled by its disastrous inability even to acknowledge the truths that literature can teach us.

One of Rorty's more interesting mistakes is to suppose that, because scientific inquiry often involves linguistic shifts and innovations and relies on metaphors, science is really a genre of literature. The conclusion is bizarre; but the premise is true, and suggests a need to rethink the role of metaphors in inquiry. That is my purpose in the fourth essay, "Dry Truth and Real Knowledge"—a title drawn from Locke's splendidly metaphorical denunciation of metaphor as an abuse of language intolerable in serious discourse. Locke is mistaken; far from being an abuse of language, metaphor can be a tool of inquiry, playing a significant cognitive role.

One example is my metaphor of a crossword puzzle as model for the structure of evidence—a metaphor which informs the account of scientific inquiry suggested in "Puzzling Out Science" (essay 5). The Old Deferentialists, taking the rationality of science for granted, assumed that there be must a uniquely rational method of inquiry exclusive to the sciences; the New Cynics, noticing the failure of efforts to articulate what that uniquely rational method is, conclude that science is not a rational enterprise, in fact, that the whole idea of objectively better or worse conducted inquiry is ideological humbug. Neither the Old Deferentialism nor the New Cynicism will do: the former is too uncritically deferential to science, the latter too uncritically critical. Inquiry in the sciences is like other kinds of inquiry—making conjectures about some crossword entry, testing them against the clues and other completed entries—only more so: distinguished by its systematic commitment to mutual scrutiny, by division of labor, and by reliance on the findings of others in the community.

Of course, the external environment of science and its internal organization may be *more* or *less* hospitable to good, honest, thorough inquiry. Some recent sociology of science, intoxicated by the New Cynicism, has claimed to show that what theories get accepted depends on external social forces, and thus to undermine the pretensions of the sciences to give us knowledge of the world—and at the same time unintentionally undermining its own pretensions to give us knowledge of how science works. But sociology of science doesn't have to be the discreditable business it has, of late, sometimes been.

In one sense, it is true, and significant for our understanding of scientific inquiry, that science is a social enterprise. But it is other, more radical, senses that are fashionable: that social values are inseparable from scientific inquiry, that the goal of science is to improve society, that scientific knowledge, even that reality, is nothing but the product of "social negotiation," that scientific inquiry should be more democratic, that physics is subordinate to sociology.

These fashionable ideas have been adopted by some academic feminists, so that it has come to be taken for granted that not to subscribe to them is to betray complicity with sexism. This is very peculiar. In "Science as Social?—Yes and No" (essay 6), once again setting my face against the trend, I show that the idea is mistaken that a radically social conception of science is in some way distinctively feminist; and that it is no more sound feminism than it is sound philosophy of science.

There is no such connection between feminism and the theory of knowledge as the fashionable rubric "feminist epistemology" requires. One can be—I am—an epistemologist and a feminist; but "feminist epistemology" is as incongruous as it sounds: as incongruous as "Republican epistemology." In "Knowledge and Propaganda: Reflections of an Old Feminist" (essay 7), I show that one of the two possible ways of making a connection relies on old stereotypes of women as emotional and intuitive rather than logical, while the other, systematically confusing what is true with what passes for true, objectively good evidence with what passes for objectively good evidence, etc., reduces inquiry to social negotiation, knowledge to propaganda. This kind of stuff, far from helping women, will hurt humanity.

Some self-styled "feminist epistemologists" have tried to jump on the multiculturalist bandwagon. But there are different and incompatible conceptions of multiculturalism; and, as I show in "Multiculturalism and Objectivity" (essay 8), a desirable broadening of educational objectives to include learning about other cultures has been fudged into indefensible forms of tribalism or relativism.

Why, when it has supposedly been refuted again and again, is relativism so persistently attractive? In "Reflections on Relativism: From Momentous Tautology to Seductive Contradiction" (essay 9), I distinguish a whole range of more and less radical relativist views, and dismantle the arguments that have tempted Putnam to envisage a conceptual contribution to the construction of the world. But the ultimate goal is to articulate an innocent realism capable of accommodating the themes that make relativism seem attractive—linguistic innovation, the interpretiveness of perception, the lack of a privileged vocabulary.

Other reasons for the disenchantment with truth are less intellectual than social. Reflecting on affirmative action in the academy in "The best man for the job may be a woman . . ." (essay 10), frustrated by the This-or-Nothingism of the usual debates on the topic and the foam-rubber language in which they have come to be conducted, obliged to reflect on the vicissitudes of my own career in disturbing ways, I try to think through the consequences of preferential hiring in my profession. One, I fear, is that well-intentioned but ill-conceived attempts to make a person's sex or race matter less to our judgment of the quality of his or her mind, and to welcome women and blacks as full participants in the life of the intellect, seem to have encouraged the idea that truth, evidence, reason, are tools of their oppression: an idea as tragic as it is bizarre.

And then there's preposterism. "Valuing knowledge," as Barzun puts it, "we preposterize the idea and say, 'everyone must produce written research in order to live, and it shall be deemed a knowledge explosion.'" Preposterism has become the way of academic life; and in the concluding essay, "Preposterism and Its Consequences," I explore how conceptions of productivity more appropriate to a manufacturing plant than to the pursuit of truth have encouraged pseudo-inquiry, diverted us into scientistic or anti-scientific exaggerations, and fed those feminist extravagances.

In these essays I have tried to expose the flaws of recent fads, fashions, and false dichotomies: *either* scientistic philosophy, *or* philosophy as "just a kind of writing"; *either* metaphor as an abuse of language, *or* metaphor as ubiquitous and philosophy, even the sciences, as genres of literature; *either* the Old Deferentialism, *or* the New Cynicism; *either* scientific knowledge as a mere social construction, *or* a denial of the significance of the internal organization and external context of scientific work; *either* the scholastic rigidities of analytic epistemology, *or* wild or wooly "feminist epistemology"; *either* preferential hiring of women, etc., *or* the Old Boy Network; and so forth and so on.

The fads, fashions, and false dichotomies at which I take aim are philosophical; but these essays are intended not only for philosophical readers, but for all those—literary or legal scholars, scientists, historians, etc.— who, troubled by these irrationalist tendencies, are ready to listen to "the still small voice that whispers, 'bosh!'" I hope this book will serve not only as a protest against the irrationalist tendencies of our times, but also as a step on the path back to "the calm sunlight of the mind."

Confessions of an Old-Fashioned Prig

"In order to reason well . . . ," C. S. Peirce wrote a century or so ago, "it is absolutely necessary to possess . . . such virtues as intellectual honesty and sincerity and a real love of truth."[1] Forty or so years ago, C. I. Lewis observed that "we presume, on the part of those who follow any scientific [it is clear from the context that he means, 'intellectual'] vocation, . . . a sort of tacit oath never to subordinate the motive of objective truth-seeking to any subjective preference or inclination or any expediency or opportunistic consideration."[2]

Of late, however, it is not unusual to hear such ideas denigrated as naive, confused, out of date. Stephen Stich professes a sophisticated disillusionment, writing that "once we have a clear view of the matter, most of us will not find any value . . . in having true beliefs."[3] Richard Rorty, who tells us that he "does not have much use for notions like . . . 'objective truth'"—after all, to call a statement true "is just to give it a rhetorical pat on the back"—describes philosophers who think of themselves as seeking the truth as "lovably old-fashioned prigs."[4] Jane Heal, pointing out that "there is no goddess, Truth, of whom academics and researchers can regard themselves as priests or devotees,"[5] hints that this reveals the hollowness of the ideal of the disinterested pursuit of truth.

Call me old-fashioned if you like; but I think Peirce and Lewis had some insight into what the life of the mind demands, while Stich, Rorty, and Heal reveal a startling failure, or perhaps refusal, to grasp what concern for truth is, or why it is important. So I shall try in what follows to articulate what it means to care about truth, what intellectual integrity is and why we value it, and what has gone wrong in the thinking of those who deny its importance. In the process I hope to have something to say about the meaning of truth; and something to say, also, about how it comes about that we find philosophers of the classical pragmatist tradition defending the importance of intellectual integrity, and self-styled neo-pragmatists taking it upon themselves to unmask this supposed ideal.

TO BELIEVE THAT things are thus and so is to hold it true that things are thus and so; i.e.—very briefly and very roughly—to have a complex of dispositions including a disposition to speak (etc.), and act, as if things are thus and so.[6] Pseudo-belief, however, is a very common phenomenon; think of those familiar psychological states of obstinate loyalty to a proposition you half-suspect is false, or of sentimental attachment to a proposition you have given little thought or none at all (when, still very briefly and roughly, your verbal behavior is apt to be too vehement, and your nonverbal behavior unstable). Samuel Butler puts it better than I could when, after describing Ernest Pontifex's sudden realization that "few care two straws about the truth, or have any confidence that it is righter or better to believe what is true than what is untrue," he continues, "yet it is only those few who can be said to believe anything at all; the rest are simply unbelievers in disguise."[7]

And to inquire is to try to discover the truth of some question. But pseudo-inquiry is a phenomenon no less common than pseudo-belief; so much so that, when the government or our university institutes an Official Inquiry into this or that, some of us reach for our scare quotes.

The difference between pseudo-inquiry and the real thing lies, as Peirce once put it, in "the motive."[8] The distinguishing feature of genuine inquiry is that what the inquirer wants is *to find the truth of some question.* The proximal motive, that is; the inquiry is still genuine if some further consideration, of utility or of ambition, motivates the inquirer to seek the truth. The distinguishing feature of pseudo-inquiry is that what the "inquirer" wants is not to discover the truth of some question but *to make a case for some proposition determined in advance.*

Peirce identifies one kind of pseudo-inquiry when he writes of "sham reasoning":[9] making a case for the truth of some proposition your commitment to which is already evidence- and argument-proof. He has in mind philosophers who devise elaborate metaphysical underpinnings for theological propositions which no evidence or argument would induce them to give up. I think of Philip Gosse's tortured efforts to reconcile the evidence Darwin adduced in favor of the theory of evolution with the literal truth of the book of Genesis—and of the advocacy "research" and politi-

cally motivated "scholarship" of our own times. The cha
of sham inquiry is the "inquirer's" *prior and unbudgeal*
the proposition for which he tries to make a case.

Another kind of pseudo-inquiry is fake reasoning:
some proposition advocating which you believe will a
also a familiar phenomenon when, as in some areas of contemporary aca
demic life, a clever defense of a startlingly false or impressively obscure idea
can be a good route to reputation and advancement. Peirce's exasperated
observations about "studying in a literary spirit"[10]—that preoccupation
with style over content, argument, and evidence to which he thought some
contemporaries of his had succumbed—reveal that, though he did not
identify it specifically, he was aware of the possibility of fake reasoning
as well as of the sham. The characteristic feature of fake reasoning is the
"inquirer's" *indifference to the truth-value* of the proposition for which he
seeks to make a case (the mark, as Harry Frankfurt observes, of the bull-
shitter).[11]

There is a large difference between fake reasoning and genuine inquiry
motivated by the hope of fame or fortune. In the case of fake reasoning,
the truth-value of the proposition advocated—though not its publicity-
value—is irrelevant to achievement of the "inquirer's" goal; while in the
case of genuine inquiry undertaken in the pursuit of fame or fortune, the
ultimate goal can be achieved (or the inquirer believes it can be achieved)
only by discovering the truth. James Watson tells us in *The Double Helix*[12]
how he dreamed of winning the Nobel Prize; that helped motivate him to
work so hard on his "smashingly important problem," the structure of
DNA (p. 49). He was an ambitious inquirer; but not, for all that, any less
a genuine inquirer.

One might say, as Peirce does, that the genuine inquirer has a love of
truth; but this is nothing like the love of a collector for the antique furniture or the exotic stamps he collects, nor is it like the religious person's
love of God. The genuine inquirer is not a collector of true propositions,
nor is he a worshiper of an intellectual ideal. But he does want the true
answer to his question: if he is inquiring into whether cigarette smoking
causes cancer, he wants to end up believing that cigarette smoking causes
cancer if cigarette smoking causes cancer, and that it doesn't if it doesn't
(and that it's a lot more complicated than that if it's a lot more complicated
than that); if he is inquiring into who committed the murder, he wants to
end up believing that the butler did it if the butler did it, that the maid did
it if the maid did it, . . . ; and so on.

In one sense of "disinterested," the word is redundant as it appears in sinterested inquirer" or "disinterested inquiry." But the word has several senses: (i) uninterested; (ii) not having an interest (especially, not having a financial interest) in an inquiry's coming out this way rather than that; or (iii) not motivated by the desire that the inquiry come out this way rather than that. ("Interested," naturally, is ambiguous in the same ways.)

The first of the senses of "interested" and "disinterested" is not much to the purpose here—except perhaps for its contribution to encouraging the idea that disinterested inquiry is impossible. Some seem to have been tempted to suppose that, since a person would hardly bother to inquire if he had no interest [sense (i)] in the question at issue, disinterested inquiry [sense (iii)] is impossible. Others seem to have been tempted to suppose that, since any inquirer is interested [sense (i)] only in certain, selected aspects of the question he investigates—as florists and botanists are interested in different aspects of roses, daisies, etc.—disinterested inquiry [sense (iii)] is impossible. In both cases, as my annotations reveal, an equivocation has been committed.

The second sense is more germane, but chiefly because of its connection with the third. It is human nature to hope that a question will come out the way it would be in your interests for it to come out; that is why we want to know who paid for this study of the health benefits of oat bran, or that study of the effects of smoking, or this research into the effectiveness of target schools, etc., etc.[13] It is, however, neither necessarily nor invariably the case that someone who has an interest in an inquiry's coming out this way rather than that will not really try to discover the truth of the matter.

To be disinterested in the third and most relevant of the senses of the word is to be impartial, i.e., not motivated by the desire to arrive at a certain conclusion. This is the sense in which "disinterested inquiry" is a pleonasm, and "interested inquiry" an oxymoron (an attempt to show that cigarette smoking is harmless just *isn't* an inquiry into whether cigarette smoking is or isn't harmful). Peirce's description of the genuine inquirer as seeking the truth of some question, "regardless of what the color of that truth may be,"[14] is exactly right.

To describe someone as intellectually honest, a person of intellectual integrity, is to attribute a standing disposition, a trait of character. An intellectually dishonest person is given to deceiving himself about where evidence points, temperamentally disposed to wishful and fearful thinking; while a person of intellectual integrity—the suggestion of wholeness, of unity, is just right—is someone whose will and whose intellect, instead of pulling in opposite directions, act in concert. So an intellectually honest person, if he thinks some question needs looking into, is disposed genuinely to inquire, not to busy himself with pseudo-inquiry.

Thus far, however accurate conceptually, the picture I have sketched is psychologically crude. In real life people are more or less intellectually honest, of more or less solid intellectual integrity; more or less genuinely seeking the truth of this or that question, perhaps motivated in part, but not wholly, by the desire to find out, more or less willing to follow the evidence where it leads, more or less ready to modify their beliefs in the face of evidence; perhaps more inclined to self-deception and wishful thinking in some areas than in others, or capable of intellectual honesty in an environment that encourages it, but vulnerable to temptation by opportunities for advancement through fake reasoning.[15] And people are capable of so many kinds and degrees of pseudo-belief and self-deception—think of how a fake reasoner struggling to disguise his charlatanism from himself may manage to become a true believer and transform himself into a sham reasoner.

It can be hard, very hard, just to admit that you were wrong, that the investment of time, energy, and ego you have put into some question hasn't paid off. It can be hard, too, just to admit that you don't know; most of us like to have opinions, even on questions where we are in no position to know. Perhaps no one is ever a fully, unreservedly genuine inquirer; and surely none of us is of absolutely rock-solid, across-the-board intellectual integrity. But it doesn't follow, and neither is it true, that the difference between a more-or-less honest inquirer and an outright sham or fake, or between a high degree of intellectual integrity and none, doesn't matter. Far from it.

But now I need to get beyond tautologies—that sham and fake reasoners aren't really inquiring, that an intellectually honest person, if he thinks some question needs looking into, is disposed really to inquire—to see what, substantively, is wrong with sham and fake reasoning, and why we value intellectual integrity.

A genuine inquirer wants to get to the truth of the matter that concerns him, whether or not that truth comports with what he believed at the outset of the investigation, and whether or not advancing the proposition in question is likely to get him tenure, or make him rich, famous, or popular. So he is motivated to seek out all the relevant evidence he can and weigh it as fairly as possible, to acknowledge, to himself as well as others, where his evidence seems shakiest or his articulation vaguest, to go with the evidence even to conclusions that will make him unpopular or that under-

mine his formerly deeply held convictions; and if the evidence begins to
disfavor what he originally thought, he will change his belief, or the degree
of his belief, appropriately. To borrow Peirce's words again, a genuine inquirer will be a "contrite fallibilist," prepared to "dump his whole cartload
of beliefs"[16] if the evidence goes against them.

In real life it's a lot messier, but the essential points still hold. As, again,
he reports in *The Double Helix*, when Wilkins and Franklin came from
London to look at his early model for the structure of DNA, and pointed
out that it contained only a tenth of the water content of Franklin's sam-
ples, Watson flirted briefly with the idea of fudging it by squeezing the
water molecules in somehow—but soon admitted that his model just
couldn't be right (p. 94). Later, when Jerry Donohue pointed out that another model, which Watson had hailed as the solution in a letter already
mailed to Max Delbrück, relied on mistaken chemical assumptions, once
again he admitted he'd been wrong, and went back to the drawing board
(p. 190).

Thinking about Crick and Watson's reaction to the "long-feared news"
that Linus Pauling had a structure for DNA, and their relief when it turned
out that Pauling's structure couldn't be right (pp. 156, 163), I realize there
is a significant difference between wanting *to know the truth* with respect
to some question, and wanting *to be the person who discovers that truth*. If,
like those parents in the movie *Lorenzo's Oil*, you just want to know the
cure for your child's disease, you will be happy whoever finds it; but if, like
Watson, you want to discover the structure of this molecule and to win the
Nobel Prize for doing so, you won't be exactly delighted if someone else
finds it first. Perhaps Jowett was right that "the way to get things done is
not to mind who gets the credit of doing them."[17] All the same, human
nature being what it is, people *do* mind who gets the credit; so putting ego
in the service of creativity and respect for evidence is no bad thing.

The closer someone approximates the completely genuine inquirer, the
harder he will try to find out the truth of the question that concerns him.
The closer he approximates the sham or the fake reasoner, however, the
more selective he will be in seeking out evidence (which reveals the connection between the two senses of "partial," "incomplete," and "biased":
bias is served by paying attention only to that part of the evidence which
points in the desired direction); and the more disposed to try to explain
any awkward evidence away. The more of a sham he is, the more disinclined he will be to budge in his convictions; the more of a fake, the more
inclined to fudge as best he can to make himself look good.

Other things being equal, the more intellectually honest you are, the better inquirer you will be—more zealous in seeking out evidence, more scrupulous in weighing it, more responsive to where it points. ("Other things being equal" because, however honestly you want the truth, you won't have much success in discovering it if you lack such other necessary conditions of successful inquiry as intelligence and imagination.) Intellectual integrity is a disposition to honesty in inquiry: to do your best to extend your evidential reach, to scrutinize your evidence with care and patience, to stretch your imaginative powers. It is epistemically valuable because it advances inquiry.

In a community of inquirers, competition between proponents of rival theories may compensate for individuals' reluctance to give up a theory on which their reputation rests, or on which they have worked for years—provided all those involved are not shamming to such a degree that nothing would budge them. (Think of Linus Pauling "conceding the race" to discover the structure of DNA on recognizing the undeniable biological merits of Crick and Watson's model.)[18] This is one of the mechanisms by which natural-scientific inquiry has managed to sustain respect for evidence despite human beings' imperfect intellectual integrity.

In a court of law, there is competition between opposing attorneys: a model which may have encouraged some to suppose that disinterestedness is altogether dispensable. Counsel, however, are not inquirers; nor is a legal proceeding an inquiry into whether the defendant did it. The jury *is,* however, trying to figure out whether the defendant's guilt is established to the required degree by the admissible evidence presented. And a juror will perform this role better, the closer he approximates the genuine inquirer.

Intellectual honesty, I said, is epistemically valuable because it advances inquiry. But why, you may ask, should we care about that? After all, in some circumstances you may be better off not inquiring, better off having an unjustified belief than a justified, better off having a false belief than a true. Some truths are boring, trivial, unimportant, not worth the effort of investigating. And, yes, there is always the possibility that inquiry by a madman bent on destroying the planet might succeed—and bring further inquiry to an end. Nevertheless, there is instrumental value in intellectual integrity, because in the long run and on the whole it advances inquiry, and successful inquiry is, by and large, instrumentally valuable. Compared with other animals, we humans are not especially fleet or strong; our forte is a capacity to figure things out, and hence to anticipate and avoid danger. Granted, this is by no means an unmixed blessing; as shrewd old Thomas Hobbes put it long ago, the same capacity that enables men, unlike brutes, to engage in ratiocination, also enables men, unlike brutes, "to multiply one untruth by another"[19] (and, I might add, to busy themselves with pseudo-inquiry, not to mention making up elaborate arguments why concern for truth doesn't matter!). But who could doubt that our capacity to reason—imperfect as it is, and easily abused—is of instrumental value to us humans?

And, as the overlap of our vocabulary for the epistemic appraisal of character and our vocabulary for the moral appraisal of character suggests—think of "responsible," "negligent," "reckless," "courageous," "honest"—intellectual integrity is also morally valuable.

As courage is the soldier's virtue par excellence, so, one might say, oversimplifying a little, intellectual integrity is the academic's. The oversimplification is that intellectual integrity itself requires a kind of courage, the hardihood needed to give up long-standing convictions in the face of contrary evidence, or to resist fashionable shibboleths, or just to admit that you were wrong. That is why it seems almost indecent when an academic whose job is to inquire denies the intelligibility or denigrates the desirability of the ideal of honest inquiry.

We place a moral value on intellectual integrity in those who have a special obligation to inquire—not only academics, of course, but researchers of every kind, investigative journalists, detectives, etc., etc. (The case of someone whose job it is to inquire for morally objectionable ends—the crook paid to find out where the sewer runs so the gang can get into the bank vault, say—is, naturally, less straightforward.) But why do we value intellectual integrity more generally?

Over-belief (believing beyond what one's evidence warrants) is not always harmful; nor is it always something for which the believer is responsible. But in some case it is both; and then it is morally culpable. Think of W. K. Clifford's striking case of the shipowner who knows his ship is elderly and decaying, but doesn't check, and, managing to deceive himself into believing that the vessel is seaworthy, allows it to depart. Though Clifford is, I think, mistaken in supposing that every case of over-belief is morally culpable, he is right about this case: the shipowner's over-belief is morally culpable, and he is, as Clifford says, "verily guilty" of the deaths of passengers and crew when the ship goes down.[20] The same argument applies, mutatis mutandis, for under-belief (not believing when one's evidence warrants belief).

Not all of us are employed to inquire. But all of us are sometimes in a position where, if we believe irresponsibly, we may do damage. Though belief is never straightforwardly voluntary, it is sometimes willful; sometimes, as the saying goes, the wish *is* father to the thought. And it is precisely when your over- or under-belief is not only harmful, but also some-thing for which you can be held responsible because it results from self-deception, from a lack of intellectual integrity, that it is morally culpable. Intellectual dishonesty, a habit of reckless or feckless belief-formation, puts you at chronic risk of morally culpable over- and under-belief.

That is why intellectual integrity is not only an epistemic virtue (i.e., as the etymology of "virtue" suggests, an epistemic strength), but also a moral virtue. To be sure, intellectual integrity is not sufficient by itself, any more than courage is, or kindness, to make you a good person; to be sure, like courage, intellectual integrity may prove useful in the pursuit of morally undesirable projects as well as desirable ones. And, yes, you might be in other respects a decent person, kind to your wife and dog, even honest in your tax returns, and so forth, while lacking in intellectual honesty. But, to my ear at least, "he is a good man but intellectually dishonest," if not quite an oxymoron, really does need an "otherwise."

SO WHAT HAS GONE WRONG in the thinking of those who denigrate concern for truth?

According to Stich, "once we have a clear view of the matter," we will realize that truth is neither an intrinsically nor an instrumentally valuable property for a belief to have.

Earlier well known for his defense of the bizarre idea that no one be-lieves anything,[21] by the time of *The Fragmentation of Reason* Stich ac-knowledges that people do, after all, have beliefs. A belief, he now tells us, is "a brain-state mapped by an interpretation function into a proposition," or, as he likes to say to make the idea vivid, a sentence inscribed in a box in one's head marked "Beliefs." Proposing a "causal/functional account of our common-sense interpretation function," i.e., of the function mapping brain states onto propositions, Stich points out that there are many pos-sible such functions. The "standard" function maps the belief he would express by "There is no water on the sun," onto the proposition that there is no H_2O on the sun, but an alternative function would map it onto the proposition that there is no H_2O or XYZ on the sun. The standard function and the alternative functions, he continues, generate different notions of reference and truth: truth, TRUTH*, TRUTH**, and so forth (pp. 109 ff.).

So, he concludes, truth is just one among many possible truth-like val-ues a belief might have. And once you grasp this, you will come to doubt that truth is intrinsically valuable, seeing that valuing truth for its own sake "is a profoundly conservative thing to do" (p. 118).

And you will also soon realize that it is no less questionable whether truth is instrumentally valuable. You have only to consider poor Harry, who believed that his plane left at 7:45 A.M.; his belief was true, but the plane crashed, and Harry died. An alternative interpretation-function would map the belief Harry would express by "my flight leaves at 7:45 A.M." onto the proposition that Harry's flight leaves at 8.45 A.M., and so make Harry's belief TRUE* (though not true). Isn't it obvious, Stich asks, that Harry would have been better off with this TRUE* belief than with his true belief? And the point generalizes to other things people value; "true beliefs are not always optimal in the pursuit of happiness or pleasure or desire satisfaction . . . [or] peace or power or love." So "the instrumental value of true beliefs is far from obvious" (pp. 123, 124).

Stich's misconstrual of what it is to believe something, studiously ignoring (or obfuscating) the internal connections between the concepts of belief and truth, encourages him to suppose that truth could be a desirable property for a belief to have only if truth is either intrinsically or instrumentally valuable. He doesn't see that truth is the internal goal of belief; to borrow James's words, that "truth is *one species of good,* . . . good in the way of belief."[22]

In any case it obviously doesn't follow from the premise that truth is only one of many semantic properties a sentence in one's head might have, that truth isn't intrinsically valuable. "Besides being true, sentence S refers to water and means the same as the French sentence 'l'eau est H_2O,'" doesn't imply "truth is not valuable." Nor does the conclusion follow from the observation that preferring true beliefs to TRUE* beliefs "is a profoundly conservative thing to do." "We have traditionally valued truth" doesn't imply "truth is not valuable."

Saying that Harry would have been better off with a TRUE* belief than a true one is just a misleading way of saying that he would have been better off had he had, instead of the true belief that his plane left at 7:45, the false belief that his plane left at 8:45. So the business about truth, TRUTH*, etc., serves only to obscure the fact that Stich's argument about instrumental value depends essentially on the assumption that there is instrumental value in having true beliefs only if in every case a true belief is optimal with respect to every goal a person might have. And this is just false; there is instrumental value in sharp ears, even though sometimes you might hear something you would be better off not knowing, and instrumental value in sharp knives, even though sometimes you might be better off with a blunt one. Perhaps it is because Stich realizes how weak his arguments are that he gradually mutes the categorical claim that truth is neither intrinsically nor instrumentally valuable into the uninteresting thesis that it "isn't obvious" that truth is either.

Heal's "The Disinterested Search for Truth," with such comments as (p. 99) "this may seem very shocking," and (p. 100) "this sounds terrible" (reminding me of Stich's boast that people sometimes think he "must be joking"),[23] gives the impression that what is to be established is very radical indeed.

"Truth is generally thought to be a Good Thing," Heal begins, but this "seeming truism" is misconstrued; "true" isn't really an evaluative term at all (p. 97). By the end of the paper she concludes that "there is no goddess, Truth, of whom academics or researchers can regard themselves as priests or devotees," and so, "as a corollary, . . . academics and researchers are not burdened with some requirement of 'intellectual integrity' or 'absolute commitment to the truth'"—notice the scare quotes cutting those supposed ideals down to size. Apparently Heal's thesis is that the disinterested search for truth is less a genuine ideal than a kind of superstition. But (again, as in Stich) there seems to be a less exciting subtext; that remark about intellectual integrity, for instance, continues, "academics and researchers are not burdened with some requirement of 'intellectual integrity' . . . over and above what is required of everyone" (p. 108). Perhaps, like Stich, Heal is at least half-aware that the arguments on offer won't take us to the advertised destination.

Evaluative terms, Heal's argument begins, have "the function of making actions intelligible by helping show us what an agent saw in those actions" (p. 97). But "true" doesn't have this function with respect to utterances: the fact that a statement is true, in and of itself, is no reason for uttering it. Nor does "true" have this function with respect to beliefs: belief-formation isn't something we do at will, and so has no aim or goal. And "true" doesn't have this function with respect to inquiry, either: the goal of an inquiry is always the answer to this or that question, never Truth-as-Such. So "true" is not evaluative; the supposed ideal of disinterested or pure inquiry is really an illusion; and the idea that intellectual integrity is especially required of academics and researchers is a confusion.

Heal is right that not every truth is worth uttering or appropriate to utter in whatever circumstances; right that not every truth is worth knowing; right that, like courage, intellectual integrity can be useful in the service of morally bad projects as well as good; and right, of course, that truth is not a goddess whom academics, etc., should worship. But from these premises, obviously, no radical conclusions follow.

Heal's account of what it is for a term to be evaluative is too narrow,

effectively ruling out the possibility of evaluative terms applicable to beliefs—such as "justified," to take only the most obvious example. As a result, Heal obscures the internal connection between the concepts of belief
and truth, and doesn't notice that, unlike moral "oughts," terms of epistemic appraisal carry no presupposition of voluntariness. In any case, her
conception of belief-formation as simply involuntary is too crude; while,
to be sure, one cannot believe at will, wishful and fearful thinking are a
problem precisely because the will *can* get in the way of our judgment of
evidence.[24] As a result, Heal obscures the reasons for the moral disapproval
we rightly feel of some quasi-voluntary unjustified beliefs.

Most consequentially, Heal apparently identifies disinterested inquiry
with "pure" inquiry, inquiry motivated exclusively by the desire for Truth-
as-Such. That, granted, is not an ideal but an illusion. But this isn't what
disinterested inquiry is: viz., impartial inquiry, not motivated by the desire
to establish some particular conclusion, but by the desire to find the true
answer "regardless of what the color of that truth may be." Heal's arguments fail to engage with the reasons for thinking that this is an ideal, or
with the reasons for thinking intellectual integrity a particular virtue in
those who have an obligation to inquire.

Heal hints, but doesn't quite say, that valuing intellectual integrity—
sorry, "intellectual integrity"!—is a kind of superstition. The idea is more
explicit in Rorty, who describes the intellectual history of the West as an
attempt "to substitute a love of Truth for a love of God."[25] When Rorty
tells us that he "does not have much use for the idea of 'objective truth,'"
however, his scare quotes reveal that he has his eye on bigger game: it is
truth—sorry, "truth"!—itself about which we are, allegedly, confused.

"It is . . . more difficult than it used to be to locate a real live metaphysical prig. [But] you can still find [philosophers] who will solemnly tell you
that they are seeking *the truth,* not just a story or a consensus but an honest-to-God, down-home, accurate representation of the way the world is."[26]
Except for its suggestion that it may be only philosophical truth about
which he is skeptical, this passage conveys the essential idea very well: a
contrast between truth-as-consensus (YES) and Truth-as-accurate-repre-
sentation (NO). Compare: "there are . . . two senses . . . of 'true' . . . the
homely use . . . to mean roughly 'what you can defend against all comers,'
. . . [and] the specifically 'philosophical' sense . . . which, like the Ideas of
Pure Reason, [is] designed precisely to stand for the Unconditioned."[27]

Rorty's dichotomy is false. On the "philosophical" side of which he dis-
approves, truth as accurate representation of Things-in-Themselves,
the metaphysical realist picture to which Putnam once subscribed, and ap-

parently (if one figures Rorty's other dismissive observations about "fact" and "correspondence" into the equation)[28] any and every version of a correspondence conception, are all run together.[29] And on the "homely and shopworn" side of which he approves, truth as "what you can defend against all comers" is said to be the conception "Tarski and Davidson are attending to."

The suggestion that Tarski, or Davidson,[30] would agree that truth is "whatever can overcome all conversational objections" seems bizarre. Perhaps Rorty first mistakes Tarski's T-schema for his definition of truth (Tarski proposed it as a material adequacy condition which any acceptable definition of truth must satisfy); then confuses this supposed definition with a conception of truth as simply a device of disquotation (Tarski's account of quotation precludes this); and then draws the conclusion that the predicate "true" is semantically superfluous, having only the rhetorical role of giving a "metaphysical pat on the back" to propositions on which we agree (perhaps Tarski's reaction to this can be inferred from his warning that semantics is not "a device for establishing that everyone except the speaker and his friends is speaking nonsense").[31]

And what Rorty calls the homely sense of "true" is not a sense of "true" at all. "True" *is* a word we apply to statements about which we agree; but that is because, if we agree that things are thus and so, we agree that it is true that things are thus and so. But we may agree that things are thus and so when it is *not* true that things are thus and so. So "true" is not a word that truly applies to all or only statements about which we agree; and neither, of course, does calling a statement true mean that it is a statement we agree about.

If calling a statement true *did* mean that it is a statement we agree about, to inquire—to try to arrive at the truth of some question—would be just to try to arrive at agreement with respect to that question. Inquiry would be more like a negotiation than an investigation. And, indeed, though Rorty continues to use the word "inquiry," it is in just this revisionary way—as "discussion" is reduced to "carrying on the conversation."

But inquiry isn't much like negotiation. Investigating the structure of DNA, Crick and Watson wanted to end up believing that DNA is a double-helical, backbone-out macromolecule with irregular bases stacked inside if DNA is a double-helical, backbone-out macromolecule with irregular bases stacked inside, to end up believing that DNA is a triple-helical, backbone-in macromolecule with like-with-like base pairs if DNA is a triple-helical, backbone-inside macromolecule with like-with-like base pairs, . . . , and so on. Yes, they had endless discussions with each other and with col-

leagues and correspondents; yes, eventually, quite some time after the publication of their paper in *Nature,* the scientific community came to agree
that their model was the right one.[32] But the goal was *to discover the structure of DNA,* not to overcome conversational objections or to reach consensus.

Of late Rorty has taken to reminding us[33] (like Paul Churchland before
him)[34] of the continuity of human cognition with the cognitive goings-on
of squid, sea slugs, etc.—which don't have representations of the world in
their heads or their whatevers. Well, no; but then squid, etc., can't talk,
write, draw maps, diagrams, etc. Why suppose, Rorty asks, that having a
belief is having a representation in one's head, rather than having a pattern
of dispositions to behave? Why indeed; so long as we don't forget that the
pattern of dispositions of a person who believes that things are thus and
so are will include dispositions to assent to/to assert sentences in some
language to the effect that things are thus and so.

And lately Rorty tells us that it makes no difference in practice whether
you aim at the truth, or aim at justified belief. This is a nasty muddle: if
"justified" is used in its ordinary sense, the contrast on which Rorty relies
is misleading, while if "justified" is used in the effete conversational sense
Rorty gives it, it makes concern for justification incomprehensible.

As I spent much of the first section of this essay explaining, the difference it makes whether you really want the truth is that, if you do, you will
want the best evidence possible; which means you will care what (competent) others think, because that is an important way to extend your evidential reach and sharpen your judgment of evidence. If you are shamming or
faking, however, you will evade, obfuscate, fudge, to avoid admitting the
force of awkward evidence.

So, in the usual sense of "justified," in which how justified you are in a
belief depends on how good your evidence with respect to that belief is,
the supposed contrast between aiming at the truth and aiming at justified
beliefs is misconceived. Yes, evidence can be misleading, and you can be
justified to some degree in believing something false; nevertheless, if you
want the truth of the matter, what you must do is go with the best evidence
you can get.

But Rorty has stripped "justification," as he has "belief," "inquiry," and
even "discussion," of essential content. Dropping any connection of justification and evidence, he assumes that to justify a belief is to defend it to
some audience or other. But it is unintelligible why anyone should care
about justification, in this anorexic sense. It mattered to Watson whether
he could defend that model of DNA to Donohue, because Donohue knew

more than he about tautomeric bonds—information crucial to the correctness or otherwise of the model. But if "justify" becomes *merely* conversational, losing its connections with evidence, with truth-indication, justifying one's beliefs is no longer an intelligible goal.

And why has Rorty stripped "justified" of its essential content? Because, if "true" just means "what you can defend against all comers," "justify" can only mean "defend against conversational objections"! He is still, after all, relying on his old, failed This-or-Nothingism.

BUT IT IS TIME to stop complaining about Rorty, and try to get clearer *what is required of the concept of truth itself* if, as I have argued, concern for truth is valuable epistemically, instrumentally, and morally.

Looking back at my explanations of what the genuine inquirer wants—to end up believing that the butler did it if the butler did it, that DNA is a double-helical, backbone-out macromolecule with like-with-unlike base pairs if DNA is a double-helical, backbone-out macromolecule, etc.—the answer is plain enough: the concept of truth must satisfy the Aristotelian Insight: to say of what is, that it is, or of what is not, that it is not, is true, etc. This is reassuring; for Aristotle's observation is so manifestly true, so far as it goes, that the goal of generalizing it so it applies to all statements regardless of form is explicit in Tarski and Ramsey, and implicit in other theories of truth.

In correspondence theories—whether of the boldly metaphysical Logical Atomist stripe, as in Wittgenstein's and Russell's conception of truth as structural isomorphism of proposition and fact, or of a more muted linguistic stripe, as in Austin's conception of truth as co-incidence of demonstrative and descriptive conventions—the Aristotelian Insight is generalized by pressing that emphatic adverb for which we sometimes reach when we say that it is true that snow is white just in case really, actually, *in fact,* snow is white, into serious theoretical service.

In Tarski's semantic theory, the idea is to generalize the Aristotelian Insight by means of a recursive definition of satisfaction which will apply to all open sentences of a language in virtue of their construction out of the simplest open sentences, and a definition of truth as satisfaction of a closed sentence by all sequences of objects.[35]

Ramsey's theory generalizes the Aristotelian Insight in the most direct way, by sentential quantification. To say that everything Socrates said was true is to say that, for all p, if Socrates said that p, then p; to say that something Plato said was true is to say that, for some p, Plato said that p, and p; and (the codicil that gave rise to the idea that Ramsey's is a redundancy theory) to say that it is true that all men by nature desire to know is to say that all men by nature desire to know. But to call this a redundancy theory is misleading, for Ramsey certainly gives "true" a substantial role; only not as a predicate of sentences, but as a natural-language device of sentential quantification, the analogue of pro*nouns,* as he says, but for sentences.[36]

Anyone who engages in reasoning at all, Peirce writes, must "certainly opine that there is such a thing as Truth." And what that means, he continues, is "that something is SO . . . whether you, or I, or anybody, thinks it is so or not."[37] This suggests that he, too, might be read as trying to generalize the Aristotelian Insight. "Every man is fully satisfied that there is such a thing as truth, or he would not ask any question," he writes elsewhere, and "*that* truth consists in a conformity to something *independent of his thinking it to be so,* or of any man's opinion on that subject."[38] This "something independent of his or any man's thinking it to be so" Peirce explains as the Final Representation, the Ultimate Opinion that would be agreed were inquiry to continue long enough.

None of these attempts to generalize the Aristotelian Insight is unproblematically successful. The Logical Atomists' version of the correspondence theory is metaphysically demanding, requiring an ontology of logically ultimate objects. Austin's version of the correspondence theory is straightforwardly applicable only where there are indexicals for the demonstrative conventions to latch onto. Tarski's method relativizes "true" to a language, and applies only to languages which are formally specifiable—which may, as Tarski thought, preclude its applicability where natural languages are concerned. Ramsey's approach—where the liberation felt with the resort to sentence letters achieves full generality only by means of sentential quantifiers—requires a new account of how such quantifiers work: for on the objectual interpretation that final "p" would stand in for the name of a sentence, needing to be made grammatically complete by the addition of a predicate, the obvious candidate being "true"; while on the substitutional interpretation "for all p, if Socrates asserted that p, then p" would be read as "every substitution-instance of 'if Socrates asserted that ——, then ——' is true."[39] And Peirce's definition faces the problem of Buried Secrets: that statements about the past which would not be settled however long inquiry were to continue must be deemed neither true nor false.

Does this mean that my defense of the value of concern for truth places impossible demands on the concept?—of course not! That we have not yet devised a completely satisfactory and fully general statement of the Aristotelian Insight is no reason to conclude that it isn't an insight at all; to suppose otherwise is to succumb to the Arrogance of Theory, to that "factitious despair" of which Bacon wrote—and "all for the miserable vainglory of having it believed that whatever has not yet been invented or discovered will not be invented or discovered hereafter."[40]

WHICH LEADS ME to the other question that bothers me: given Peirce's eloquent defense, and Lewis's sober endorsement, of the importance of intellectual integrity, how did it come about that just such a factitious despair, a wearily arrogant denigration of concern for truth, has of late come to be associated (by Stich and Rorty—Heal acknowledges no allegiances) with pragmatism? It makes you wonder ... Could Russell have been right in suspecting pragmatism of a morally debilitating tendency, of leading to "cosmic impiety," or at least to fascism?

Stich cites only James; Rorty makes frequent admiring references to James and Dewey, but dismisses Peirce as having merely given pragmatism its name. So the first diagnosis that suggests itself is that Stich and Rorty are following the wrong pragmatists—that Peirce was sound on the subject of concern for truth as James (and perhaps Dewey) was not. But this temptingly simple diagnosis won't do. For one thing, in their efforts to associate themselves with the classical pragmatist tradition, both Stich and Rorty misinterpret James.

Stich does no more than quote from "What Pragmatism Means" in a footnote. But the quotation is bowdlerized; and Stich's interpretation of it is so tendentious that it puts me in mind of James's complaints about critics who are unwilling "to read anything but the silliest of possible meanings"[41] into the pragmatists' words. The passage from James that Stich quotes in support of his claim that truth is neither intrinsically nor instrumentally valuable opens with the thesis that truth is one species of good, and goes on to argue that truth is instrumentally valuable! In the bit Stich quotes, James asks, "Ought we ever not to believe what is *better for us* to believe? and can we then keep the notion of what is better for us, and what is true for us, permanently apart?" and answers, "Pragmatism says no, and I fully agree with her." But Stich omits "if there were *no* good for life in true ideas, then the current notion that truth is divine and precious, and its pursuit a duty, could never have grown up. ... In a world like that, our duty would be to *shun* truth, rather," and the following sentence, where James observes that in *this* world, by contrast with that imagined world, true beliefs are "helpful in life's practical struggles."[42]

Perhaps Stich thinks his thesis that a justified belief is one the holding of which conduces to the believer's desires is akin to James's doctrine of the Will to Believe. But James had written: "*Our passional nature not only lawfully may, but must, decide an option between propositions, whenever it is a genuine option that cannot by its nature be decided on intellectual grounds*";[43] and insisted that critics who took him to advocate license in belief had misread him.[44]

Rorty writes that "once human desires are admitted into the criterion of 'truth,' . . . we have become pragmatists. The pragmatist's claim is that to know your desires is to know the criterion of truth."[45] But James had written: "As regards the 'Will to Believe' matter, it should not complicate the question of what one means by truth. . . . The question whether we have a right to believe anything before verification concerns not the constitution of truth, but the policy of belief."[46]

When Rorty tells us that "a pragmatist theory says . . . that Truth is not the sort of thing one should expect to have a philosophically interesting theory about,"[47] you hear a faint echo of James's urging that philosophers shift their attention from abstract Truth to concrete truths; but any affinity of Rorty's position and James's is still distant at best. In *The Meaning of Truth,* after all, James had offered this account of "truth absolute," quite reminiscent of Peirce's: "an ideal set of formulations towards which all opinions may be expected to converge in the long run of experience."[48]

"Pragmatism," Rorty tells us, "is anti-representationalism."[49] Again, the attribution seems bizarre. But then you realize that Rorty is running together three distinct and logically independent views under the single rubric, "representationalism": (1) the representative theory of perception; (2) the idea that beliefs are representations of the world, and truth a goal of inquiry; and (3) the correspondence theory of truth. All the classical pragmatists, though each in a different way, tried to transcend the representative theory of perception of the older Empiricist tradition.[50] They agreed, also, that to describe truth as correspondence with, or copying, reality is—not false exactly, but short on pragmatic meaning. But Peirce was the founder of semiotics, the theory of signs, of representation; and James's "ideal set of formulations," like Peirce's "Ultimate Representation," surely refers to something like a set of propositions.

"Since I persist in trying to interpret Davidson as the most sophisticated and radical of the American pragmatists, it suits my purposes to define pragmatism as the attempt to do something Davidson approves of";[51] now it sounds as if Rorty is admitting that he is kidnapping the word! And then you realize that Rorty may just be seizing on the fact that Davidson rejects the representative theory of perception, and has, by now, come to the conclusion that Tarski's is not a correspondence theory.

It's This-or-Nothingism again: either you accept perception-as-representative or truth-as-correspondence, or else you give up the idea that sentences represent, and become a pragmatist—a pragmatist like Bradley or Frege, I suppose!

So is it all just a misunderstanding, innocent or otherwise? This isn't quite the whole story either. Yes, Stich and Rorty misinterpret the old pragmatists they cite; yes, they are engaged in a kind of intellectual kidnapping. But remember that old joke about the soldiers passing a message down the line—beginning, "send reinforcements, we're going to advance," and ending, "send three-and-fourpence,[52] we're going to a dance." The message is laughably distorted; but if there weren't a recognizable similarity the joke wouldn't work. Similarly, I think, with Stich's and Rorty's misinterpretations of pragmatism: the message is laughably distorted; but if there weren't recognizable continuities the kidnappers wouldn't get as far as the end of the street.

In part, these new "friends" of pragmatism, like her old critics, are exploiting ambiguities and tensions in James. His efforts to disentangle the Will to Believe thesis from his pragmatism aren't altogether convincing; for his statements of the Pragmatic Maxim, blurring the two senses of "belief" (someone's believing something, versus the proposition believed), suggest that the meaning of a proposition depends on the consequences of its being believed rather than on the consequences of its being true. And sometimes James loses track of the difference between what is true, and what is accepted as true. Such observations as: "we have to live today by what truth we can get today, and be ready tomorrow to call it falsehood"[53]—which would have been true enough if only he had remembered to put in quotation marks!—make the idea that he thought that "true" is "just a word that applies to statements about which we can agree" less incomprehensible.

Peirce and James are very different kinds of thinker, and their conceptions of pragmatism are significantly different: Peirce's logical and realist, James's psychological and nominalist. Not surprisingly, a strategy of disassociating Peirce from James has been as tempting to some of Peirce's admirers as it is to his detractors among contemporary neo-pragmatists. But—now my footing is getting a little unsteady, but I will venture just a bit further—it is worth asking whether there is anything in Peirce that is recognizably distorted in contemporary Vulgar Pragmatism.

Well: Rorty's conception of truth-as-agreement sounds to me a lot like the result of stripping Peirce's account of truth of everything that anchors it in the world—distorting the Final Representation that would be agreed in the light of the fullest possible logical scrutiny of all possible evidence into "what you can defend against all comers." And Rorty's insistence that concern for truth is a kind of superstition sounds to me a lot like a reaction against the kind of rhetoric Peirce employs in its favor.

Beyond these easy steps, the path gets steeper; but it seems necessary to ask whether there are weaknesses in Peirce, as there surely are in James, that Rorty is exploiting to his cynical purposes.

Peirce's is the most articulate and serious defense of intellectual integrity I know; but there is one thing about it that bothers me a bit. He doesn't seem clearly to distinguish genuine but utility-driven inquiry from interested pseudo-inquiry.[54] Against this background, those references to the love of truth, to science as seeking "truth for truth's sake," of "the majesty of truth, as that to which, sooner or later, every knee must bow,"[55] begin to sound a bit too much like references to that goddess whom academics and researchers should worship.

And Peirce's response to the problem of Buried Secrets seems, in the end, unsatisfying. We take a shortsighted view of what inquiry might eventually be able to discover, he observes; but, as De Waal has pointed out,[56] Peirce's tychism commits him to denying the full recoverability of information about the past. We too easily assume that propositions that could never be decided however long inquiry were to continue are meaningful, Peirce tells us; but the more he must rely on denying meaningfulness, the more I worry that, though its letter is observed, the spirit of the Aristotelian Insight may have been compromised. To exclude "Hamlet sneezed three times during the three days before his death" from its scope, I feel, is one thing; to exclude "Churchill sneezed fifty-six times during the year 1942," quite another. Perhaps, after all, Peirce's unpacking of "Truth is SO, whether you or I or anybody thinks it is so or not" falls short of "to say of what is, etc., is true."

Which leads me to wonder whether Peirce sometimes seems to be tempted by a picture of the disinterested inquirer as seeking Truth-as-Such in part because his account of truth is not quite unambiguously hospitable to a more plausible conception of the genuine inquirer as simply wanting to end up believing that p if p, that not-p if not-p. Could it be that he overshoots the mark in one direction because he undershoots it in another?

I'M NOT SURE: but if it be so, so be it. "Our inquiry is to be an inquiry into truth, whatever the truth may turn out to be, and therefore, of course, is not to be influenced by any liking for pragmatism."[57] For (the words are borrowed from Stanislav Andreski, the old-fashioned prig's old-fashioned prig and a curmudgeon after my own heart—but the thought is very Peircean), "the reason why human understanding has been able to advance in the past, and may do so in the future, is that true insights are cumulative and retain their value regardless of what happens to their discoverers; while fads and stunts may bring an immediate profit to the impresarios, but lead nowhere in the long run, cancel each other out, and are dropped as soon as their promoters are no longer there."[58]

NOTES

1. C. S. Peirce, *Collected Papers,* ed. Charles Hartshorne, Paul Weiss, and Arthur Burks, Harvard University Press, Cambridge, MA, 1931–58, 2.82, 1902; references by volume and paragraph number.

2. C. I. Lewis, *The Ground and Nature of the Right,* Columbia University Press, New York, 1955, p. 34.

3. Stephen P. Stich, *The Fragmentation of Reason: Preface to a Pragmatic Theory of Cognitive Evaluation,* Bradford Books, MIT Press, Cambridge, MA, 1990, p. 101.

4. Richard Rorty, *Essays on Heidegger and Others,* Cambridge University Press, Cambridge, 1991, p. 86; "Trotsky and the Wild Orchids," *Common Knowledge,* 1.3, 1992, p. 141; *Consequences of Pragmatism,* Harvester Press, Hassocks, Sussex, 1982, p. xvii.

5. Jane Heal, "The Disinterested Search for Truth," *Proceedings of the Aristotelian Society,* 88, 1987–88, 97–108, p. 108.

6. See also my *Evidence and Inquiry: Towards Reconstruction in Epistemology,* Blackwell, Oxford, 1993, pp. 173–79.

7. Samuel Butler, *The Way of All Flesh* (1903), Signet Books, The New American Library of World Classics, New York, 1960, p. 259.

8. Peirce, *Collected Papers,* 1.34, 1869.

9. Peirce, *Collected Papers,* 1.57–58, c. 1896.

10. Peirce, *Collected Papers,* 1.33, 1869; also 5.499, c. 1905, 5.396, 1878, and MS 632, 1909. See also "As for that phrase 'studying in a literary spirit' . . . ," essay 3 in this volume.

11. H. Frankfurt, "On Bullshit," in *The Importance of What We Care About,* Cambridge University Press, Cambridge, 1989, 11–33.

12. James D. Watson, *The Double Helix*, Atheneum, New York, 1967.

13. See also Cynthia Crossen, *Tainted Truth: The Manipulation of Fact in America*, Simon and Schuster, New York, 1994.

14. Peirce, *Collected Papers*, 7.605, 1902.

15. See also "Preposterism and Its Consequences," essay 11 in this volume.

16. Peirce, *Collected Papers*, 1.14, c. 1897 ("contrite fallibilism"); 1.55, c. 1896 ("ready to dump his whole cartload of beliefs").

17. My source is *The Oxford Book of Aphorisms*, ed. John Gross, Oxford University Press, Oxford, 1983, p. 100; no specific reference is given.

18. Watson, *The Double Helix*, pp. 218–19.

19. Thomas Hobbes, *Human Nature* (1650), in *Hobbes Selections*, ed. J. E. Woodbridge, Charles Scribner's Sons, New York, 1930, p. 23. Compare Peirce, "Those whom we are so fond of referring to as the 'lower animals' reason very little. Now I beg you to observe that those beings very rarely commit a *mistake*, while we ———!" (1.626, 1898).

20. W. K. Clifford, "The Ethics of Belief" (1877), in *The Ethics of Belief and Other Essays*, Watts and Company, London, 1947, p. 70. See also Haack, "'The Ethics of Belief' Revisited," in *The Philosophy of R. M. Chisholm*, ed. Lewis Hahn, Open Court, La Salle, IL, 1997, 129–44.

21. Stephen P. Stich, *From Folk Psychology to Cognitive Science*, Bradford Books, MIT Press, Cambridge, MA, 1983; see also my *Evidence and Inquiry*, pp. 158–81.

22. William James, "What Pragmatism Means," in *Pragmatism: A New Name for Some Old Ways of Thinking* (1907), ed. Frederick Burkhardt and Fredson Bowers, Harvard University Press, Cambridge, MA, 1975, p. 42.

23. Stich, *The Fragmentation of Reason*, p. 101.

24. See also *Evidence and Inquiry*, p. 76.

25. Richard Rorty, *Contingency, Irony, and Solidarity*, Cambridge University Press, Cambridge, 1979, p. 22.

26. Rorty, *Essays on Heidegger and Others*, p. 86.

27. Richard Rorty, *Philosophy and the Mirror of Nature*, Princeton University Press, Princeton, NJ, 1979, pp. 308–9.

28. Richard Rorty, "The Priority of Democracy to Philosophy," in Merrill D. Petersen and Robert C. Vaughn, eds., *The Virginia Statute for Religious Freedom*, Cambridge University Press, Cambridge, 1988, 257–82, p. 271; *Consequences of Pragmatism*, p. xvii.

29. See also "Reflections on Relativism: From Momentous Tautology to Seductive Contradiction," essay 9 in this volume.

30. I won't attempt to trace the various shifts in Davidson's position since Rorty began to try to "appropriate" him, except to note that in "True to the Facts" (1969), in *Inquiries into Truth and Interpretation*, Oxford University Press, Oxford, 1984, 37–54, Davidson had suggested calling Tarski's a correspondence theory, a suggestion he withdrew in "Afterthoughts, 1987" [to 'A Coherence Theory of Truth and Knowledge,' 1983]," in *Reading Rorty*, ed. Alan R. Malachowski, Blackwell, Oxford,

1990, 134–37. See also Davidson, "The Myth of the Subjective," in *Relativism: Interpretation and Confrontation,* ed. Michael Krausz, University of Notre Dame Press, Notre Dame, IN, 1989, 159–72; "The Structure and Content of Truth," *Journal of Philosophy,* 87, 1990, 279–328; and "The Folly of Trying to Define Truth," *Journal of Philosophy,* 93.6, 1996, 263–78.

31. Alfred Tarski, "The Semantic Conception of Truth," *Philosophy and Phenomenological Research,* 4, 1944; reprinted in Herbert Feigl and Wilfred Sellars, eds., *Readings in Philosophical Analysis,* Appleton-Century Crofts, New York, 1949, 52–84, p. 56.

32. See Francis Crick, *What Mad Pursuit?* Basic Books, New York, 1988, pp. 71–74.

33. Richard Rorty, "Is Truth a Goal of Enquiry? Davidson vs. Wright," *Philosophical Quarterly,* 45.180, 1995, 281–300.

34. Paul Churchland, "Folk Psychology and the Explanation of Behaviour," *Proceedings of the Aristotelian Society,* Supplement, 62, 1988, 209–22; and in *A Neurocomputational Perspective: The Nature of Mind and the Structure of Science,* Bradford Books, MIT Press, Cambridge, MA, 1989, 111–27. See also *Evidence and Inquiry,* pp. 168–70.

35. On pp. 53–54 of "The Semantic Conception of Truth," Tarski makes the goal of generalizing the Aristotelian Insight explicit.

36. F. P. Ramsey, *On Truth* (1927–29), ed. Nicholas Rescher and U. Majer, Kluwer, Dordrecht, The Netherlands, 1990. The "redundancy" interpretation was the standard one, found in, among many other places, my *Philosophy of Logics,* Cambridge University Press, Cambridge, 1978, before the publication of these papers of Ramsey's.

37. Peirce, *Collected Papers,* 2.135, 1902.

38. Peirce, *Collected Papers,* 5.211, 1903. (I leave aside consideration of what modification might be needed for the case of a person's beliefs about his own beliefs.)

39. See Dorothy Grover, *A Prosentential Theory of Truth,* Princeton University Press, Princeton, NJ, 1992; C. J. F. Williams, *Being, Identity, and Truth,* Clarendon Press, Oxford, 1992, and "A Prosentential Theory of Truth," *Reports on Philosophy,* 15, 1995, Jagiellonian University, Krakow; and M.-J. Frápolli, "The Logical Enquiry into Truth," *History and Philosophy of Logic,* 17.5, 1996, 179–97.

40. Francis Bacon, *The New Organon* (1620), Book I, Aphorism LXXXVIII.

41. James, "Pragmatism's Conception of Truth," *Pragmatism,* p. 112.

42. Stich, *The Fragmentation of Reason,* p. 160; James, "What Pragmatism Means," *Pragmatism,* pp. 42–43.

43. William James, "The Will to Believe" (1896), in *The Will to Believe and Other Essays* (1897), Dover, New York, 1956, p. 11.

44. See, for example, Ralph Barton Perry, *The Thought and Character of William James,* Little, Brown, Boston, 1935, volume 2, chapter 66.

45. Rorty, *Essays on Heidegger and Others,* pp. 30–31.

46. James, letter to Horace Kallen, August 1, 1907; in Perry, *The Thought and Character of William James,* volume 2, p. 249.

47. Rorty, *Consequences of Pragmatism,* p. xiii.

48. William James, *The Meaning of Truth* (1909), ed. Frederick Burkhardt and Fredson Bowers, Harvard University Press, Cambridge, MA, 1975, p. 143. (Peirce's conception is expressed in terms of a hypothetical consensus, however, not convergence.)

49. Richard Rorty, "Introduction" to J. P. Murphy, *Pragmatism from Peirce to Davidson,* Westview Press, Boulder, CO, 1990, 1–6, p. 1.

50. Cf. Haack, "How the Critical Common-sensist Sees Things," *Histoire, Epistemologie, Langage,* 16.1, 1994, 9–34.

51. Richard Rorty, "Realism, Anti-Realism, and Pragmatism: Comments on Alston, Chisholm, and Davidson," in Christopher Kulp, ed., *Realism/Antirealism and Epistemology,* Rowman and Littlefield, Lanham, MD, 1997, 149–72, p. 149.

52. 3/4d: a small sum of money in the old, predecimal British currency.

53. James, "Pragmatism's Conception of Truth," *Pragmatism,* p. 107.

54. An omission of which I was guilty myself in "The First Rule of Reason" (1992), in *The Rule of Reason: The Philosophy of Charles Sanders Peirce,* ed. Jacqueline Brunning and Paul Forster, University of Toronto Press, Toronto, 1997, 241–61.

55. Peirce, *Collected Papers,* 1.44, c. 1896; 8.136, 1901.

56. Cornelis de Waal, "The Quest for Reality: Charles S. Peirce and the Empiricists," Ph.D. dissertation, University of Miami, 1997.

57. Peirce, *Collected Papers,* 5.34, 1903.

58. Stanislav Andreski, *Social Sciences as Sorcery,* St. Martin's Press, New York, 1972, p. 17.

TWO

"We Pragmatists . . .":
Peirce and Rorty in Conversation

SUSAN HAACK: Let me begin by asking Professor Rorty to explain how he feels about philosophers like you, Mr Peirce, who take themselves to be seeking the truth.*

RICHARD RORTY: It is . . . more difficult than it used to be to locate a real live metaphysical prig. [But] you can still find [philosophers] who will solemnly tell you that they are seeking *the truth*, not just a story or a consensus but an honest-to-God, down-home, accurate representation of the way the world is . . . lovably old-fashioned prigs (EHO, p. 86).

SUSAN HAACK: Mr Peirce?

CHARLES SANDERS PEIRCE: In order to reason well . . . , it is absolutely necessary to possess . . . such virtues as intellectual honesty and sincerity and a real love of truth (2.82). The cause [of the success of scientific inquirers] has been that the motive which has carried them to the laboratory and the field has been a craving to know how things really were . . . (1.34). [Genuine inquiry consists] in diligent inquiry into truth for truth's sake (1.44), . . . in actually drawing the bow upon truth with intentness in the eye, with energy in the arm (1.235).

[When] it is no longer the reasoning which determines what the conclusion shall be, but . . . the conclusion which determines what the reasoning shall be . . . this is sham reasoning. . . . The effect of this shamming is that men come to look upon reasoning as mainly decorative. . . .

---

*Charles Sanders Peirce (1839–1914) was the founder, with William James, of Pragmatism; Richard Rorty (b. 1931) is the most influential of contemporary neo-"Pragmatists."

The result of this state of things is, of course, a rapid deterioration of intellectual vigor . . . (1.57–58).

RR: "Justification" [is] a social phenomenon rather than a transaction between "the knowing subject" and "reality" (PMN, p. 9), . . . not a matter of a . . . relation between ideas (or words) and objects, but of conversation, of social practice. . . . We understand knowledge when we understand the social justification of belief, and thus have no need to view it as accuracy of representation (p. 170).

CSP: The result [as I said] is, of course, a rapid deterioration of intellectual vigor. This is just what is taking place among us before our eyes. . . . Man loses his conceptions of truth and of reason (1.58, continued, and 1.59).

RR: I do not have much use for notions like . . . "objective truth" (TWO, p. 141). [The] pragmatist view [is] of rationality as civility, . . . [as] respect for the opinions of those around one, . . . of "true" as a word which applies to those beliefs upon which we are able to agree . . . (SS, pp. 44, 40, 45).

CSP: [As I was saying,] man loses his conceptions of truth and of reason. If he sees one man assert what another denies, he will, if he is concerned, choose his side and set to work by all means in his power to silence his adversaries. The truth for him is that for which he fights (1.59, continued).

RR: Truth [is] entirely a matter of solidarity (ORT, p. 32). There is nothing to be said about either truth or rationality apart from descriptions of the familiar procedures of justification which a given society—*ours*—uses (SS, p. 42).

CSP: You certainly opine that there is such a thing as Truth. Otherwise, reasoning and thought would be without a purpose. What do you mean by there being such a thing as Truth? You mean that something is SO . . . whether you, or I, or anybody thinks it is so or not. . . . The essence of the opinion is that there is *something* that is SO, no matter if there be an overwhelming vote against it (2.135). Every man is fully satisfied that there is such a thing as truth, or he would not ask any question. *That* truth consists in a conformity to something *independent of his thinking it to be so,* or of any man's opinion on that subject (5.211).

Truth [is] overwhelmingly forced upon the mind in experience as the effect of an independent reality (5.564). The essence of truth lies in its resistance to being ignored (2.139).

RR: Some philosophers . . . insist that natural science discovers truth rather than makes it. . . . Other philosophers [like myself] . . . have concluded that science is no more than the handmaiden of technology (CIS, pp. 3–4).

CSP: There are certain mummified pedants who have never waked to the truth that the act of knowing a real object alters it. They are curious specimens of humanity, and . . . I am one of them (5.555).

RR: My rejection of traditional notions of rationality can be summed up by saying that the only sense in which science is exemplary is that it is a model of human solidarity (SS, p. 46).

CSP: Other methods of settling opinion have [certain advantages] over scientific investigation. A man should consider well of them; and then he should consider that, after all, he wishes his opinions to coincide with the fact . . . (5.387).

RR: . . . I think that the very idea of a "fact of the matter" is one we would be better off without (PDP, p. 271).

CSP: . . . he should consider that, after all, he wishes his opinions to coincide with the fact, and . . . there is no reason why the results of those . . . [other] methods should do so (5.387, continued).

RR: "True sentences work because they correspond to the way things are" . . . [is an] empty metaphysical compliment, . . . [a] rhetorical pat on the back. . . . [The pragmatist] drops the notion of truth as correspondence with reality altogether (CP, p. xvii).

CSP: Truth is the conformity of a representamen to its object, *its* object, ITS object, mind you (5.554).

[However,] that truth is the correspondence of a representation to its object is, as Kant says, merely the nominal definition of it. Truth belongs exclusively to propositions. A proposition has a subject (or set of subjects) and a predicate. The subject is a sign; the predicate is a sign; and the proposition is a sign that the predicate is a sign of that of which the subject is a sign. If it be so, it is true. But what does this correspondence . . . of the sign to its object consist in? The pragmaticist answers this question as follows. . . . If we can find out the right method of thinking and can follow it out . . . then truth can be nothing more nor less than the last result to which the following out of this method would ultimately carry us (5.553).

RR: There are . . . two senses apiece of 'true' and 'real' and 'correct representation of reality,' . . . the homely use of 'true' to mean roughly 'what you can defend against all comers,' . . . [the] homely and shopworn sense [and] the specifically 'philosophical' sense . . . which, like the Ideas of Pure Reason, [is] designed precisely to stand for the Unconditioned (PMN, pp. 308–9.)

CSP: That to which the representation should conform, is itself . . . utterly unlike a thing-in-itself (5.553).

RR: A pragmatist theory . . . says that Truth is not the sort of thing one should expect to have a philosophically interesting theory about . . . (CP, p. xiii). Pragmatists think that the history of attempts to . . . define the word "true" . . . supports their suspicion that there is no interesting work to be done in this area (p. xiv).

CSP: Truth is that concordance of an abstract statement with the ideal limit towards which endless investigation would tend to bring scientific belief. . . . The truth of the proposition that Caesar crossed the Rubicon consists in the fact that the further we push our archaeological and other studies, the more strongly will that conclusion force itself on our minds forever—or would do so, if study were to go on forever. . . . The same definitions equally hold in the normative sciences (5.565–66).

RR: I do not think . . . that [your account] is defensible . . . [It] uses a term—'ideal'—which is just as fishy as 'corresponds' (PDT, pp. 337, 338).

CSP: A false proposition is a proposition of which some interpretant represents that, on an occasion which it indicates, a percept will have a certain character, while the immediate perceptual judgment on that occasion is that the percept has not that character. A true proposition is a proposition belief in which would never lead to such disappointment so long as the proposition is not understood otherwise than it was intended (5.569).

Prof. Royce [like you] seems to think that this doctrine is unsatisfactory because it talks about what would be. . . . It may be he is right in this criticism; yet to our apprehension this "would be" is readily resolved . . . (8.113). [The] most important reals have the mode of being of what the nominalist calls "mere" words, that is, general types and would-bes. [His] "mere" reveals a complete misunderstanding . . . (8.191). The *will be's*, the actually *is's*, and the *have beens* are not the sum of the reals. . . . There are besides *would be's* and *can be's* that are real (8.216).

SH: I suspect, Professor Rorty, that your sympathies lie with the nominalist . . .

RR: Nominalists like myself—those for whom language is a tool rather than a medium, and for whom a concept is just the regular use of a mark or noise . . . see language as just human beings using marks and noises to get what they want (EHO, pp. 126–27).

The right idea, according to us nominalists, is that "recognition of meaning" is simply ability to substitute sensible signs . . . for other signs, . . . and so on indefinitely. This . . . doctrine is found . . . in [your writings] (TMoL, p. 211).

CSP: The nominalistic *Weltanschauung* has become incorporated into what I will venture to call the very flesh and blood of the average modern mind (5.61). Modern nominalists are mostly superficial men (5.312).

[A] realist is simply one who knows no more recondite reality than that which is represented in a true representation (5.312, continued). I am myself a scholastic realist of a somewhat extreme stripe (5.470). Nomenclature involves classification; and classification is true or false, and the generals to which it refers are either reals in the one case, or figments in the other (5.453).

Pragmaticism could hardly have entered a head that was not already convinced that there are real generals (5.503).

SH: I wonder how Professor Rorty feels about your references to "true representations" . . .

RR: Pragmatism [is] anti-representationalism (PPD, p. 1).

CSP: REPRESENT: to stand for, that is, to be in such a relation to another that for certain purposes it is treated by some mind as if it were that other. . . . When it is desired to distinguish between that which represents and the . . . relation of representing, the former may be termed the "representamen," the latter the "representation" (2.273).

A sign, or *representamen*, is something which stands to somebody for something in some respect or capacity. It . . . creates in the mind of that person an equivalent sign, or perhaps a more developed sign. That sign which it creates I call the *interpretant* of the first sign. The sign stands for something, its *object* . . . in reference to a sort of idea, which I have sometimes called the *ground* of the representamen (2.228).

RR: The notion of "accurate representation" is simply an . . . empty compliment which we pay to those beliefs which are successful in helping us do what we want to do (PMN, p. 10).

CSP: It is as though a man should address a land surveyor as follows: "You do not make a true representation of the land; you only measure lengths from point to point . . . you have to do solely with lines. But the land is a surface. . . . You, therefore, fail entirely to represent the land." The surveyor, I think, would reply, "Sir, you have proved that . . . my map *is not* the land. I never pretended that it was. But that does not prevent it from truly representing the land, as far as it goes" (5.329).

SH: I am beginning to think that you may disagree with each other not only about nominalism, but about the nature and status of metaphysics . . .

RR: The pragmatist . . . does not think of himself as *any* kind of a metaphysician (CP, p. xxviii).

CSP: [The Pragmatic Maxim] will serve to show that almost every proposition of ontological metaphysics is either meaningless gibberish—one word being defined by other words, and they by still others, without any real conception ever being reached—or else is downright absurd; so that all such rubbish being swept away, what will remain of philosophy will be a series of problems capable of investigation by the observational methods of the true sciences. . . . So, instead of merely jeering at metaphysics . . . the pragmaticist extracts from it a precious essence (5.423).

We should expect to find metaphysics . . . to be somewhat more difficult than logic, but still on the whole one of the simplest of sciences, as it is one whose main principles must be settled before very much progress can be gained either in psychics or in physics. Historically we are astonished to find that it has been a mere arena of ceaseless and trivial disputation. But we also find that it has been pursued in a spirit the very contrary of that of wishing to learn the truth, which is the most essential requirement. . . . *Metaphysics* is the proper designation for the third, and completing department of coenoscopy. . . . Its business is to study the most general features of reality and real objects. But in its present condition it is . . . a puny, rickety and scrofulous science. It is only too plain that those who pretend to cultivate it carry not the hearts of true men of science within their breast (6.4–6).

Here let us set down almost at random a small specimen of the questions of metaphysics which press . . . for industrious and solid investigation: Whether or no there be any real indefiniteness, or real possibility and impossibility? Whether there be any strictly individual existence? Whether there is any distinction . . . between fact and fancy? Or between the external and the internal worlds? What general . . . account can be given of the different qualities of feeling . . . ? Do all possible qualities of sensation . . . form one continuous system . . . ? . . . Is Time a real thing . . . ? How about Space . . . ? . . . Is hylozoism an opinion, actual or conceivable, rather than a senseless vocable . . . ? . . . What is consciousness or mind like . . . ? (6.6).

RR: Metaphysicians see [books] as divided according to disciplines, corresponding to different objects of knowledge. [We] ironists see them as divided according to traditions (CIS, pp. 75–76).

CSP: All science is either, A. Science of Discovery; B. Science of Review; or C. Practical Science. . . . Science of Discovery is either, I. Mathematics; II. Philosophy; or III. Idioscopy. . . . Philosophy is divided into *a*. Phenomenology; *b*. Normative Science; *c*. Metaphysics. . . . Phenomenology is . . . a single study. Normative Science has three widely separated divisions: i. Esthetics; ii. Ethics. iii. Logic. . . . Metaphysics may be divided into, i, General Metaphysics, or Ontology; ii, Psychical, or Religious, Metaphysics, concerned chiefly with the questions of 1, God, 2, Freedom, 3, Immortality; and iii, Physical Metaphysics, which discusses the real nature of time, space, laws of nature, matter, etc. (1.181–92).

RR: [You really are just] one more whacked-out triadomaniac . . . (PP, p. 93)

SH: Professor Rorty, *please!* Perhaps you would be so kind as to explain your reference to "ironists" . . . ?

RR: [Ironists] take naturally to the line of thought developed in . . . [my] book. . . . The opposite of irony is common sense. (CIS, p. 74).

CSP: Pragmaticism will be sure to carry critical common-sensism in its arms (5.499).

RR: Sentences like . . . "Truth is independent of the human mind" are simply platitudes used to inculcate . . . the common sense of the West (CIS, pp. 76–77).

CSP: The Critical Common-sensist holds that all the veritably indubitable beliefs are *vague* . . . (5.505); [that they] refer to a somewhat primitive mode of life . . . (5.511); [he] has a high esteem for doubt (5.514); [he] criticizes the critical method (5.523).

RR: [We ironists emphasize] the spirit of playfulness . . . (CIS, p. 39). [We are] never quite able to take [our]selves seriously (p. 73).

CSP: [The Critical Common-sensist] is none of those overcultivated Oxford dons—I hope their day is over—whom any discovery that brought quietus to a vexed question would evidently vex because it would end the fun of arguing around it and about it and over it (5.520).

RR: . . . I have spent forty years looking for a coherent . . . way of formulating my worries about what, if anything, philosophy is good for (TWO, p. 146).

CSP: It is true that philosophy is in a lamentably crude condition at present; . . . most philosophers set up a pretension of knowing all there is to know—a pretension calculated to disgust anybody who is at home in any real science. But all we have to do is to turn our backs upon all such truly vicious conduct, and we shall find ourselves enjoying the advantages of having an almost virgin soil to till, where a given amount of really scientific work will bring in an extraordinary harvest . . . of very fundamental truth of exceptional value from every point of view (1.128).

SH: How do you feel about Mr Peirce's description of philosophy as "scientific work," Professor Rorty?

RR: [One] side of pragmatism has been scientific. . . . Let me call the claim that there is [a] "reliable [scientific] method" "scientism." . . . If one takes the core of pragmatism to be its attempt to replace the notion of true beliefs as representations . . . and instead to think of them as successful rules for action, then it becomes . . . hard to isolate a "method" that will embody this attitude (PWM, pp. 260–62).

CSP: It is far better to let philosophy follow perfectly untrammeled a scientific method. . . . If that course be honestly and scrupulously carried out, the results reached, even if they be not altogether true, even if they be grossly mistaken, can not but be highly serviceable for the ultimate discovery of truth (1.644). [R]ational methods of inquiry . . . will make that result as speedy as possible (7.78).

The first problems to suggest themselves to the inquirer into nature are far too complex . . . for any early solution. . . . What ought to be done, therefore, . . . is at first to substitute for those problems others much . . . more abstract. . . . The reasonably certain solutions of these last problems will throw a light . . . upon more concrete problems. . . . This method of procedure is that Analytic Method to which modern physics owes all its triumphs. It has been applied with great success in psychical sciences also. . . . It is reprobated by the whole Hegelian army, who think it ought to be replaced by the "Historic Method," which studies complex problems in all their complexity, but which cannot boast any distinguished successes.

There are in science three fundamentally different kinds of reasoning, Deduction, . . . Induction, . . . and Retroduction . . . Analogy combines the characters of Induction and Retroduction (1.63–66).

SH: Do you share Mr Peirce's high regard for logic, Professor Rorty?

RR: [R]igorous argumentation . . . is no more *generally* desirable than blocking the road of inquiry is generally desirable (CP, p. xli).

CSP: There are two qualifications which every true man of science possesses. . . . First, the dominant passion of his whole soul must be to find out the truth in some department. . . . Secondly, he must have a natural gift for reasoning, for severely critical thought (7.605). Logic is the theory of *right* reasoning, of what reasoning ought to be (2.7).

RR: We no longer think of ourselves as having reliable "sources" of knowledge called "reason" or "sensation" (OE, p. 531).

CSP: The data from which inference sets out and upon which all reasoning depends are the *perceptual facts,* which are the intellect's fallible record of the *percepts,* or "evidence of the senses" (2.143).

RR: Eventually I got over [my] worry about circular argumentation by deciding that the test of philosophical truth was overall coherence, rather than deducibility from unquestioned first principles. But this didn't help much (TWO, p. 145).

CSP: The reader will, I trust, be too well grounded in logic to mistake . . . mutual support for a vicious circle in reasoning (6.315).

    Philosophy ought . . . to trust . . . to the multitude and variety of its arguments. . . . Its reasoning should not form a chain which is no stronger than the weakest link, but a cable whose fibers may be ever so slender, provided they are sufficiently numerous and intimately connected (5.265).

RR: But [as I said] this didn't help much. For coherence is a matter of avoiding contradictions, and St Thomas' advice, "When you meet a contradiction, make a distinction," makes that pretty easy (TWO, p. 145).

SH: How do you feel about Professor Rorty's observation that making distinctions is "pretty easy," Mr Peirce?

CSP: . . . Kant's conception of the nature of necessary reasoning is clearly shown by the logic of relations to be utterly mistaken, and his distinction between analytic and synthetic judgments, . . . which is based on that conception, is so utterly confused that it is difficult or impossible to do anything with it (5.176).

SH: Perhaps, while we are on the subject of logic, you could explain your attitude to the principle of bivalence . . .

RR: The pragmatist . . . should not succumb to the temptation to . . . take sides on the issue of "bivalence" (CP, p. xxvi).

CSP: Triadic logic is universally true (*Logic Notebook* for 1909).

SH: Perhaps, Professor Rorty, it would be helpful if you would explain how you see the relation of philosophy to science . . .

RR: The pragmatist is betting that what succeeds the "scientific," positivist culture which the Enlightenment produced will be *better* (CP, p. xxxviii). Science as the source of "truth" . . . is one of the Cartesian notions which vanish when the ideal of "philosophy as strict science" vanishes (p. 34). Pragmatism . . . views science as one genre of literature—or, put the other way around, literature and the arts as inquiries, on the same footing as scientific inquiries (p. xliii). Philosophy is best seen as a kind of writing. It is delimited, as is any literary genre, not by form or matter, but by tradition. . . . Philosophy as more than a kind of writing—is an illusion. . . . [One] tradition takes scientific truth as the center of philosophical concern (and scorns the notion of incommensurable scientific world-pictures). It asks how well other fields of inquiry conform to the model of science. The second [pragmatist] tradition takes science as one (not especially privileged nor interesting) sector of culture, a sector which . . . only makes sense when viewed historically (pp. 92–93). Literature has now displaced religion, science, and philosophy as the presiding discipline of our culture (p. 155).

SH: Mr Peirce?

CSP: [I] desire to rescue the good ship Philosophy for the service of Science from the hands of lawless rovers of the sea of literature . . . (5.449).

RR: A few [lovably old-fashioned prigs] will even claim to write in a clear, precise, transparent way, priding themselves on manly straightforwardness, on abjuring "literary" devices (EHO, p. 86).

CSP: As for that phrase "studying in a literary spirit" it is impossible to express how nauseating it is to any scientific man . . . (1.33).

RR: As soon as a program to put philosophy on the secure path of science succeeds, it simply converts philosophy into a boring academic specialty (PMN, pp. 384–85).

CSP: In order to be deep it is requisite to be dull. . . . The new pragmatists . . . are *lively* . . . (5.17). The apostle of Humanism [like you] says that professional philosophists "have rendered philosophy like unto themselves, abstruse, arid, abstract, and abhorrent." But I conceive that some branches of science are not in a healthy state if they are *not* abstruse, arid, and abstract, in which case, . . . it will be as Shakespeare said . . .
    "Not harsh and crabbèd, as dull fools suppose,
    But musical as is Apollo's lute," . . . (5.537).
The reader may find the matter [of my "Minute Logic"] so dry, husky and innutritious to the spirit that he cannot imagine that there is any human good in it. . . . But the fault is his. It shall not be more tedious than the multiplication table, . . . and as the multiplication table is worth the pains of learning, . . . so shall this be (2.15).

SH: Professor Rorty, your view of philosophy as a genre of literature puzzles me; surely pragmatism is a form of empiricism?

RR: Pragmatism has gradually broken the historical links that once connected it to empiricism (PPD, p. 4).

CSP: The kind of philosophy which interests me and must, I think, interest everybody is that philosophy, which uses the most rational methods it can devise, for finding out the little that can as yet be found out about the universe of mind and matter from those observations which every person can make in every hour of his waking life . . . laboratory-philosophy (1.126, 129).

RR: From the radically anti-representationalist viewpoint I . . . commend

. . . pragmatism can be seen as gradually . . . escaping from scientism (PPD, p. 4).

CSP: [Philosophical theories] have the same sort of basis as scientific results have. That is to say, they rest on experience—on the total everyday experience of many generations. . . . Such experience is worthless for distinctively scientific purposes . . . although all science . . . would have to shut up shop if she should manage to escape accepting them. No "wisdom" could ever have discovered argon; yet within its proper sphere, . . . the instinctive result of human experience ought to have so vastly more weight than any scientific result, that to make laboratory experiments to ascertain, for example, whether there be any uniformity in nature or no, would vie with adding a teaspoonful of saccharine to the ocean in order to sweeten it (5.522).

RR: The basic motive of pragmatism was . . . a continuation of the Romantic reaction to the Enlightenment's sanctification of natural science (EHO, p. 18).

CSP: [Science] embodies the epitome of man's intellectual development (7.49). Iconoclastic inventions are always cheap and often nasty (4.71).

SH: May we go back for a minute to Professor Rorty's reference to Romanticism?

RR: The Platonist and the positivist share a reductionist view of metaphor: They think metaphors are either paraphrasable or useless for the one serious purpose which language has, namely, representing reality. By contrast, the Romantic has an expansionist view. . . . Romantics attribute metaphor to a mysterious faculty called the "imagination," a faculty they suppose to be at the very center of the self (CIS, p. 19).

CSP: When a man desires ardently to know the truth, his first effort will be to imagine what that truth can be. . . . there is, after all, nothing but imagination that can ever supply him an inkling of the truth. . . . For thousands of men a falling apple was nothing but a falling apple; and to compare it to the moon would by them be deemed "fanciful." It is not too much to say that next after the passion to learn there is no quality so indispensable to the successful prosecution of science as imagination. . . . There are, no doubt, kinds of imagination of no value in science, mere artistic imagination, mere dreaming of opportunities for gain. The scientific imagination dreams of explanation and laws (1.46–48).

Cuvier said that Metaphysics is nothing but Metaphor. . . . If metaphor be taken literally to mean an expression of a similitude when the sign of predication is employed instead of the sign of likeness—as when we say this man *is* a fox instead of this man is like a fox,—I deny entirely that metaphysicians are given to metaphor . . . but if Cuvier was only using a metaphor himself, and meant by metaphor broad comparison on the ground of characters of a formal and highly abstract kind,—then, indeed, metaphysics professes to be metaphor (7.590).

RR: [A] philosopher . . . like myself . . . thinks of himself as auxiliary to the poet rather than to the physicist. . . . Interesting philosophy is . . . a contest between an entrenched vocabulary which has become a nuisance and a half-formed new vocabulary which vaguely promises great things. (CIS, pp. 7–9).

SH: But I don't think Mr Peirce would deny the importance of linguistic innovation . . .

CSP: Every symbol is a living thing, . . . its meaning inevitably grows, incorporates new elements and throws off old ones. . . . Science is continually gaining new conceptions; and every new *scientific* conception should receive a new word. . . . Different systems of expression are often of the greatest advantage (2.222).

RR: It is a feature of . . . science that the vocabulary in which problems are posed is accepted by all those who count as contributing to the subject. The vocabulary may be changed, but that is only because a new theory has been discovered. . . . The vocabulary in which the *explicanda* are described has to remain constant (CP, pp. 141–42).

CSP: How much more the word *electricity* means now than it did in the days of Franklin; how much more the term planet means now than it did in the time [of] Hipparchus. These words have acquired information (7.587).

Symbols grow. . . . In use and in experience, [the] meaning [of a symbol] grows. Such words as *force, law, wealth, marriage,* bear for us very different meanings from those they bore to our barbarous ancestors (2.302).

SH: I gather, Professor Rorty, from your references to "irony" and "playfulness," that you disapprove of too solemn an attitude to philosophy as a profession . . .

RR: I would welcome a culture dominated by "the Rich Aesthete, the Manager and the Therapist" so long as *everybody* who wants to gets to be an aesthete . . . The ironic, playful intellectual is a desirable character-type (FMR, pp. 16, 15).

SH: Mr Peirce?

CSP: We remark three classes of men. The first consists of those for whom the chief thing is the qualities of feelings. These men create art. The second consists of the practical men . . . The third class consists of men to whom nothing seems great but reason. . . . Those are the natural scientific men (1.43).

It is infinitely better that men devoid of genuine scientific curiosity should not barricade the road of science with empty books and embarrassing assumptions (1.645).

RR: Intellectual gifts—intelligence, judgment, curiosity, imagination, . . . kinks in the brain . . . provide these gifts . . .(CIS, pp. 187–88).

CSP: There is a kink in my damned brain that prevents me from thinking as other people think.

RR: As we look about at the manly, aggressive and businesslike academics of our . . . time, . . . the well-funded professors, jetting home after a day spent advising men of power . . . [we see that the] American academic mind has long since discovered the joy of making its own special enterprise "greater and better organized and a mightier engine in the general life" (CP, p. 61).

CSP: Wherever there is a large class of academic professors who are provided with good incomes and looked up to as gentlemen, scientific inquiry must languish. Wherever the bureaucrats are the more learned class, the case will be still worse (1.51).

SH: And how do you see the relation of philosophy to society?

RR: Pragmatism must be defined as the claim that the function of inquiry is, in Bacon's words, to "relieve and benefit the condition of man" (EHO, p. 27).

CSP: A modern reader who is not in awe of [Bacon's] grandiloquence is chiefly struck by the inadequacy of his view of scientific procedure. . . . "He wrote on science like a Lord Chancellor," indeed, as Harvey, a genuine man of science said (5.361).

RR: Philosophy [is] *in the service* of democratic politics . . . (CIS, p. 196). We pragmatists commend our antiessentialism and antilogocentrism on the ground of its harmony with the practices and aims of a democratic society (EHO, p. 135).

CSP: I must confess that I belong to that class of scallawags who purpose, with God's help, to look the truth in the face, whether doing so be conducive to the interests of society or not. Moreover, if I should ever attack that excessively difficult problem, 'What is for the true interest of society?' I should feel that I stood in need of a great deal of help from the science of legitimate inference . . . (8.143). [A]gainst the doctrine that social stability is the sole justification of scientific research . . . I have to object, first, that it is historically false . . . ; second, that it is bad ethics;

and, third, that its propagation would retard the progress of science (8.135).

RR: [There have been in our century] three conceptions of the aim of philosophizing. They are the Husserlian (or 'scientistic') answer, the Heideggerian (or 'poetic') answer, and the pragmatist (or 'political') answer (EHO, p. 9).

CSP: In my opinion, the present infantile condition of philosophy . . . is due to the fact that . . . it has chiefly been pursued by men who have not . . . been animated by the true scientific *Eros;* but who have . . . been inflamed with a desire to amend the lives of themselves and others . . . (1.620). The two masters, *theory* and *practice,* you cannot serve (1.642).

SH: It seems to me that the two of you have radically different conceptions of what pragmatism is. . .

RR: "Pragmatism" is a vague, ambiguous and overworked word (CP, p. 160).

CSP: Many writers, . . . in spite of pragmatists' declarations, unanimous, reiterated, and most explicit, still remain unable to "catch on" to what we are driving at, and persist in twisting our purpose and purport all awry. . . . [Pragmatism] is merely a method of ascertaining the meanings of hard words and of abstract concepts (5.464).

RR: The pragmatist . . . must struggle with the positivist for the position of radical anti-Platonist. . . . At first glance he looks like just another variety of positivist. (CP, p. xvii).

CSP: Pragmaticism is a species of prope-positivism (5.423).

RR: My first characterization of pragmatism is that it is simply anti-essentialism applied to notions like "truth," "knowledge," "language," "morality," and similar objects of philosophical theorizing. . . . There is no wholesale, epistemological way to direct, or criticize, or underwrite, the course of inquiry (CP, p. 162). [A] second characterization of pragmatism might go like this: there is no epistemological difference between truth about what ought to be and truth about what is, nor any metaphysical difference between facts and values, nor any methodological difference between morality and science (p. 163). . . . The pragmatists tell us, it is the vocabulary of practice rather than of theory . . . in which one can say something useful about truth (p. 162). [A] third . . . characterization of pragmatism [is]: it is the doctrine that there are no constraints on inquiry save conversational ones. . . . The only sense in which we are constrained to truth is that, as [you] suggested, we can make no sense of the notion that the view which can survive all objections might be false.

But objections—conversational constraints—cannot be anticipated (p. 165).

CSP: To satisfy our doubts, . . . it is necessary that a method should be found by which our beliefs may be determined by nothing human, but by some external permanency—by something upon which our thinking has no effect. . . . It must be something which affects, or might affect, every man. . . . The method must be such that the ultimate conclusion of every man shall be the same. Such is the method of science (5.384).

RR: Once human desires are admitted into the criterion of "truth," . . . we have become pragmatists. The pragmatist's claim [is] that to know your desires is to know the criterion of truth (EHO, pp. 30–31).

CSP: It is necessary to note what is essentially involved in the Will to Learn. . . . I can excuse a person who has lost a dear companion and whose reason is in danger of giving way under the grief, for trying, on that account, to believe in a future life. . . . [But] I myself would not adopt a hypothesis . . . simply because the idea was pleasing to me. . . . That would be a crime against the integrity of . . . reason (5.583, 598).

RR: What I am calling "pragmatism" might also be called "left-wing Kuhnianism" (SS, p. 41).

CSP: An opinion which has of late years attained some vogue among men of science, [is] that we cannot expect any physical hypothesis to maintain its ground indefinitely even with modifications, but must expect that from time to time there will be a complete cataclysm that shall utterly sweep away old theories and replace them by new ones. As far as I know, this notion has no other basis than the history of science. Considering how very, very little science we have attained, and how infantile the history of science still is, it amazes me that anybody should propose to base a theory of knowledge upon the history of science alone. An emmet is far more competent to discourse upon the figure of the earth than we are to say what future millennia and millionennia may have in store for physical theories . . . The only really scientific theory that can be called old is the Ptolemaic system; and that has only been improved in details, not revolutionized (2.150).

RR: [Your] contribution to pragmatism was merely to have given it a name (CP, p. 161).

CSP: It has probably never happened that any philosopher has attempted to give a general name to his own doctrine without that name's soon acquiring in common philosophical usage, a signification much broader than was originally intended. . . . [My] word "pragmatism" . . . begins to be met with occasionally in the literary journals, where it gets abused in the merciless way that words have to expect when they fall into literary clutches. ... So, then, the writer, finding his bantling "pragmatism" so promoted, feels that it is time to kiss his child good-by and relinquish it to its higher destiny; while to serve the precise purpose of expressing the original definition, he begs to announce the birth of the word "pragmaticism," which is ugly enough to be safe from kidnappers (5.143–44).

It is good economy for philosophy to provide itself with a vocabulary so outlandish that loose thinkers shall not be tempted to borrow its words. ... Whoever deliberately uses a word ... in any other sense than that which was conferred upon it by its sole rightful creator commits a shameful offence against the inventor of the symbol and against science, and it becomes the duty of the others to treat the act with contempt and indignation (2.223–24).

RR: Revolutionary movements within an intellectual discipline require a revisionist history of that discipline (CP, p. 211).

CSP: It seems to me a pity [that the pragmatists of today] should allow a philosophy so instinct with life to become infected with seeds of death in such notions as that of ... the mutability of truth ... (6.485).

BIBLIOGRAPHY

Except where otherwise indicated, Peirce's contributions are taken from:

Collected Papers, ed. Charles Hartshorne, Paul Weiss, and Arthur Burks, Harvard University Press, Cambridge, A, 1931–58; references by volume and paragraph number.
Peirce's comment about the kink in his brain is reported by E. T. Bell in *The Development of Mathematics,* McGraw-Hill, New York and London, 1949, p. 519.
The quotation Peirce attributes to Shakespeare is actually from Milton's *Comus.*

Rorty's contributions to the conversation are taken from:

CIS: *Contingency, Irony, and Solidarity,* Cambridge University Press, Cambridge, 1989.
CP: *Consequences of Pragmatism,* Harvester, Hassocks, Sussex, 1982.
EHO: *Essays on Heidegger and Others,* Cambridge University Press, Cambridge, 1991.

FMR: "Freud and Moral Reflection," in J. H. Smith and W. Kerrigan, eds., *Pragmatism's Freud,* Johns Hopkins University Press, Baltimore and London, 1986, 1–27.

OE: "On Ethnocentrism: A Reply to Clifford Geertz," *Michigan Quarterly Review,* 25, 1986, 525–34.

ORT: *Objectivity, Relativism, and Truth,* Cambridge University Press, Cambridge, 1991.

PDP: "The Priority of Democracy to Philosophy," in Merrill D. Peterson and Robert C. Vaughn, eds., *The Virginia Statute for Religious Freedom,* Cambridge University Press, Cambridge, 1988, 257–82.

PDT: "Pragmatism, Davidson, and Truth," in E. Lepore, ed., *Truth and Interpretation: Perspectives on the Philosophy of Donald Davidson,* Blackwell, Oxford, 1986, 333–54.

PP: "The Pragmatist's Progress," in Stefan Collini, ed., *Interpretation and Overinterpretation,* Cambridge University Press, Cambridge, 1992, 89–108.

PPD: "Introduction" to J. P. Murphy, *Pragmatism from Peirce to Davidson,* Westview Press, Boulder, CO, 1990, 1–6.

PMN: *Philosophy and the Mirror of Nature,* Princeton University Press, Princeton, NJ, 1979.

PWM: "Pragmatism without Method," in Paul Kurtz, ed., *Sidney Hook: Philosopher of Democracy and Humanism,* Prometheus Books, Buffalo, NY, 1938, 259–74.

SS: "Science as Solidarity," in John S. Nelson, Allan Megill, and Donald M. McCloskey, eds., *The Rhetoric of the Human Sciences,* University of Wisconsin Press, Madison, WI, 1987, 38–52.

TMoL: "Two Meanings of 'Logocentrism,'" in Reed Way Dasenbrock, ed., *Redrawing the Lines: Analytic Philosophy, Deconstruction, and Literary Theory,* Minnesota University Press, Minneapolis, MN, 1989, 204–16.

TWO: "Trotsky and the Wild Orchids," *Common Knowledge,* 1.3, 1992, 140–53.

THREE

As for that phrase "studying in a literary spirit" . . .

Peirce aspires, he tells us, to "rescue the good ship Philosophy for the service of Science from the hands of lawless rovers of the sea of literature" (5.449).[1] "As for that phrase 'studying in a literary spirit,'" he writes, "there is nothing more nauseating to a scientific man" (1.33).

Those who, like myself, feel a little queasy when Rorty tells them that "philosophy is delimited, as is any literary genre, . . . by tradition," and that "philosophy as more than a kind of writing—is an illusion,"[2] will probably find Peirce's curmudgeonliness refreshing.

Still, for all their curmudgeonly charm, Peirce's observations might well give the impression that he is as scientistic and as denigratory of literature as Rorty is dilettantish[3] and denigratory of science. One purpose of this essay is to show that this impression is false on both counts: Peirce's conception of the relation of philosophy to the natural sciences is complex and subtle, naturalistic but not at all scientistic; and his harsh words about "studying in a literary spirit" are no indication of any hostility to literature, nor to the study of literature.

But my ultimate purpose is not exegetical but philosophical. Of late, two contrasting departures from the analytical mainstream—both, ironically enough, described by their protagonists as "pragmatism"—have become fashionable: the displacement of philosophy by the natural sciences epitomized by the Churchlands' theme of "neurophilosophy," and the displacement of philosophy by the literary epitomized by Rorty's theme of philosophy as "just a kind of writing." Both are disastrous. My goal is, with Peirce's help, to articulate a conception of what philosophy is and does which allows a more robustly plausible account of the relation of philosophy to the sciences, and of its relation to literature, than either.

PEIRCE'S ASPIRATION to "rescue the good ship Philosophy for the service of science" should not be taken as suggesting that philosophy is parasitic on, or that it could be replaced by, the natural sciences. The point is, rather, that philosophy should become scientific. And this means not only that it should use the method of science, but also, even more importantly, that it should be undertaken with "the scientific attitude."

"Scientific," here, needs careful handling; neither the scientific attitude nor the scientific method, as Peirce conceives them, is the exclusive prerogative of scientists, in the ordinary sense in which that term includes, inter alia, physicists and chemists, and excludes, inter alia, detectives, investigative journalists, historians—and philosophers. Part of the point of Peirce's insistence that philosophy should become scientific is, precisely, that there is an attitude of mind and a method of inquiry, manifested, not invariably or exclusively, but primarily, by natural scientists, which *all* inquirers can and should adopt. Peirce's observation that science "embodies the epitome of man's intellectual development" must be read in the light of passages like: "[science] does not so much consist in *knowing,* not even in 'organized knowledge,' as it does in diligent inquiry into truth for truth's sake, without any sort of axe to grind, . . . from an impulse to penetrate into the reason of things" (7.49, 1.44).

Peirce also describes the scientific attitude as "a craving to know how things really are" (1.34); the "passion to learn" (1.47); "an intense desire to find things out" (1.14); "a great desire to learn the truth" (1.235); the "Will to Learn" (5.583). In more prosaic words, it is the attitude of disinterested truth-seeking. This is the attitude, Peirce believes, that has made the natural sciences possible; and philosophy should be conducted in the same spirit. It should be *genuine, disinterested* truth-seeking, a good-faith effort to discover the truth of some question ("whatever the color of that truth may be," 7.605).

As "without any sort of axe to grind" prefigures, Peirce contrasts the scientific attitude with "sham reasoning," meaning efforts to make a case for some proposition one's commitment to which is already evidence- and argument-proof. And he complains that when, as in his day, philosophy is largely in the hands of theologians, sham reasoning—in the form of elaborate attempts to devise metaphysical systems to support theological principles which nothing would induce the reasoner to give up—is only to be expected. Hence his contrast of "laboratory" with "seminary" philosophy: "In my opinion the present infantile condition of philosophy . . . is due to the fact that in this century it has chiefly been pursued by men who have not been nurtured in dissecting rooms and other laboratories, and who consequently have not been animated by the true scientific *Eros;* but who have on the contrary come from theological seminaries, . . . radically unsuiting them for the task of scientific investigation" (1.620); "[metaphysics] has been pursued in a spirit the very contrary of that of wishing to learn the truth" (6.5). And hence, also, his wry comment that "it will sometimes strike a scientific man that the philosophers have been less intent on finding out . . . , than on inquiring what belief is most in harmony with their system" (5.406).

The "scientific man" needs, not only a genuine desire to discover the truth, but also a "well-considered method" for finding it out (1.235). Scientific philosophy will use the method of science, of experience and reasoning. Peirce contrasts the scientific method with the a priori method; and his insistence that the method of science should also be the method of philosophy is intimately connected with a conception of philosophical theories as, not wholly conceptual, but partly experiential. This is intimately connected, in turn, with the theses that the meanings of our words grow as our knowledge grows, and that the analytic cannot be identified with the trivially verbal.

"Experiential" requires no less careful handling than "scientific." Peirce sometimes distinguishes the various sciences by reference to the kinds of special apparatus on which they rely for obtaining observations—from the microscope to the questionnaire; and, in line with this, he describes what is distinctive about philosophical inquiry in terms of the kinds of observation on which *it* relies: not, like physics or chemistry or psychology, on recherché observations which it requires special apparatus to contrive, but on features of our ordinary, everyday experience so commonplace that the difficulty is to become distinctly aware of them. Contrasting laboratory and seminary philosophies, he writes that "the kind of philosophy which interests me and must, I think, interest everybody, is that philosophy which uses the most rational methods it can devise for finding out the little that can as yet be found out about the universe of mind and matter *from those observations which every person can make in every hour of his waking life*" (1.126, my italics). And again: ". . . by philosophy I mean that department of Positive Science . . . which does not busy itself with getting facts, but merely with *learning what can be learned from that experience which presses in upon every one of us hourly and daily*" (5.120, my italics). Hence his interest in phenomenology, or "phaneroscopy."

Another important aspect of Peirce's conception of the method of science is his stress on its being the work of a community of inquirers, within and across generations. Thus, he observes how, in contrast to "the present state of [philosophy]," in the natural sciences "investigators, instead of contemning each the work of most of the others as misdirected from beginning to end, cooperate, stand upon one another's shoulders . . ." (5.413).

Now it is time to articulate what Peirce does *not* mean when he urges that philosophy become scientific.

First, though pragmat[ic]ism is, as Peirce puts it, a form of prope-positivism, it is not, like Logical Positivism, anti-philosophical. "Ontological metaphysics," as Peirce dubs the bad, unscientific, kind, he regards as "gibberish," devoid of pragmatic meaning.[4] But far from suggesting that philosophy should be abandoned in favor of the natural sciences, he also envisages a good, scientific, kind of metaphysics. "Instead of merely jeering at metaphysics, the pragmatist extracts from it a precious essence" (5.423); and this scientific metaphysics, Peirce anticipates, will "bring in an extraordinary harvest . . . of very fundamental truth" (1.128).

Second, the scientific philosophy Peirce envisages will retain its distinctness from the natural sciences. Philosophy requires, not the specialized, contrived experience on which the natural sciences depend, but attention to "the total everyday experience of many generations." And far from suggesting that philosophical problems could be handed over to the natural sciences to resolve, Peirce expressly comments on the absurdity of the idea: "to make laboratory experiments to ascertain, for example, whether there be any uniformity in nature or no, would vie with adding a teaspoonful of saccharine to the ocean in order to sweeten it" (5.522). The last point is important when considering whether Peirce's own metaphysical work is itself of the good, scientific kind; as is his picture of philosophical arguments as, not a chain, but a cable of mutually reinforcing threads, and the reconception of the analytic/synthetic distinction motivated by his thesis that meaning grows as our knowledge grows. To look for the laboratory experiment that would constitute the crucial test of agapism, synechism, or tychism, say, would be to misunderstand what Peirce means by "scientific metaphysics." Better to look to the phaneroscopic considerations he advances that his categories, firstness, secondness, thirdness, everywhere infuse our everyday experience, or to his account of perception as at once direct and interpretive.

Peirce's "extreme scholastic realism," the thesis that there are real generals, i.e., laws and natural kinds independent of how you or I or anybody thinks them to be, provides another instructive example. That theatrical business with the stone is not intended as a direct experimental test of scholastic realism. Peirce's point is rather that if his audience believes (as of course they do) that they can predict what will happen when he lets go of the stone, then they accept that there are real generals. For otherwise they could have no grounds to expect this stone to behave now as other stones have done; prediction, induction, explanation, science itself would be impossible. It is in this characteristically oblique connection to our everyday experience that we *are* sometimes able to predict—as well as in its characteristic insistence that *which* generals are real cannot be read off our language, but must be investigated by the sciences—that Peirce's scholastic realism redeems its claim to be scientific.

The fundamental ideas behind Peirce's conception of a reformed, scientific philosophy are really startlingly simple: first, that philosophy is a kind of inquiry, of truth-seeking; a kind of inquiry, second, that depends, albeit partially and obliquely, on experience; not, however, third, on the recherché, contrived sorts of experience needed by the natural sciences, but on close attention to the character of everyday experience. It is the first of these, as will shortly become clear, that informs his unkind remarks about "studying in a literary spirit."

WHEN PEIRCE URGES that philosophy be kept out of the hands of the "lawless rovers of the sea of literature," there are two main themes at work, both apparent in this characteristic passage:

> [The] scientific spirit has been . . . misunderstood as it is found in the schoolmen. They have been . . . found fault with because they do not write a literary style and do not "study in a literary spirit." The men who make this objection cannot possibly comprehend the real merits of modern science. If the words *quidditas, entitas,* and *haecceitas* are to excite our disgust, what shall we say of the Latin of the botanists, and the style of any technically scientific work? As for that phrase, "studying in a literary spirit" it is impossible to say how nauseating it is to any scientific man, yes even the scientific linguist. (1.33)

Now "the scientific spirit" is being contrasted with "the literary spirit." The schoolmen "remind us less of the philosophers of our own day than of the men of science," Peirce had observed just before, on account of their respect for authority, and, he continues shortly afterwards, on account of their willingness to submit their theories to searching test. The rest of the passage indicates the second theme: "studying in a literary spirit" induces the wrong attitude to philosophical terminology.

Thus far, it is clear only that the contrast between the scientific attitude and the literary spirit is different from the more familiar contrast between the scientific attitude and sham reasoning. A second passage gives the best clue to what Peirce has in mind:

> Among *dilettanti* it is not rare to find those who have so perverted thought to the purposes of pleasure that it seems to vex them to think that the questions upon which they delight to exercise it may ever get finally settled; and a positive discovery which takes a favorite subject out of the arena of literary debate is met with ill-concealed dislike. This disposition is the very debauchery of thought. (5.396)

"Studying in a literary spirit" contrasts with the scientific attitude not because, as with sham reasoning, the answer is determined in advance, but because no answer is really desired. The purpose is, rather, to enjoy the exercise of cleverness, and, above all, to write a pleasing paper. "Studying in a literary spirit," as Peirce conceives it, is one form of what I call "fake reasoning";[5] unlike sham reasoning, of which the characteristic feature is the "reasoner's" prior and unbudgeable *commitment* to the propositions for which he seeks to make a case, its characteristic feature is the "reasoner's" *indifference* to the truth-value of the propositions he propounds.

It is clear enough why Peirce associates sham reasoning with doing philosophy from a theological perspective; the theologian has, so to speak, a professional commitment to the truth of certain propositions which puts him in the frame of mind characteristic of the sham reasoner. But it may not be so clear why Peirce associates another kind of pseudo-inquiry, fake reasoning, with "studying in a literary spirit." Part of the explanation, presumably, is his low opinion of the literary journals of his time, as filled with elegant but pointless debate. But, as is clear from his accusing certain "overcultivated Oxford dons" of the same dilettantish attitude (5.520), Peirce doesn't think fake inquiry is the exclusive prerogative of literary types, any more than he thinks genuine inquiry is the exclusive prerogative of "scientific men." Less superficially sociological is the thought that "studying in a literary spirit" ("studying in a belletrist spirit" might have been a better choice of words) implies a preoccupation with what is aesthetically pleasing that diverts attention from inquiry and pulls against what ought to be the highest priorities of philosophical writing: not elegance, euphony, allusion, suggestiveness, but clarity, precision, explicitness, directness.

This begins to bring into focus the second theme of Peirce's objections to "the literary spirit" in philosophy, its conflict with the ethics of terminology. Since all thought is in signs, Peirce writes, thinking well and using good terminology are scarcely distinguishable; and so "it is wrong to say that a good language is *important* to good thought, merely; for it is of the essence of it"; the more so, he continues, as inquiry advances. And since scientific inquiry must unavoidably be the work of many, within and across generations, communication, and hence *agreement* in terminology, is vital. But it won't do to impose terminological agreement by sheer authority, for "the health of the scientific community requires the most absolute mental freedom," while "the scientific and philosophical worlds are infested with pedants . . . endeavoring to set up a sort of magistrature over thoughts and other symbols." What is needed is principles of good terminological practice that will bring about agreement "by the power of rational principles over the conduct of men" (2.220).

The first "rational princip!e" Peirce proposes is that every branch of science should have a vocabulary of cognate words for each conception, each word to have "a single exact meaning"; this, he adds, should not be taken to call for absolute fixity (which would be to forget that symbols are "living things," constantly taking on and putting off meaning), but for keeping "the *essence*" of the term the same. Though each term should have one meaning, he goes on, it can be an advantage to have more than one system of expression for the same conceptions. The person responsible for introducing a new idea has the duty and the privilege of introducing a suitable term for it; and those who follow have a duty not to use his term in another sense (2.222–23).

The case of philosophy is peculiar, according to Peirce, since alone among the sciences it actually needs "a body of words of vague significations with which to identify those vague ideas of ordinary life which it is its business to analyze. . . . In no other science is there a scientific need of terms whose meanings are required to be vague." This doesn't mean, however, that philosophy has no need of a precise, technical, vocabulary; it needs that too, for its the chief task, in its present stage, is to express the meanings of its vague vocabulary in terms of a precise technical terminology (MS 280).

No doubt choosing the literary-sounding phrase deliberately, Peirce writes that "*the first rule of good taste in writing* is to use words whose meanings will not be misunderstood; and if a reader does not know the meaning of the words, it is infinitely better that he should know he does not know it." Hence his insistence that ugliness in philosophical terminology is positively a good thing, that "vocables [which] have no . . . sweetness or charm [to] tempt loose writers to abuse them" are actually to be preferred (2.223, my italics). Philosophers' "submission to that ordinary rule of rhetoric that forbids departure from polite usage, as if it were not exempt from its application, is . . . in *the worst of bad taste*" (MS 280, my italics).

Of the many illustrations of Peirce's ethics of terminology to be found in his writings,[6] I shall mention three, all of which also illustrate his attitude to "studying in a literary spirit." The first is his neologism, "pragmaticism." The new term is cognate with "pragmatism," but the "ic" indicates its narrower sense; and, famously, Peirce hopes aloud that it is "ugly enough to be safe from kidnappers." The context in which it is introduced reveals that Peirce's purpose is not (as is often supposed) to distinguish his style of pragmatism from James's, or even from Schiller's; rather:

> At present, the word ["pragmatism"] begins to be met with occasionally in the literary journals, where it gets abused in the merciless way that words have to expect when they fall into literary clutches. . . . So, then, the writer, finding his bantling "pragmatism" so promoted, feels it is time to kiss his child good-by . . . while, to serve the purpose of expressing the original definition, he begs to announce the birth of the word "pragmaticism," which is ugly enough to be safe from kidnappers. (5.414)

The second is Peirce's distinction of "precission" versus "precision," "preciss" versus "precise," etc., which illustrates how different but related conceptions are to be represented by distinct but cognate words; and which is introduced as follows:

> If we desire to rescue the good ship Philosophy for the service of Science from the hands of lawless rovers of the sea of literature, we shall do well to keep prescind, preciss, precission and precissive on the one hand, to refer to dissection in hypothesis, while precide, precise, precision and precisive are used so as to refer exclusively to an expression of determination which is made either full or free for the interpreter. (5.449)

The third (already encountered earlier) is Peirce's defense of the scholastic terminology of *quidditas, haecceitas*, etc., which, if it does not go quite so far as to claim that the ugliness of these terms is a good thing, makes it clear that it is no serious objection to them, and derides the "literary spirit" of those who think it is.

Peirce's realism, which he traces back to those schoolmen whose jargon he is defending and whose scientific spirit he commends, is, again, an instructive example. In the review of Fraser's edition of the works of Berkeley in which he first declares for realism, Peirce argues that the key difference is that nominalists and realists *have different conceptions of the real* (8.12). His articulation of realism requires him to make a technical distinction of "real" versus "exists," and to press "general" into service as a noun. You might wonder why he doesn't introduce new terms—until you remember his observation that "real" is quite modern, a thirteenth-century word, and his proposal that, as modern botanical terminology goes back to Linnaeus, so modern philosophical terminology should go back to Scotus.

Now it is time to articulate what Peirce does *not* mean when he urges that philosophy be rescued from the "lawless rovers of the sea of literature."

I see no evidence that he means to denigrate the worth of literature. Recall: "Bad poetry is false, I grant; but nothing is truer than true poetry" (1.315). His barbs are reserved for "studying in a literary spirit," for the "lawless rovers" who infest the literary journals.[7] And his translation from Goethe's *Torquato Tasso*, and his commentary ("It is not a hankering after applause and success nor a regard for his interests which make the artist of genius work. It is solely hankering to give shape to the work of art that exists in his mind. The true poet does not versify because he will but because he must"),[8] suggest that, though he was, to be sure, "a scientific man," he was not without literary sensibility.[9]

It is sometimes supposed that only a literary conception of philosophy can truly acknowledge the importance of linguistic innovation, of metaphor, of imagination. Peirce would think this a misunderstanding both of science and of scientific philosophy. Far from denying the importance of linguistic or conceptual innovation, he insists upon it. The ethics of terminology, though it demands one sense for each term, does not require that sense to be absolutely fixed, which would be incompatible with the way symbols take on meaning as our knowledge grows. And Peirce sees those shifts of meaning, not as an obstacle to scientific inquiry, but as contributing to its progress (7.587).

Again, far from denigrating figurative language, Peirce regards metaphor as a significant source of conceptual innovation (2.222); and, noting that metaphysics "has been said contemptuously to be a fabric of metaphors," replies that "not only metaphysics, but logical and phaneroscopical concepts need to be clothed in such garments" (MS 283). I think of his metaphor of a cable of reasons, adapted from Reid, replacing the Cartesian metaphor of a chain; of his metaphor of the mind as a lake, of which the cognitive is only the thinnest surface; of the metaphor of inquirers as storming the fortress of knowledge, borrowed from Locke, to which Peirce adds the figure of later inquirers climbing on the corpses of those who have gone before.

And, far from denying the importance of imagination in scientific inquiry, philosophy included, Peirce insists upon it in the strongest terms: "when a man desires ardently to know the truth, his first effort will be to imagine what that truth can be. . . . It is not too much to say that next after the passion to learn there is no quality so indispensable to the successful prosecution of science as imagination." He goes on: "there are, no doubt, kinds of imagination of no value in science, mere artistic imagination, mere dreaming of opportunities for gain. The scientific man dreams of explanations and laws" (1.46–48). Here, implicitly, he makes a crucial distinction between the imaginative and the imaginary: for the laws of which the scientist dreams, if he is successful, are real.

The fundamental ideas behind Peirce's harsh words about "studying in a literary spirit" are as startlingly simple as the ideas behind his conception of a reformed, scientific philosophy: that philosophy should be bona fide inquiry, not fake reasoning; and that the highest priority in philosophical writing should be to communicate as clearly, precisely, directly, and explicitly as possible, which sometimes—specifically with respect to technical terminology—conflicts with literary priorities.

IT IS ALREADY CLEAR how the scientific philosophy to which Peirce aspires differs from the analytic paradigm: though it shares the analytic concern for clarity and rigor, it is neither to be purely conceptual nor to use the method of "what is agreeable to reason."[10] Looking back at that last sentence, though, I will add that "analytic philosophy" refers to a complex congeries of ideas differing in important ways among themselves, and that a Peircean critical common-sensism could add a new dimension to Austin's observation that ordinary language embodies the wisdom of generations.

It is equally clear how Peircean naturalism differs from the revolutionary scientism of those who, like the Churchlands (and Quine some of the time), would replace philosophical inquiries by natural-scientific projects, as well as from the reformist scientism of those who, like Goldman (and Quine some of the time), propose to hand over philosophical problems to the natural sciences to answer.[11]

But a suspicion may linger that Peirce is not innocent of another kind of scientism, that his stress on the need for technical terminology, not to mention his Dismal Dictum, "in order to be deep it is necessary to be dull"

(5.17), suggests that kind of philosophical aping of the manner of the natural sciences which mistakes technicality for rigor[12]—a fault of which contemporary analytic philosophy has sometimes, not without some justice, been accused.

A brisk way with this objection would be to point out that Peirce does not say that in order to be deep it is necessary *always* to be dull, let alone that in order to be deep it is *sufficient* to be dull; and to wonder aloud whether those whose hackles rise at the sight of technical terminology may not be guilty of mistaking woolliness for profundity. But a better response requires a short detour, back to Peirce's remarks about the social character of scientific inquiry and his anticipation of a time when philosophers, also, will "cooperate, and stand on one another's shoulders." That, too, read unsympathetically and in isolation, might convey the impression of a kind of scientism, the kind that would have philosophers ape the organization of the research team in physics or cellular biology. But now listen to Peirce on the subject of "the German method in philosophy," which "puts great stress upon cooperation and solidarity in research even in the early stages of a branch of science, when independence of thought is the wholesome attitude, and gregarious thought is really sure to be wrong" (3.425). His point, evidently, is that though the hope is that eventually philosophy will reach a stage where genuinely cooperative work is possible and desirable, it is not yet at that stage, and, until it is, cooperative work is a sort of sham, and positively a hindrance to inquiry. And so, too, with technical terminology in philosophy, which is desirable when expressing genuinely well-thought-out concepts and distinctions, but otherwise an undesirable sham.

This puts one in mind of Bacon's choosing to present his *New Organon* as a series of aphorisms rather than a systematic treatise, precisely as a way of emphasizing its exploratory, provisional character: a choice of which, in view of his comments on "the German method in philosophy," Peirce could, and should, entirely have approved.

As factitious sociality is a kind of disguised collusion in mutual promotion, so pseudo-precision is a kind of affected obscurity.[13] And the two points are connected in a second way also. Success in presentation is of course audience-relative; and Peirce's ideas about the style of writing appropriate to scientific philosophy are most plausible if understood as concerning the best style of presentation to one's fellow inquirers, to other "scientific men."

As these reflections allow me to articulate a Peircean conception of philosophy innocent of this subtle kind of scientism, they also supply a starting point for articulating a Peircean account of the relation of philosophy to literature: "Peircean," rather than "Peirce's," because from here on some substantive amplification will be required beyond what Peirce himself made explicit.

By my lights, and I think by Peirce's too, while "philosophy," like "chemistry," "geography," etc., picks out a kind of inquiry, "literature" does not. I get the impression that for Peirce "studying in a literary spirit" is something like an oxymoron; but for its bringing Quine's mathematical cyclist irresistibly to mind, I might suggest as analogy, "calculating in a athletic spirit"—"innovating in a bureaucratic spirit," suggested by Migotti, conveys the idea.

To say that "literature" does not refer to a kind of inquiry is not to deny that novelists, playwrights, etc., engage in inquiry. Of course they do; and not just in the kind of historical or geographical research required by, say, a Michener saga, but also in the kind of informal observation of and pondering about human nature which imaginative literature often expresses. Hence the occasional striking coincidence of the results of a novelist's informal observation and pondering and of a psychologist's more formal investigation—as of Alison Lurie's and Leon Festinger's of cognitive dissonance, for example.[14] Nor is it to deny that literary works may make, or convey, true claims—historical, geographical, psychological, . . . philosophical—and in a perfectly ordinary sense of "true." (I don't mean that a novelist's statements about a fictional Mr. N. N. are true claims about a non-existent person, but that such statements may convey truths about what makes real people tick.)

But the fact that novelists, etc., engage in historical, geographical, psychological, . . . , philosophical inquiry, and sometimes make or convey historical, geographical, psychological, . . . , philosophical claims, is no more a threat to the distinction between philosophy and literature than it is to the distinction between geography and literature. Though writers engage in inquiry, *"literature" picks out the writing, not the inquiry.* And, though chemists, astrophysicists, etc., engage in writing, *"science" picks out the inquiry, not the writing.* As does "philosophy."

The inquiry in which novelists, etc., engage is sometimes philosophical, and so works of literature sometimes express philosophical insights. And—the other side of the same coin—the writing in which philosophers engage is sometimes of a literary kind. Hence, the philosophical novel, play, dialogue, etc.

It is quite compatible with the proposed modest interpretation of Peirce's claims about philosophical style to acknowledge that, if the philosophical ideas to be presented fall short of systematic development, or if the intended audience is, not the author's fellow inquirers, but educated readers generally, such literary forms may be, not merely appropriate, but even ideal. The point is only that, where it is a matter of communicating developed philosophical ideas to one's fellow inquirers, the more direct, the better; aesthetic concerns cannot take the highest priority. A genuine inquirer, remember, *really wants the truth;* so he doesn't need to be jollied or charmed into paying attention.

On the suggested interpretation of Peirce's claims about philosophical style, there is no real tension with the not-infrequent literary flourishes one finds in his own writing (as there is with the figurative language in which Locke announces that where "dry truth and real knowledge" are concerned, figures of speech are an abuse of language not to be tolerated).[15] I think, for example, of the dialogue in which Peirce explains to two imaginary objectors, Drs. X and Y, the connections between pragmatism and critical common-sensism; and of his remarkable presentation of the strengthened Liar paradox, matching form (two columns of print) with content (two arguments, each leading to a conclusion that contradicts the other).

And then there are those literary flourishes used to make a point about literary flourishes. For example, at 5.537, twitting the new pragmatists as too "lively," and citing Schiller's complaint that professional philosophers have made their subject "abstruse, arid, abstract and abhorrent," Peirce writes:

> I conceive that some branches of science are not in a healthy state if they are *not* abstruse, arid and abstract, in which case, like the Aristotelianism which is this gentleman's particular *bête noire,* it will be as Shakespeare said (*of it,* remember)
> "Not harsh and crabbèd, as dull fools suppose,
> But musical as is Apollo's lute," etc.

(Actually, he has it wrong; it was Milton, not Shakespeare.)[16]

And then there is the simply playful, such as that mock-Platonic dialogue in which Gorgias "proves" that some black is white (5.338). This illustrates Peirce's theme of the "deceptive sophisms" which teach us about the nature of logic—as well as giving Gorgias, for once, all the good lines, and reducing Socrates, for once, to "how very true, Gorgias," etc. But it should not escape notice that, immediately before, Peirce has spelled out the point, about existential import in syllogistic reasoning, in a carefully explicit way.

Mentioning Plato prompts me to articulate a couple of points about what I do *not* mean by my qualified endorsement of Peirce's observations about philosophical style.

To say, as I have, that the priorities in philosophical writing are different from, and sometimes conflict with, literary priorities, is not to say that those works of philosophy that are also works of literature cannot be great philosophy. Of course, some are. Nor do I mean to deny that reading such works may call for the same kinds of skills and sensibilities as reading other works of literature. Of course, it does.

But, in an oblique way, this seems to confirm Peirce's essential point about philosophical style. To communicate with your fellow inquirers, the first priority is to say what you mean as explicitly and unequivocally as possible. (That is why reading works of philosophy written in the carefully devised technical vocabulary that is sometimes essential demands quite different skills and sensibilities than reading literary philosophy, and why Peirce fulminates against the ruinous "literary habit," warning wryly that it won't do to "peruse" his philosophical writing as one might a novel (MS 632).) In works of literature, by contrast, doubleness or multiplicity of meaning, allusion, verbal play, are to be appreciated and enjoyed. "In nearly all poetry," I. A. Richards writes, "the sound and feel of the words ... get to work first, and the senses in which the words are later more explicitly taken are subtly influenced by this fact." In contrast, he continues, "science ... endeavours with increasing success to bar out these factors. We believe a scientist because he can substantiate his remarks, not because he is eloquent. ... In fact, we distrust him when he seems to be influencing us by his manner."[17]

Now I see that it is better to talk, not in terms simply of clarity and rigor (to which literary, no less than scientific, writing aspires, but in a different way), but of *explicitness, directness,* and *univocality* (the qualities peculiarly desirable in scientific, and philosophical, writing). And I begin to understand how the aphorism, or the few lines of poetry or of a novel with which I sometimes feel it appropriate to open or close a paper, may express in a compressed and lapidary way what I am struggling to articulate and argue for explicitly and in detail. Discerning an ambiguity in a philosophical text, however, is often the first step in discovering that the author has confused something true but trivial with something interesting but false; and unpacking what is implicit in a philosophical text is often the first step in discovering that a claim or distinction rests on mistaken presuppositions.

If my interpretation is correct, Peirce's hope of "rescuing the good ship Philosophy for the service of Science" is in no way scientistic, and his harsh remarks about the "lawless rovers of the sea of literature" are neither indicative of hostility to literature as such nor incompatible with considerable concessions about literary style in philosophical writing and about philosophical content in literature. Indeed, his references to science and to literature are secondary to his central and essential point: *that philosophy can and should be genuine inquiry.*

This central and essential point is, however, radically at odds with Rorty's metaphilosophy, which, as I shall argue, would precisely reduce philosophy to that "studying in a literary spirit"—fake inquiry—which Peirce rightly deplores.

RORTY SOMETIMES CLAIMS that his literary conception of philosophy is the pragmatist conception, sometimes that it is the conception of a new, enlightened brand of pragmatism which has thrown off the scientism of its precursor. The first claim is false not only of Peirce but of the other classical pragmatists; including Schiller, who, though Russell described him as "the literary protagonist"[18] of pragmatism because of his penchant for philosophical limericks and playlets, surely did not think of philosophy as "just a kind of writing." (Those limericks and playlets, not so incidentally, all poke fun at other philosophers' excesses, as: "A staid fellow of Merton named B[radley]/ Fell in love with the Absolute, madly/ . . .") Rorty's second claim is perhaps best regarded as a not-very-convincing attempt to present himself as representative of a new and supposedly enlightened wing of pragmatism.

Further complications arise with Rorty's later observation that "there have been three conceptions of philosophy in our century: the Husserlian (or 'scientistic') answer, the Heideggerian (or 'poetic') answer, and the pragmatist (or 'political') answer."[19] Giving up his earlier hope of finding a philosophy that would "hold reality and justice in a single vision,"[20] he seems to have moved toward a conception of philosophy as Heideggerian or poetic on its "private" side, and pragmatist or political on its "public" side; besides beginning to emphasize the political elements in and relevance of literature. But the new claim about the pragmatist tradition is as misleading as the earlier ones—and, again, not only of Peirce, but of the other classical pragmatists; including Dewey, who, though indeed much concerned with social and political issues, stressed the importance of using the method of science to discover what is really conducive to human flourishing, the need for inquiry as the basis of wise and effective social change.

Rorty's remarks about philosophy being a genre of literature identified "by tradition" may give the impression that his point is just that who counts as a philosopher—whether Addison, say, or Santayana, or Emerson, qualifies—is optional, that we might, perhaps that we should, include such "easy and obvious" philosophers as well as the "accurate and abstruse" (to use that distinction of Hume's of which you will already have heard echoes in Peirce's interchange with Schiller). But the question, whether this novelist or that essayist is *really* a philosopher, seems to me to lose much of its interest once it is acknowledged that works of literature may express philosophical insights. And in any case, when Rorty writes that "revolutionary movements within an intellectual discipline require a revisionist history of that discipline,"[21] it seems he is proposing, not simply a revisionary list of who is to count as a philosopher, but a history of philosophy which is revisionary in the much stronger sense revealed by his breezy observation that "since I persist in trying to interpret Davidson as the most sophisticated and radical of the American pragmatists, it suits my purposes to define pragmatism as the attempt to do something Davidson approves of. . . ."[22]

Rorty sometimes suggests that only a literary conception can acknowledge the importance of imagination, linguistic innovation, and metaphor in philosophy; but this is seen to be false as soon as one recognizes, as Peirce does, that imagination, linguistic innovation, metaphor, etc., are by no means the exclusive prerogative of literature, but also play important roles in science—and would have the same important roles in a scientific philosophy.

But something even deeper is at issue: the very possibility, not only of philosophical inquiry,[23] but of inquiry of any kind. Rorty writes that he "views science as one genre of literature," or, he continues, "put the other way around [*sic*], literature and the arts as inquiries, on the same footing as scientific inquiries."[24] The idea of chemistry or astrophysics as genres of literature is nothing short of laughable. Even the idea of chemical reports, or the proceedings of the astrophysical society, as genres of literature is pretty strange[25] (though they are, to be sure, kinds of writing, as are bus timetables, and *could* be read somewhat as one reads literature—as one might notice happy alliterations or rhymes in the bus schedule). When Rorty, as he says, puts this the other way round, what he gives us is a different proposition altogether: that literature is a kind of inquiry. This is not ludicrous; but it is, as the considerations articulated earlier suggest, false.

What really lies behind Rorty's strange observations about science being a genre of literature, and/or vice versa, is *a disillusionment with the very idea of inquiry.* The "anti-representationalism" with which Rorty sometimes identifies his "pragmatism"[26] repudiates the idea that "true" is anything more than "a word which applies to those beliefs upon which we are able to agree";[27] and hence, by Peirce's lights or mine, is committed to repudiating the idea of inquiry as well. (Peirce's pioneering work in semiotics, and his conception of truth as concordance with the ultimate representation, puts him about as far from "anti-representationalism" as it is possible to be; but Rorty is relying on one of those startlingly false dichotomies: *either* truth is Mirroring the Unconditioned, *or* "true" just means "what you can defend against all comers.")[28] Rorty continues to use the word "inquiry"; but it has taken on a revisionist sense, no longer meaning "attempt to arrive at the truth," but "attempt to arrive at the 'truth,'" i.e., "attempt to arrive at agreement."

If Rorty's more radical pronouncements are to be taken seriously,[29] his position is that even the sciences don't come up with objective truths, or for that matter falsehoods, about the world; "anti-representationalism" has dispensed with that naive idea. "How does having knowledge differ from making poems and telling stories?" he asks rhetorically.[30] "Science as the source of 'truth,'" he assures us, "is one of the Cartesian notions which will vanish when the ideal of 'philosophy as strict science' vanishes"[31]—which, one gathers, in view of his observation that he "doesn't have much use for notions like . . . 'objective truth,'"[32] can't be too soon for him. Scientists just come up with the incommensurable theories which constitute their conversation, as successive genres constitute the literary conversation. The only thing exemplary about science is that it is a model of "human solidarity."[33] Even science isn't inquiry, in Peirce's or my (or Webster's)[34] sense.

Rorty's radical claims about truth, representation, etc., are radically false. To be sure, if we agree that p, we agree that p is true. But we may agree that p when p is *not* true (and we may not agree that p when p is true). So "true" is not a word that truly applies to all or only statements about which we agree; and calling a statement "true" certainly doesn't mean that we agree about it. Reducing Peirce's complex and difficult definition of truth to "whatever can survive all conversational objections,"[35] Rorty has transmuted inquiry into "conversation," evidence into "objections," an indefeasible consensus determined by "some external permanency" (5.384) into "solidarity"; and, confusing what is true with what passes for true,[36] has sacrificed the idea that truth "is SO—whether you or I or anybody thinks it is so or not," that "the essence of truth lies in its resistance to being ignored" (2.135, 2.139), that truth "consists in a conformity to something *independent of [your] thinking it to be so,* or of any man's opinion on the subject" (5.211).

You see the radical effect of these radically false claims not only in Rorty's philosophy, but also when he writes about literature. The effect is particularly striking when he writes about a work in which truth is itself a theme: as in his discussion of *Nineteen Eighty-Four*,[37] from which (since Rorty is anxious to persuade us that truth "drops out") O'Brien's insistence that "whatever the party holds to be truth, is truth" is notable by its absence; as, true to anti-representationalist form, is any mention of Newspeak.

But the disaster is quite general. To suppose, like Rorty, that to call a statement true "is just to give it a rhetorical pat on the back,"[38] is to induce a factitious despair of the possibility of real inquiry of any kind—scientific, historical, forensic, . . . , as well as philosophical; to misprize the truths that literature expresses, whether about truth or anything else; and to undermine the hope of knowing what would truly improve the condition of society. This is the very opposite of edifying.

In a revealing recent piece of intellectual autobiography, Rorty tells us that, looking as a young man for "a way to be . . . a nerdy recluse and a fighter for justice," he has "spent forty years looking for a coherent . . . way of formulating [his] worries about what, if anything, philosophy is good for."[39] I recall that Peirce thought such motives, however admirable in themselves, the wrong motives for inquiry: "if a man occupy himself with investigating . . . for some ulterior purpose, such as to make money, or amend his life, or to benefit his fellows, he may be ever so much better than a scientific man . . . but he is not a scientific man" (1.45); and even, protesting about being obliged to lecture on "Vitally Important Topics," predicted that the result of philosophizing from such motives would be unedifying.[40]

Be that as it may, Rorty's worry is well founded; if philosophy really could be no more than his radical metaphilosophy allows, it would, indeed, be good for nothing: "the very debauchery of thought." And—to return to the main themes of this essay—Rortyesque dilettantism, leaving room only for "conversation," fake reasoning, can do justice neither to science nor to literature. A scientific conception of philosophy, in Peirce's subtle sense, is more robust not only on the former, but also on the latter, score. It is—dare I say it?—ironic.

NOTES

1. Unless otherwise indicated, quotations from Peirce are from *Collected Papers*, ed. Charles Hartshorne, Paul Weiss, and Arthur Burks, Harvard University Press, Cambridge, MA, 1931–58; references by volume and paragraph number.

2. Richard Rorty, *Consequences of Pragmatism*, Harvester, Hassocks, Sussex, 1982, pp. 92–93.

3. Recall Rorty's observation that philosophers (with a small p) will be "all purpose intellectuals . . . ready to offer a view on pretty much anything" (*Consequences of Pragmatism*, p. xxxix).

4. Though his terminology might suggest otherwise, it is clear that Peirce does not mean that good, scientific metaphysics will eschew ontology.

5. First in "The First Rule of Reason" (1992), in *The Rule of Reason: Essays in the Philosophy of Charles Peirce*, ed. Jacqueline Brunning and Paul Forster, Toronto University Press, Toronto, 1997, 241–61; then in "Confessions of an Old-Fashioned Prig" (essay 1) and "Preposterism and Its Consequences" (essay 11) in this volume.

6. Which is not to suggest that he never violates those principles.

7. Among those "overcultivated [Harvard] dons," Gérard Déledalle suggests, Peirce had in mind Santayana, of the first two volumes of whose *The Life of Reason* he wrote that they are "all that Boston has of the most *précieux*. They are also extremely handy and agreeable to the eyes" (*Peirce's Contributions to The Nation*, ed. Kenneth Lane Ketner, volume 3, pp. 221–21). Deledalle adds that Santayana got his revenge later, writing that up to 1925, the only valuable book in American philosophy was Anita Loos's *Gentlemen Prefer Blondes*!

8. MSS. 1517, 1118; quoted in C. S. Peirce, *New Elements of Mathematics*, ed. Carolyn Eisele, Mouton, The Hague, The Netherlands/Humanities Press, Atlantic Highlands, NJ, 1976, volume 1, p. vii.

9. Jaime Nubiola drew to my attention Peirce's attempt at fiction, the "Tale of Thessaly"; see Max Fisch's "Introduction" to *Writings of C. S. Peirce*, volume 2, Indiana University Press, Bloomington, IN, 1984, p. xxxiv, and his "Peirce's Arisbe," in *Peirce, Semeiotic, and Pragmatism*, Indiana University Press, Bloomington, IN, 1986, pp. 243–44 and note 39.

10. See Hilary Putnam's critique of David Lewis's reliance on the method of "what is agreeable to reason," *Renewing Philosophy*, Harvard University Press, Cambridge, MA, and London, 1992, pp. 135–36.

11. See also Haack, *Evidence and Inquiry*, Blackwell, Oxford, 1993, chapters 6 (Quine), 7 (Goldman), and 8 (Churchland); and "Between the Scylla of Scientism and the Charybdis of Apriorism," in *The Philosophy of Sir Peter Strawson*, ed. Lewis Hahn, Open Court, La Salle, IL, 1998, 49–63.

12. A shrewd phrase due, I believe, to Renford Bambrough.

13. The phrase is from John Locke, *An Essay Concerning Human Understanding* (1690), III.xi.6.

14. Alison Lurie, *Imaginary Friends*, Coward-McCann, New York, 1967; Leon Festinger, *A Theory of Cognitive Dissonance*, Row, Peterson, Evanston, IL, 1957. (It is possible, of course, that the agreement is not a coincidence, but the result of Lurie's having read Festinger.)

15. *Essay Concerning Human Understanding*, III.x.34. See also "'Dry Truth and Real Knowledge': Epistemologies of Metaphor and Metaphors of Epistemology," essay 4 in this volume.

16. *Comus* (1634), lines 477–78. The line before runs, "How charming is divine philosophy!"

17. I. A. Richards, *Science and Poetry*, Kegan Paul, Trench, and Trubner, London, 1926; p. 29 in second, 1935, edition.

18. Bertrand Russell, *Sceptical Essays*, W. W. Norton, New York, 1928, p. 6.

19. *Essays on Heidegger and Others*, Cambridge University Press, Cambridge, 1991, p. 9.

20. A phrase of Yeats's used by Rorty in "Trotsky and the Wild Orchids," *Common Knowledge*, 1.3, 1992, 140–153, pp. 143, 147.

21. *Consequences of Pragmatism*, p. 211.

22. "Realism, Anti-Realism, and Pragmatism: Comments on Alston, Chisholm, Davidson, Harman, and Searle," in Christopher Kulp, ed., *Realism/Antirealism and Epistemology*, Rowman and Littlefield, Lanham, MD, 1997, 149–72, p. 149.

23. James, commenting on the limits of what can be achieved by theorizing about ethics, observes that, to the extent that books on ethics really touch upon the moral life, they are akin to "novels and dramas of the deeper sort" ("The Moral Philosopher and the Moral Life," *International Journal of Ethics*, 1891; reprinted in Graham Bird, ed., *Selected Writings*, Everyman, London, 1995, 298–319, p. 316). But Rorty's position, which rests not on doubts about what can be achieved by theorizing in some, or even all, areas of philosophy, but of repudiation of the very idea of inquiry, in philosophy or any other area, is far more radical.

24. *Consequences of Pragmatism*, p. xliii.

25. We speak of "reading the literature" on this or that technical topic; but to depend on this usage to show that chemical or astrophysical reports are "literature" in the sense at issue in this essay would be at best a bad pun.

26. Richard Rorty, Introduction to J. P. Murphey, *Pragmatism from Peirce to Davidson*, Westview Press, Boulder, CO, 1990, 1–6, p. 1; see also "Confessions of an Old-Fashioned Prig," essay 1 in this volume.

27. "Science as Solidarity," in John S. Nelson, A. Megill, and D. M. McCloskey, eds., *The Rhetoric of the Human Sciences*, University of Wisconsin Press, Madison, WI, 38–52, p. 45.

28. *Philosophy and the Mirror of Nature*, Princeton University Press, Princeton, NJ, 1979, p. 308.

29. The "if" clause is intended, of course, to indicate that Rorty doesn't always sound this radical; just very often.

30. *Consequences of Pragmatism*, p. 129.

31. *Consequences of Pragmatism,* p. 34.

32. "Trotsky and the Wild Orchids," p. 141.

33. "Science as Solidarity," p. 46.

34. In 1961, anyway, "*inquiry:* search for truth . . ."; but I note with some dismay that in my newer (1991) edition this has disappeared, replaced by "a systematic investigation."

35. *Consequences of Pragmatism,* p. 165.

36. A confusion evident in this comment on rival commentators who hold "that Orwell teaches us to set our faces against all those sneaky philosophers who try to tell us that truth is not 'out there,' that what counts as a possible truth is a function of the vocabulary you use, and *what counts as a truth* is a function of the rest of your beliefs" (*Contingency, Irony, and Solidarity,* Cambridge University Press, Cambridge, 1989, p. 172, my italics).

37. *Contingency, Irony, and Solidarity,* chapter 8, "The Last Intellectual in Europe: Orwell on Cruelty," 169–88. See also Cora Diamond, "Truth: Defenders, Despisers, Debunkers," in Leona Toker, ed., *Commitment in Reflection,* Garland Press, New York, 1994, 195–221.

38. *Consequences of Pragmatism,* p. xvii.

39. "Trotsky and the Wild Orchids," pp. 143, 146.

40. "In philosophy , . . . the investigator who does not stand aloof from all intent to make practical applications will . . . endanger his own moral integrity and that of his readers" (1.619).

"Dry Truth and Real Knowledge": Epistemologies of Metaphor and Metaphors of Epistemology

Locke is eloquent in defense of plain speech. In a famous, or notorious, chapter of the *Essay*,[1] "Of the Abuse of Words," though he admits that "since wit and fancy find easier entertainment than dry truth and real knowledge, figurative speeches and allusions in language will hardly be admitted as an imperfection of it," Locke insists that nevertheless, "if we would speak of things as they are, we must allow that all the art of rhetoric, besides order and clearness; all the artificial and figurative applications of words eloquence hath invented, are for nothing else than to insinuate wrong ideas, move the passions, and thereby mislead the judgement; and so indeed are perfect cheats." Figurative language may be appropriate in "harangues and popular addresses"; but, Locke continues, it is "certainly, in all discourses that pretend to inform and instruct, wholly to be avoided; and where truth and knowledge are concerned, cannot but be thought a great fault, either of the language or person that makes use of them."

However, if figurative use of language is indeed, at least where "dry truth and real knowledge" are concerned, an abuse of language, then it is an abuse of which Locke himself is hardly innocent. At the close of this long paragraph deploring the figurative, Locke observes that it will no doubt be thought "great boldness" in him to speak out against figures of speech; for "eloquence, like the fair sex, has too prevailing beauties in it to suffer itself ever to be spoken against" (III.x.34). And a few pages earlier in the same chapter, deploring the "affected obscurity" of "the wrangling and disputing philosophers," Locke comments that "there is no such way to gain admittance, or give defence to . . . absurd doctrines, than to guard them about with legions of obscure, doubtful and undefined words." "Which," he continues, "if it be hard to get them out of, it is not for the strength that is in them, but the briars and thorns, and the obscurity of the thickets they are beset with" (III.x.9).

And Locke's use of metaphor is not always, as no doubt it is here, purely in the service of vividness; certain metaphors play a role in his philosophy much deeper than mere picturesqueness of speech: the metaphor of the philosopher as underlaborer to the sciences, for example, and the metaphors of the mind as an empty cabinet, blank sheet of paper, wax tablet.

Locke is by no means the only philosopher who manifests this kind of pragmatic inconsistency between his official attitude to figurative language, and his use of it. Hobbes, almost as notoriously, regards it as an abuse of speech to use words metaphorically, "that is," as he puts it in *Leviathan,* "in another sense than they are ordained for; and thereby deceive"; though he admits that "Metaphors, ar.d Tropes of speech" are less dangerous than other kinds of inconstancy of meaning, "because they profess their inconstancy." But even when he is explaining why metaphors are an abuse of speech, he uses them: "Metaphors . . . are like *ignes fatui*; and, reasoning upon them, is wandering among innumerable absurdities." Again: the man who seeks precise truth, Hobbes argues, needs definitions; otherwise he will "find himselfe entangled in words, as a bird in lime-twigges; the more he struggles, the more belimed." Again: without language, he remarks, a man could be neither "excellently wise" nor "excellently foolish," "for words are wise man's counters, they do but reckon by them: but they are the mony of fooles. . . ."[2] In Hobbes, too, metaphors play a more than decorative role; most notable, of course, is "*Leviathan*" itself.

For now I will add only one more name to the list of "plain Englishmen"[3] whose official condemnation of metaphor is at odds with their use of it. J. S. Mill classifies metaphor as a kind of ambiguity, differing from ordinary ambiguity such as that of "file" or "post" or "box" only in that "a name . . . is predicated of two things, not univocally, . . . but in significations somewhat similar, derived one from another."[4] And this kind of ambiguity, Mill remarks, where the senses, though different, are related, is especially likely to tempt one into fallacies of equivocation.

Compared to Hobbes or Locke, Mill is a dry, literal writer; yet even he, not long after issuing this warning against metaphor, in a discussion of one of the most philosophically consequential fallacies of equivocation, the confusion of "is," meaning "exists," with the "is" of predication, observes: "the fog which rose from this narrow spot diffused itself at an early period over the whole surface of metaphysics."[5]

These writers' hostile attitude to figurative language will strike modern readers as quaint, perhaps, but surely as indefensible. In this regard, intellectual fashion has changed dramatically. Today virtually all writers on metaphor agree that it has a legitimate place not only in "harangues and public addresses," not only in literary writing, but also where "dry truth and real knowledge" are concerned; indeed many go so far as to claim that metaphor plays not only a legitimate or a useful but an essential role in theoretical inquiry.

To this extent, at least, I concur: if the question is, given the tension between Hobbes's, Locke's, and Mill's official condemnation of metaphor and their use of it, whether the conclusion one should draw is that their practice falls regrettably short of their legitimately high standards of what language is appropriate in serious discourse, or that their practice is quite legitimate and their repudiation of metaphor ill-motivated—the latter answer is clearly the better. These writers' use of metaphor is, after all, in general harmless and on occasion positively illuminating, so it must be their repudiation of metaphor that is repudiated.

But this response, though correct as far as it goes, provides no simple or straightforward answers about the epistemology of metaphor. In the passage quoted, Locke seems to take it for granted that figurative language is confusing and emotive; this should be read in the light of the passage earlier in the *Essay* where he distinguishes *wit,* the operation of "assemblage of ideas ... with quickness ... wherein can be found any resemblance or congruity, thereby to make up pleasant pictures and agreeable visions in the fancy," from *judgement,* the operation of discerning ideas, "thereby to avoid being misled by similitude, and by affinity to take one thing for another" (II.xi.2). Hobbes takes metaphor to be a kind of ambiguity which, while not the most virulent, can lead to a dangerous instability of meaning. Mill construes metaphor as ambiguity of a particularly treacherous kind. In other words, their agreement that metaphor is inappropriate in serious discourse does not derive from their subscribing to the same theory about how metaphor works, nor to the same diagnosis of why it is inappropriate.

It is hard to deny, of course, that emotive language, ambiguity, instability of meaning are indeed all unwelcome in serious discourse; so, one is tempted to argue, none of these accounts of metaphor can be correct. Well, no, not *entirely* so; but it is surely no less hard to deny that metaphorical language *may* function to arouse emotion, or *may* give rise to something like equivocation if (by accident or design) it is taken literally.

Hobbes, Locke, and Mill agree that metaphor is to be deplored, but not about why. Virtually all modern writers agree that metaphor is to be welcomed—but, still, not about why. Not only do they not agree about how metaphor plays the significant role in inquiry they agree it *does* play; some—and a fashionable party, at that!—insist on the importance of metaphor while denying it "cognitive content."[6] It is all very confusing, to put it mildly.

Both the friends and the enemies of metaphor, it seems to me, exaggerate. Metaphors are sometimes cognitively vital; not seldom illuminating; perhaps more often than not at least harmless. Metaphors can also be feeble; can be exploited to the purpose of persuading by emotional appeal rather than strong evidence or good argument; can serve as lazy substitutes for adequate theoretical articulation; can lead inquiry into what turns out to be quite the wrong direction. Metaphor is neither a Good Thing nor a Bad Thing in and of itself; it is, rather, a linguistic device capable of being put to good or bad use, sometimes a help, sometimes harmless, sometimes a hindrance. An adequate theory of how metaphor works, therefore, ought to suggest an explanation *both* of its usefulness *and* of its dangers.

THE BEST STARTING POINT for such a theory is the traditional account, the account found in Aristotle, Cicero, and Quintilian:[7] metaphors are elliptical similes. This idea is hopelessly out of fashion; nevertheless, it has not only an honorable ancestry, but also an undeniable intuitive appeal.

It is also strikingly consonant with a noteworthy feature of some of the examples given earlier: a shift from metaphor to corresponding simile, or vice versa, within a single sentence. Hobbes begins by remarking that the man who seeks precise truth needs definitions to avoid finding himself entangled in words "*as* a bird in lime-twigges" [simile] and continues with the comment, "the more he struggles, the more belimed" [metaphor]. Locke, after observing that "there is no such way to . . . give defense to . . . absurd doctrines, as to guard them round about with legions of obscure, doubtful and ill-defined words" [metaphor], continues by remarking that to do so is to "make these retreats *more like* the dens of robbers or the holes of foxes . . . than the fortresses of fair warriors" [simile].

Present fashion has it that the traditional account faces insuperable difficulties, and that one or another rival theory (a semantic-interaction theory, as in Richards and Black;[8] or a speaker-meaning theory, as developed by Searle; or, most fashionably of all, perhaps, the "fecund falsity" theory, as urged by Davidson) is clearly superior. So I shall be swimming against the tide; for my view is that the idea that metaphor is elliptical simile can be elaborated in a way that avoids the difficulties fashionably supposed insuperable, and that, so elaborated, it can accommodate what is most plausible in the theories fashionably supposed to be its rivals. I shall be swimming against the tide, but not without assistance; here, happily, I can rely in considerable measure on arguments to be found in Fogelin's admirable *Figuratively Speaking*,[9] in defense of what he calls the "comparativist" position.

A metaphor is an elliptical simile; the difference between the two is that the latter does in a grammatically explicit way what the former does implicitly. (The difference is significant; it explains, for instance, why metaphor permits much greater grammatical flexibility than simile.) To say this, however, is to say relatively little; before it amounts to anything that merits the title "theory" it needs to be amplified by some account of what similes are, how they work.

The first moves are easy enough. Similes are, manifestly, statements which compare one thing with another; they are given the special title "simile" and classified among figures of speech because they make figurative or *tropical* comparisons. This leaves two further questions: how do ordinary, non-figurative statements of comparison work, and what is peculiar about figurative, tropical comparisons?

The ordinary statements of comparison with which metaphors have the closest affinity are those which are *unspecific* and *context-dependent*: statements which indicate that the things compared are alike in significant but unspecified respects, which respects are significant depending on the context. This much is true alike of such literal comparisons as "Tomatoes are like apples" (which might, depending on context, be taken as telling us that both are fruit, or that both contain vitamin C, or that both can be ripened artificially, etc.) and of figurative ones like "My love is like a red, red rose," or "Reading Heidegger is like wading knee-deep through treacle."

The etymology of "trope" (from the Greek, *tropos*, turn) offers a clue to what makes non-literal comparisons non-literal: the things compared figuratively are in significant respects *unlike* each other, the comparison is on the face of it *incongruous*, and to figure out the respects of likeness calls for an imaginative twist.[10]

Consider this very fine exchange of insults from *A Midsummer Night's Dream* (Act 3, Scene 2): Puck has anointed the wrong Athenian's eyes with the love potion; Lysander, Hermia's lover, has fallen in love with Helena. But Helena, lovesick for Demetrius, thinks that Lysander is making declarations of love to mock her, and that Hermia is part of the cruel plot:

HERMIA:	O me! you juggler! you canker-blossom!
	You thief of love! What! Have you come by night,
	And stolen my love's heart from him?
HELENA:	Fine, i'faith!

.　.　.

	Fie! Fie! you counterfeit, you puppet you!
HERMIA:	'Puppet!' why so? Ay, that way goes the game.
	Now I perceive that she has made compare
	Between our statures; she hath urged her height;
	And with her personage, her tall personage,
	Her height forsooth, she hath prevailed with him.
	And are you grown so high in his esteem
	Because I am so dwarfish and so low?
	How low am I, thou painted maypole?

.　.　.

HELENA:	O, when she is angry, she is keen and shrewd;
	She was a vixen when she went to school;
	And though she be but little, she is fierce.
HERMIA:	'Little' again! Nothing but 'low' and 'little'!

.　.　.

LYSANDER:	Get you gone, you dwarf!
	You minimus, of hind'ring knot-grass made;
	You bead, you acorn.

Helena isn't as tall as a maypole, or made of wood, or perfectly cylindrical in shape, or painted in stripes. The insulting suggestion is something like: she is too tall, too stiff and gawky, lacking in feminine curves—and she "paints" (i.e., wears makeup). Hermia isn't a small furry animal with a pointed nose and sharp teeth. This time the insulting suggestion is spelled out for us: "though she be but little, she is fierce."

It goes without saying that these comments miss most of the intricacies and subtleties of a very intricate and subtle interchange—the shift from a literal comment on Helena's height ("she hath urged her height") through an ironical juxtaposition of terms ("with her personage, her *tall* personage") to a play on a metaphorical use of "high" ("and are you grown so high in his esteem?"), for example. But they make, albeit crudely, the point that is at issue; that there has to be a kind of editing of the features of a maypole, or a vixen, to find those that might be the relevant respects of comparison here.

Initial incongruity being, I suppose, a matter of degree, so too, I take it, is the distinction of figurative and literal comparisons.

By setting the comparativist position in the context of Grice's theory of conversation, Fogelin is able to present comparative statements (presumably, that is, the unspecific ones) as indirect, in the sense that their utterance conveys more than is said; and figurative comparisons as, additionally, non-literal in virtue of being made with the mutually recognized intention on the speaker's part that the hearer should not take the words uttered at face value, but adjust them so as to square with the context.

And borrowing from Tversky's discussion of comparisons and similarity,[11] he is able to present the process of adjustment as a matter of selecting, among the salient features of Gs (where "G" is the predicate of the comparison statement) those appropriate to Fs (the subject). This applies rather neatly to the example just discussed: we select, among the salient features of maypoles, or vixen, those applicable to persons, specifically to young women.

It is compatible with the idea of metaphor as elliptical simile, then, to acknowledge that metaphor is better regarded as a phenomenon of use than as a peculiarity of words or sentences—live metaphor, that is; metaphorical usages may, through being conventionalized or, as Searle puts it, "frozen," eventually enter the language in petrified form as a kind of ambiguity (as "foot the bill," "ruminate over a problem," "grasp an idea," "taken aback")[12] or idiom (as "kick the bucket," "bite the bullet," "three sheets to the wind"). The briefest reflection, or the most superficial skimming of the dictionary, reveals how ubiquitous is the formerly, and the still barely, metaphorical.

"Conventionalization" being a matter of degree, so too, I take it, is the distinction of live and dead metaphor—though one might take the occurrence of a secondary sense in a dictionary as a rule of thumb to distinguish the definitely dead from the merely moribund. Perhaps it will be felt that there is tension between treating the distinction of live versus dead metaphor as a matter of degree, and treating dead metaphor as a matter of semantics while treating live metaphor as a phenomenon of use; but I am willing to grasp this nettle (or bite this bullet!) and acknowledge that the line between semantic phenomena and phenomena of use is not sharp.

By treating (live) metaphor as a phenomenon of use, I am suggesting a development of the traditional conception in a somewhat contemporary style. I agree with Searle and Davidson, in other words, in regarding metaphor as belonging rather to pragmatics than to semantics. My disagreement with them could be summed up, rather crudely, like this: Searle focuses too exclusively on speakers' intentions; Davidson focuses too exclusively and too indiscriminately on the effect of a metaphorical utterance on its hearers.

Searle explains metaphor in terms of speaker's, as distinct from linguistic, meaning. (So in his account metaphor is a kind of ambiguity, but a non-standard kind; there are two meanings, but in two senses of "meaning.") Speaker's meaning is characterized in terms of the utterer's intentions, and Searle provides a list of principles by which to compute "which similarities are metaphorically intended by the speaker."[13] What makes me uneasy about this is the idea that the speaker's intentions necessarily exhaust the interpretation of the metaphor.

The problem isn't that Searle holds that metaphorical meaning is always completely determinate; in fact, he allows a category of "open-ended metaphor" where "a speaker says S is P but means an indefinite range of meanings, S is R_1, S is R_2, etc."[14] It is, rather, that his account of metaphorical meaning as constituted by the speaker's intentions implies that any interpretation of the metaphorical utterance by a hearer which specifies respects, however appropriate, which the speaker didn't specifically have in mind is a *mis*interpretation. And this seems wrong.

It may be that Searle fails to see this because of an ambiguity in his formula: read as "a speaker says S is P but means metaphorically 'S is R_1, or S is R_2, or . . . ,'" it has the consequence that any interpretation that makes the respects of comparison more detailed or determinate than the speaker had in mind is a misinterpretation; read as "a speaker says S is P but means metaphorically 'S is R_1,' or means metaphorically 'S is R_2,' or means metaphorically—well, something else," it doesn't. But on the reading on which it doesn't have the undesired consequence it also fails to do what Searle wants it to do—give a criterion to determine the metaphorical meaning of an utterance.

Davidson urges that we "give up the idea that a metaphor carries a message, that it has a content or meaning (except, of course, its literal meaning)."[15] Unlike Searle's, which focuses on the speaker's intentions, Davidson's account is focussed on the effects of a metaphorical utterance on its audience. A metaphorical utterance is an utterance of a sentence which is, taken literally, strikingly anomalous (usually glaringly false, but sometimes simply trivial). And such an utterance "can, like a picture or a bump on the head, make us appreciate some fact—but not by standing for, or expressing, the fact."[16]

The analogy with a bump on the head might tempt you to read David-son as offering a brutally causal account: a metaphorical utterance just causes the audience to think this or that, as a loud noise might do. But this can't be right; Davidson stresses that it is the anomalous character of the sentence uttered which alerts us to its being a metaphor, and suggests that making a metaphor is something like joking or lying, so he can't be taken as suggesting a purely causal account, an account in which the (literal) meaning of the words uttered has no role at all.

One way of putting what bothers me would be to say, simply, that Da-vidson doesn't tell us what that role is. A better way, perhaps, would be to say that the meaning of the words uttered could have a causal role in bring-ing about an effect on an audience in any of a number of ways, only one of which is characteristic of metaphor; and that it is hard to avoid the suspicion that Davidson is either relying on a mistaken assimilation of metaphorical to some other perlocutionary effects, or else offering no ac-count at all of how the words uttered affect what a metaphorical utterance "evokes" or "intimates."

An utterance of certain words may evoke a response in an audience by means of simple association of ideas (I believe it was Titchener who re-ported that "but" brought to his mind the image of the back of the head of a colleague of his who sat in front of him at departmental seminars, and regularly opened the discussion, "But . . ."). This isn't how metaphors work. An obviously anomalous utterance may evoke a response in an audi-ence by provoking them to work out what the speaker could have been trying to do (as the startling opening sentence of chapter 5 of Ursula Le Guin's *The Left Hand of Darkness*,[17] "My landlady was a voluble man," prompts the reader to figure out that the apparent mix-up of genders is a device to draw one's attention to the fact that the inhabitants of the world in which the story is set are neither male nor female, but hermaphrodite). This isn't how metaphors work either—as Davidson must be aware, since he observes, correctly, that the effect of metaphor cannot be explained simply in terms of the hearer's figuring out the speaker's intentions.

These remarks about Searle and Davidson may provoke the question: how, if metaphor is a phenomenon of use, can it fail to be *either* a matter of the speaker's intentions (as Searle has it) *or* a matter of the effect on the hearer (as Davidson has it)? Fogelin's account shows us that there is a third possibility. Metaphor is an interactive phenomenon, in the sense that it is an utterance which a speaker intends his hearer to amplify and adjust.[18]

THOUGH IT IS NOT a semantic phenomenon, metaphor certainly is a *lin-guistic* phenomenon, a phenomenon of the use of language. An under-standing of its cognitive role, therefore, calls for some thought about the role of language in inquiry; and this leads rather directly to the hoary old problem of The Relation of Thought to Language.

One way to read Locke's critique of figurative language is to take it as focused on the inappropriateness of figures of speech *to certain kinds of discourse:* in discourse intended simply to persuade, one might take Locke to be saying, figurative language may be appropriate, but in discourse in-tended to instruct it is inappropriate. The distinction implicit in this read-ing between persuasive and instructive discourse (i.e., discourse intended to persuade and discourse intended to instruct) may seem quite artificial, occluding the possibility that a speaker might intend to persuade an audi-ence of some truths. But despite its artificiality, the distinction does high-light an important point: that simply inducing one's hearer to believe that p, even if it is true, doesn't necessarily count as having brought him to the knowledge that p; that requires that he be induced to believe that p by being made aware of good reasons for thinking it true. Locke's allusion to "real knowledge" may be an indication that he is aware of this point. Nevertheless, construed as a claim about the language appropriate to in-structive discourse, Locke's position is mistaken; metaphor may be a very useful device of instructive discourse. A metaphorical presentation may, for example, make "dry truth" more palatable, by representing it in terms more familiar to the audience, and/or more memorable, by presenting it in a way that calls for the audience to participate.

Perhaps, though, Locke intends an allusion to the distinction he had made in "Of the Imperfection of Words," between the *civil* and the *philo-sophical* use of words: the former is "such a communication of thoughts and ideas by words, as may serve for the upholding of common conver-sation and commerce," the latter "such a use [of words] as may serve to convey the precise notions of things, and to express in general propositions certain and undoubted truths, which the mind may rest upon and be satis-fied with in its search after true knowledge" (III.x.2). On this reading, Locke's point would be that figurative language is inappropriate for a par-ticular kind of instructive discourse; for, as one might say in a more con-temporary idiom, the most strictly scientific discourse.[19] Construed in this way, as a claim about the language appropriate for the ideally precise and specific articulation and presentation of scientific or philosophical theo-ries, Locke's position is, I think, correct. Metaphorical presentation is allusive, open-ended, unspecific; it lacks the specification, the precision, which theoretical articulation aspires eventually to reach.

But Locke is saying not only that figurative language is inappropriate to serious (on the most plausible reading, to "philosophical") *discourse*, but also that it is an impediment to genuine *inquiry*. In the passage I discussed at the beginning, he comments that by moving the passions, metaphors are liable to "cloud the judgement." And in the *Epistle to the Reader* he had observed that one of the tasks of the philosophical underlaborer is to remove the rubbish that stands in the way of inquiry; and he specifically mentions, among this rubbish, the "vague and insignificant forms of speech, and abuse of language" that "have so long passed for mysteries of science." So chapters ix and x of Book III of the *Essay*—"Of the Imperfection of Words," "Of the Abuse of Words"—are precisely intended to contribute to the whole project by removing the linguistic rubbish which, according to Locke, is a significant "hindrance of true knowledge."

Though Locke is wrong to hold that figurative language is always an abuse, and that it is inevitably a hindrance to inquiry, he is right to take for granted that the language one uses and the way one uses it may— will—affect one's success in inquiry. For all that Book III of the *Essay*, with its stress, from the beginning, that the purpose of language is to express and communicate ideas, seems officially to make language dependent on thought, Locke's conception of abuses of language as hindrances to knowledge reveals his awareness that, conversely, thought may also depend on language.[20]

A correct picture of the relation of thought and language will involve quite complex relations of interdependence. Whether or not one wants to say that a languageless creature can have thoughts, one had better acknowledge that the possession of language is intellectually enabling, in the sense that it makes it possible for adult humans to engage in complex and sophisticated mental processes which would not otherwise be possible for them. But language is not an unmixed blessing. Recall Hobbes again, after observing that the possession of language makes men, unlike brutes, capable of "ratiocination," observing that it also makes men, unlike brutes, capable of "multiplying one untruth by another."[21]

It would be an oversimplification to assume that possession of language is a simple matter of yes or no; it is a matter of degree both in breadth (e.g., in vocabulary or mastery of complex constructions) and in depth (e.g., in completeness of understanding of complex or deeply theoretical terms, in skill in indirect and figurative uses of language). It would be another oversimplification to think of language mastery as a matter of fluency in some language or languages conceived as fixed; at least at the higher levels of intellectual sophistication, where theoretical inquiry is concerned, it is also a matter of capacity for linguistic innovation (e.g., of disambiguation of terms in common usage, and of devising novel vocabulary). And it would be another oversimplification again to suppose that the possession of language is intellectually enabling *only* because, as Hobbes observes, it is an aid to the memory and the means of learning from others; it is also potentially intellectually enabling because it makes it possible to think thoughts that would otherwise be too complex or subtle to grasp.

But the points most relevant to the argument of the present paper are simple enough. First: language and thought are *interdependent,* in the sense that cognitive capacity and linguistic sophistication can be mutually reinforcing. But, second: though the capacity for language is surely cognitively *en*abling, linguistic imperfections or abuses may no less surely be cognitively *dis*abling; just as richness of and scrupulousness in the use of linguistic resources can advance inquiry, poverty or abuse of linguistic resources can impede it.[22] Locke's glorious tirade against affected obscurity in the "holes of foxes" passage is a shrewd diagnosis of an endemic disease of philosophy.[23]

To COMPLETE MY PICTURE of the epistemology of metaphor, another piece has to be put into place alongside the account of metaphorical usage and the account of the relation of language to thought. This concerns the stages of inquiry, and requires a revision of the familiar dichotomy of the context of discovery versus the context of justification. Relying on a distinction between a stage at which an inquirer comes up with a theory in the first instance and the stage at which the theory is subsequently subjected to testing strongly suggests a picture in which an inquirer arrives at a stroke, as it were, at a full-blown theory. And this is surely extremely rare, at best. A better picture would include something like an initial phase in which an inquirer forms a vague idea for a possible theory, and subsequent phases of exploration and articulation, testing, modification, presentation; a better picture again would avoid the suggestion of a simple sequence of phases and acknowledge that the exploration and articulation, testing, modification, presentation of an initial vague idea can take place together, or in an up-and-back order. Unlike the discovery/justification distinction, the more elaborate distinctions suggested here would have the advantage that they need not rely, explicitly or implicitly, on there being precise and well-motivated criteria for the individuation of theories. This more complicated picture is a bit more realistic about what inquiry is really like; it is also more hospitable to the idea that metaphors have a significant role in inquiry—in the pursuit of "dry truth and real knowledge."

I shall be arguing that the most interesting cognitive role of metaphor is in the exploratory phases of inquiry. First, though, I want to amplify some points anticipated earlier about the role of metaphor in the presentation of theories.

Success or failure in presentation is, obviously, audience-relative; what succeeds, or is appropriate, for one audience, may fail, or be inappropriate, for another. A popular account of a scientific or philosophical theory will presumably aim to make the essentials of the theory (sufficiently) clear to a lay audience, whereas a presentation in a professional journal will aim to spell out the detailed workings of the theory as explicitly as possible. The previous discussion has suggested a distinction, first, of persuasive and instructive discourse, and then, within the category of instructive discourse, a continuum from the popular through the professional to the ideally explicit, specific, and detailed.

The role of metaphor in instructive discourse might reasonably be expected to be larger, and more appropriate, when the audience is lay or less expert, and smaller, and less appropriate, when the audience is of the inquirer's peers. Within this picture, what Locke calls "philosophical" discourse would represent a kind of ideal limit, and his thesis that metaphorical presentation is to be avoided in philosophical discourse would become the near-tautology that in the limit case where presentation is to be as explicit and specific as possible, the metaphorical, being implicit and unspecific, is to be avoided.

A metaphorical presentation can be helpful to the goal of instruction if it makes a theory comprehensible to an audience unfamiliar with its technical vocabulary, or insufficiently sophisticated in its logical, mathematical, or experimental techniques, to understand it in a literal presentation; or if, by inviting the audience to participate in figuring out the significant respects of comparison, it improves their understanding of the theory and memory for its details. It can on the other hand be a hindrance to the goal of instruction if there is any unclarity about what is or isn't to be taken literally; or if it is no more than a lazy evasion of the task of spelling out essential details; or if it gets the audience to accept the theory primarily by associating it metaphorically with some emotively appealing idea.

But what about the role of metaphor in the development of a theory? Berggren comments that "the difference between a metaphorical popularization of science and the creative use of metaphor by scientists themselves is a difference of degree only, not of kind."[24] There is truth in this, but it clearly requires some explanation.

Happily, the necessity of explaining how this can be coincides with the necessity of answering a question prompted by my account of metaphor. The account suggested of how metaphor works has looked to an interaction of speaker and hearer. This means that, while the role of metaphor in *presenting* a theory looks to fit neatly enough into place, the role of metaphor in other stages of inquiry faces a difficulty. The initial conception of a theory is an individual matter, and the exploration, articulation, testing, and modification of a theory may also be undertaken by one individual working alone; so how, if metaphor is in this sense an interactive process, could it fit into those phases? (And an objector pressing this point could be expected to add that the presentation stage is a stage "of inquiry" only by courtesy; that the other phases are the core, and it peripheral at best.)

The difficulty can be overcome if it is acknowledged that working out a problem, developing a theory, is well construed as involving a kind of inner dialogue. An inquirer tries out a conjecture; imagines possible objections and devises possible replies; figures out consequences and puts himself in the position of a hypothetical objector, . . . and so on. I should be very surprised to find that I am the only philosopher who, for instance, sometimes writes down a conjecture and returns to it after a while "to see if it still looks true," or who makes lists of potential objections, responses, responses to responses, etc.

A conception of the inquirer as engaging in inner dialogue permits an interesting partial explanation of how it is that linguistic development can contribute to cognitive development: crudely, as you get better at talking, you get better at talking to others, of course, but also at talking to yourself, at the inner dialogue which helps you to think through problems and figure out solutions. This conception also permits a plausible response to the difficulty about how metaphor fits in: in the inner dialogue of inquiry, the inquirer plays the role both of speaker and of hearer, and his metaphorical musings are an invitation to himself—as metaphorical utterances are an invitation to others—to seek out the similarities between the prima facie disparate phenomena implicitly compared. (It is worth noting that an approach like Searle's, by conceiving of metaphorical meaning as exhausted by the speaker's intentions, precludes this kind of exploratory role for metaphor.)

The invitation is especially useful in the exploratory stages of inquiry, as one is trying to develop an initial, usually very sketchy, idea into something worthy of the title "theory." Part of what is useful about a metaphor in this context lies in its combination of lack of specificity and directedness. Something merely vague might represent where you are at well enough, but would offer no help about how to advance; a metaphor invites you to look in certain directions. This much, however, is true of many literal comparisons, as well as of metaphors; so an account of the usefulness of metaphor, of figurative comparisons, calls for something more. The thought, crudely, is that metaphor is conducive to innovative, creative thinking because, by inviting a comparison of the phenomenon of which one is exploring a theory, and some other apparently *incongruous* phenomenon, it directs one's attention in what are likely to be hitherto-*unexplored* directions.

Eventually we want a theory to be as specific, as detailed, as precise as possible; but in the process of developing a specific, detailed, precise theory a vague idea may be a very useful stage along the way. A figurative comparison is well fitted to serve in this capacity because it is open-ended and unspecific, but at the same time invites a certain process of specification and filling in of details (a search for salient features of the thing or phenomenon with which the comparison is being made which are also features of the thing or phenomenon a theory of which one is exploring); and because, being initially incongruous, a metaphorical comparison is apt to direct one's attention along so far unexplored paths.

Perhaps one could make a connection between Aristotle's comparison of metaphors to puzzles, and his observation that an educated person will not expect more precision than the subject (I should prefer to say, than the stage the inquiry has reached) permits. At any rate, a metaphor's lack of specificity, combined with its directedness and novelty, is indeed what makes it useful in the early, fumbling-around phases of inquiry.

MY TITLE PROMISES some thoughts not only about the epistemology of metaphor, but also about metaphors of epistemology. I shall try to fulfill this undertaking by way of a selection of examples from epistemological inquiry which illustrate some of the suggestions made about the cognitive role of metaphor.

In epistemological writing, as elsewhere, metaphor, simile, analogy are ubiquitous: from Plato's analogies of the Sun, the Cave and the Divided Line, through Sextus's comparison of the skeptic's arguments to a ladder he climbs and then throws away, through Locke's metaphors of the philosopher as underlaborer and the mind as a wax tablet, to Neurath's simile likening inquirers to sailors rebuilding their ship while sailing in it, and his metaphor of the web of belief,[25] made famous by Quine—and developed by Putnam in his figure of science as a fleet of ships, from which sailors call to one another and borrow materials.[26]

The figures I have mentioned are clearly more than devices of presentation; though of course they are indeed that, as one is reminded by Quine's delight in playful variations on Neurath's theme: "I see philosophy and science as in the same boat—a boat which, to revert to Neurath's figure as I so often do, we can rebuild only at sea while staying afloat in it."[27] To call these figures "theory-constitutive" would be overstating it a bit; but they are, at the least, so deeply embedded in their authors' theories that it is reasonable to speculate that, just as they serve as what one might call "interpretive instruments" to the reader trying to figure out Plato's or Sextus's or Locke's or Neurath's or Quine's theories of knowledge, so also they served for their authors as "speculative instruments" (Berggren's term) or as sketch maps for the exploratory phase of inquiry.

Perhaps a few words are in order about my "metaphor, simile, analogy" a couple of paragraphs back. Metaphors are elliptical similes; similes and metaphors are figurative comparisons. Comparisons are figurative, rather than literal, to the extent that there is a prima facie *in*congruity between the things or phenomena compared. "Analogy" seems to suggest itself in preference to "metaphor" or "simile" for comparisons which are relatively closer to literal comparisons, and where the comparison invited focuses on *structural* features. It is not surprising that this is the kind of figure which seems most often to play a significant cognitive role in epistemological (and other) theory-exploration.

Part of what I have had to say is that metaphor is neither a good thing nor a bad thing in and of itself, that it may be helpful, harmless, or a hindrance to inquiry. No doubt philosophers sometimes use metaphor in ways that exploit their emotive associations. Nietzsche opens the preface to *Beyond Good and Evil*[28] by asking "Suppose Truth is a woman—what then?" The overt point is that philosophers have been clumsy and inexpert in their wooing; a covert point, maybe a denigration of the object of their pursuit—to knock Truth off her pedestal. Sometimes confusion may arise from, or advantage be taken of, the possibility of mistaking a figurative use for a literal. I am thinking, for example, of Davidson's critique of experientialist foundationalism, of the idea that some beliefs are justified, not by the support of other beliefs, but by the subject's experience.[29] Such a theory requires, Davidson suggests, a "confrontation" of belief and experience, would have us "getting outside our skins" to "compare" belief and experience; it is hard to avoid the suspicion that Davidson is taking advantage of the fact that we cannot *literally* get outside our skins, cannot *literally* confront our beliefs with experience, to ease the reader into accepting that experience can have no relevance to justification. And sometimes again, no doubt, epistemologists have been guilty of reliance on metaphor as a substitute for detailed theoretical articulation, or as an evasion, more or less conscious, of difficulties which would be revealed were such an articulation made. This, ironically enough, is the burden of T. H. Green's critique of Locke's metaphor of experience as making impressions on the wax tablet of the understanding.[30]

When examples are taken from the epistemological literature, there is the difficulty that—since what is studied is some philosopher's *presentation* of his theory—the question of the *cognitive* role of his metaphors, similes, and analogies, of their role in the process by which his theory was worked out, becomes a matter of speculation—at least usually, though occasionally a philosopher reports on this process, as Quine does in "Two Dogmas in Retrospect": "my [*sic*] metaphor [of the web of belief] needed unpacking, and that was largely my concern in the ten years between 'Two Dogmas' and *Word and Object*."[31] Anyhow, I hope it is not inappropriate for me to conclude with some observations of an autobiographical character about the role of an analogy which has come to play a central part in my own epistemological work; for here, at least, I can minimize the element of speculation.

Convinced that neither of the traditionally rival theories of epistemic justification—foundationalism and coherentism—would do, I at first advanced only so far as to introduce a word ("foundherentism") for the kind of intermediate theory I believed was required, and to sketch some of the desiderata it should satisfy: unlike foundationalism, it should not make relations of evidential support exclusively one-directional, but should allow for pervasive mutual support; unlike coherentism, it should allow the relevance of the subject's experience to the justification of his empirical beliefs. Ruminating on how to satisfy the first (and perhaps inspired by Polanyi's analogy between the social aspects of scientific inquiry and a roomful of people doing a huge jigsaw puzzle) it struck me that the way a person's beliefs about the world support one another is rather like the intersecting entries in a crossword. Furthermore, there was an analogue for the needed distinction between experiential evidence and reasons for a belief, in the different roles of the clue and of other already-completed intersecting entries in supporting an entry in a crossword.

The analogy has sustained me through subsequent stages of exploration and articulation of the vague idea with which I began. The reasonableness of an entry in a crossword depends on three factors: how well it is supported by its clue and any already-completed intersecting entries; how reasonable those intersecting entries are, independent of the support given them by the belief in question; and how much of the crossword has been completed. This led to a three-dimensional account of the determinants of degree of justification of a belief: how well it is supported by the subject's experiential evidence and reasons; how justified he is, independently of the support of the belief in question, in believing those reasons; and how comprehensive his evidence is.

The second criterion, which I called "independent security," presented an initial appearance of regressiveness, since "justified," the *explicandum*, occurs in this second part of the *explicans*. Were it not for the fact that the mutual dependence of entries in a crossword puzzle is obviously neither viciously circular nor infinitely regressive, this might have led me to abort the embryo theory. Instead, however, the analogy enabled me to articulate the theory further, and to avoid the apparent problem: in assessing the reasonableness of an entry in a crossword, you eventually reach a point where the question turns, not on how well an entry is supported by other entries, but on how well some entry is supported by its clue. Just so, I argued, in assessing the degree of justification of an empirical belief, eventually you reach a point where the question turns, not on how well a belief is supported by other beliefs, but on how well some belief is supported by the subject's experience; and here the question of justification no longer arises.

But didn't this mean that I had avoided a regress at the price of turning the theory back into a form of foundationalism? No. "Justified" eventually drops out of the *explicans* as we reach the question, how well some belief(s) is (are) supported by experiential evidence; but this doesn't require that any beliefs be justified exclusively by experiential evidence, nor, a fortiori, that all other justified beliefs be justified by the support of such beliefs.[32]

Explicitness is a desideratum of theory; in this, Locke is quite correct. My goal, as I spell out the foundherentist theory, is a specific, detailed, fully literal articulation. But the crossword analogy has been an indispensable aid in my progress toward that goal.

Davidson opens "What Metaphors Mean" by observing that "metaphors are the dreamwork of language." I shall close more prosaically, though no less metaphorically, by observing that metaphors can be the training wheels of inquiry.

NOTES

1. John Locke, *An Essay Concerning Human Understanding* (1690), III.x.34; references by book, chapter, and section number.

2. Thomas Hobbes, *Leviathan* (1651), ed. C. B. McPherson, Penguin Books, Harmondsworth, Middlesex, 1968; the quotations are from pp. 102, 110, 107, 105, 106. The *OED* defines *leviathan* as "sea monster [Bibl]; huge ship; anything very large of its kind; person of formidable ability, power or wealth"; *ignes fatuus* as "Will-o'-the-wisp, phosphorescent light seen on marshy ground; delusive hope or gain"; and *lime* as "sticky substance made from holly bark for catching small birds."

3. Baron William de Traci, the third knight in T. S. Eliot's *Murder in the Cathedral*, describes himself and his fellow assassins as "four plain Englishmen."

4. John Stuart Mill, *A System of Logic* (1843), new impression, Longmans, London, 1970, pp. 28–29.

5. Mill, *A System of Logic*, p. 50. The distinction Mill is making is between, for example, the "is" in "God is" (meaning "God exists") and the "is" in "God is good."

6. See Donald Davidson's influential statement in "What Metaphors Mean," *Critical Inquiry*, 5, 1978, 31–47; reprinted in *Inquiries into Truth and Interpretation*, Clarendon Press, Oxford, 1984, 245–64. Davidson's theme is taken up by, for example, David Cooper, *Metaphor*, Blackwell, Oxford, 1986, and Richard Rorty, "Unfamiliar Noises: Hesse and Davidson on Metaphor," *Proceedings of the Aristotelian Society, Supplement*, 61, 1987, 283–396. See also F. C. T. Moore, "On Taking Metaphor Literally," in David Miall, ed., *Metaphor: Problems and Perspectives*, Harvester Press, Sussex, and Humanities Press, Atlantic Highlands, NJ, 1982, 1–13, for a position remarkably close to, but arrived at independently of, Davidson.

7. Aristotle, *Rhetoric, Works*, XL, Oxford University Press, Oxford, 1952, 1406b, 1410b; Cicero, *de Oratore*, trans. H. Racham, Harvard University Press, Cambridge, MA, vol . 2, 3.38.156–39.157; Quintilian, *Institutio Oratoria*, Heinemann, London, 1922, Book 7, vi, 8–9.

8. I. A. Richards, *The Philosophy of Rhetoric*, Oxford University Press, Oxford, 1936; reprinted by Galaxy Press, New York, 1965, lecture 5; Max Black, "Metaphor," *Proceedings of the Aristotelian Society*, 55, 1954–55, 273–94.

9. Robert Fogelin, *Figuratively Speaking*, Yale University Press, New Haven, CT, 1988.

10. Though I do not subscribe to his theory, I borrow a happy phrase from

Beardsley's, "The Metaphorical Twist," *Philosophy and Phenomenological Research,* 22, 1962, 293–307; reprinted in Wayne Shibles, ed., *Essays on Metaphor,* Language Press, Whitewater, WI, 1972, 73–91.

11. Amos Tversky, "Features of Similarity," *Psychological Review,* 84, 1977, 67–78.

12. The *OED* defines *aback* as "backwards; (Naut) of square sails pressed against mast by headwind; taken ——, of ship w. sails in that state, (fig) surprised."

13. John Searle, "Metaphor," in *Expression and Meaning,* Cambridge University Press, Cambridge, 1979; reprinted in Andrew Ortony, ed., *Metaphor and Thought,* Cambridge University Press, Cambridge (1979), second edition, 1993, 83–111, pp. 102 ff. of the latter.

14. Searle, "Metaphor," p. 110.

15. Davidson, "What Metaphors Mean," p. 261.

16. Davidson, "What Metaphors Mean," p. 262.

17. Ursula Le Guin, *The Left Hand of Darkness,* Ace Books, New York, 1969.

18. My use of "interactive," which is pragmatic, referring to an interaction of speaker and hearer, should not be confused with the semantic sense in which Black uses the word. A later paper of Davidson's, "A Nice Derangement of Epitaphs" (in E. Lepore, ed., *Truth and Interpretation,* Blackwell, Oxford, 1986, 433–46), is much more hospitable to the pragmatic-interaction approach suggested here than his earlier work, in which his noncognitivist attitude to metaphor was, if not determined, at least strongly indicated by his emphasis on semantics of a strictly Tarskian stripe.

19. Perhaps Locke's ubiquitous use in the *Essay* of the figurative language he officially deplores in serious discourse may be explained, not as simple inadvertence, but as an indication that he doesn't regard the *Essay* as philosophical discourse in the strictest sense. Campbell Fraser remarks in the *Prolegomena* to his edition (p. xii) that Locke's *Essay* "deals with philosophy in the inexact language of common life"; on the next page he quotes Leibniz, from the opening sentence of the preface to his *Nouveaux Essaies sure L'Entendement Humaine:* "the author of the *Essay* adapts his style more to the general reader than I pretend to do."

20. The classic expression of the interdependence of language and thought is to be found in Lev Semenovich Vygotsky, *Thought and Language,* trans. Eugenia Hanfmann and Gertrude Vakar, MIT Press, Cambridge, MA, 1962.

21. Thomas Hobbes, *Human Nature* (1650), in J. E. Woodbridge, ed., *Hobbes Selections,* Charles Scribner's Sons, New York, 1930, p. 23.

22. The classic expression of this idea is, of course, Orwell's "Newspeak."

23. A diagnosis put to use in "Preposterism and Its Consequences," essay 11 in this volume.

24. Douglas Berggren, "The Use and Abuse of Metaphor," I and II, *Review of Metaphysics,* 16, 1962, 237–58 and 450–72, p. 451.

25. Otto Neurath, "Anti-Spengler" (1921), in *Empiricism and Sociology,* ed. Marie

Neurath and Robert S. Cohen, Reidel, Dordrecht, 1973, 158–213, pp. 161 (the web) and 199 (rebuilding the ship).

26. Hilary Putnam, "Philosophers and Human Understanding," in A. H. Heath, ed., *Scientific Explanation,* Clarendon Press, Oxford, 1981, 99–121, p. 118.

27. W. V. O. Quine, "Natural Kinds," in *Ontological Relativity and Other Essays,* Columbia University Press, New York, 1969, 114–38, p. 126.

28. Friedrich Nietzsche, *Beyond Good and Evil* (1886), trans. Walter Kaufmann, Vintage Books, Random House, New York, 1966.

29. Donald Davidson, "A Coherence Theory of Truth and Knowledge," in D. Henrich, ed., *Kant Oder Hegel?* Klett-Cotta, Stuttgart, 1983, 423–38.

30. Thomas Hill Green, *Introduction to Hume's Treatise* (1874), reprinted by Thomas Y. Crowell, New York, 1968, section 9 ff.

31. W. V. O. Quine, "Two Dogmas in Retrospect," *Canadian Journal of Philosophy,* 21.3, 1991, 265–74, p. 272.

32. See my "Theories of Knowledge: An Analytic Framework," *Proceedings of the Aristotelian Society,* 83, 1982–83, 143–57; "Rebuilding the Ship While Sailing on the Water," in Robert Barrett and Roger Gibson, eds., *Perspectives on Quine,* Blackwell, Oxford, 111–27. (See also my *Evidence and Inquiry: Towards Reconstruction in Epistemology,* Blackwell, Oxford, 1993; "Puzzling Out Science" (essay 5) and "Science as Social?—Yes and No" (essay 6) in this volume; "The Puzzle of 'Scientific Method,'" *Revue Internationale de Philosophie,* 4.1997, 495–105; and "The Foundherentist Theory of Empirical Justification," in Louis Pojman, ed., *The Theory of Knowledge,* Wadsworth, Belmont, CA, second edition, 1998.)

Puzzling Out Science

Science embodies the epitome of man's intellectual development.   C. S. PEIRCE[1]

To say that man is made up of strength and weakness, of insight and blindness, of pettiness and grandeur, is not to draw up an indictment against him: it is to define him.   DENIS DIDEROT[2]

What do the natural sciences know, and how do they know it? I approach our topic with a little diffidence, since I am neither a scientist nor a historian of science, not even a specialist in the philosophy of science, but a plain epistemologist. Indeed, recalling Sheldon Glashow's reaction to an invitation to discuss what prophets of the end of science present as Grave Epistemological Issues: "forgive me if I thrash about a bit—it's not easy to beat a dead oxymoron,"[3] I feel more than a *little* diffidence! I, too, shall thrash about a bit; in my case, however, not out of pure exasperation, but in hopes of separating the chaff, the extravagances of radical critics who profess to have exposed science as a merely "subjective and relativistic project, operating out of social attitudes and ideologies,"[4] from the serious questions to which an honest epistemologist might be able to contribute something.[5]

ONCE UPON A TIME (the phrase is a warning that what follows will be cartoon history) it was taken for granted that science enjoys a peculiar epistemic authority because of its uniquely objective and rational method of inquiry. Successive efforts to articulate what that uniquely rational method might be gave rise to umpteen competing versions of what I shall call the Old Deferentialist position: science progresses inductively by accumulating true theories confirmed by empirical evidence, by observed facts; or deductively, by testing conjectures against basic statements and, as falsified conjectures are replaced by corroborated ones, improving the verisimilitude of its theories; or instrumentally, by developing theories which, though not themselves capable of truth or falsity, are efficient instruments of prediction; or, etc. Such obstacles as Quine's thesis of the underdetermination of theories even by all possible observational evidence,[6] Russell Hanson's and others' of the theory-dependence of observation,[7] Goodman's "new riddle of induction,"[8] though acknowledged as tough, were assumed to be superable, or avoidable.

It is tempting to describe these problems in Kuhnian terms, as anomalies facing the Old Deferentialist paradigm just as a rival was beginning to stir. Kuhn himself, evidently, did not intend radically to undermine the pretensions of science to be a rational enterprise;[9] but most readers of *The Structure of Scientific Revolutions,* missing many subtleties and many ambiguities, heard only: science progresses, or "progresses," not by the accumulation of well-confirmed truths, but by revolutionary upheavals; there are no paradigm-neutral standards of evidence, only the different standards of incommensurable paradigms; a scientific revolution, like a political revolution, depends on propaganda and control of resources; a scientist's shift in allegiance to a new paradigm is like a religious conversion, a conversion after which things look so different to him that he may be said to "live in a different world."

Even so, when twenty-odd years ago Feyerabend proclaimed that there is no scientific method, that appeals to "rationality" and "evidence" are nothing more rhetorical bullying, he was widely regarded—he described himself—as the "court jester" of the philosophy of science.[10] Mainstream philosophers of science mostly continued (and continue) to be convinced that the Old Deferentialism is correct in essentials, though conceding that much more work is needed on the details.

Of late, however, radical sociologists, radical feminists, radical Afrocentrists, and radical followers of (by now somewhat dated) Paris fashions in rhetoric and semiology, have turned their attention to science. Now it is commonplace to hear that science is largely or even wholly a matter of social interests, negotiation, myth-making, the production of inscriptions; that "objectivity" and "rationality" are nothing but ideological constructs disguising the exclusion of the perspective of this or that oppressed group.

"The validity of theoretical propositions in the sciences is in no way affected by factual evidence," Kenneth Gergen tells us. "The natural world," Harry Collins writes, "has a small or non-existent role in the construction of scientific knowledge." "A fact is nothing but a statement with no modality . . . and no trace of authorship," Latour and Woolgar declare. "What the [natural] sciences actually observe is . . . always nature-as-an-object of knowledge—which is always already fully encultured," Sandra Harding observes, so the natural sciences are subordinate to the social sciences.[11]

According to this new orthodoxy, not only does science have no peculiar epistemic authority and no uniquely rational method, it is really, like all purported "inquiry," just politics. "All this business about rationality and irrationality is the result of an attack by someone on associations that stand in the way," Latour assures us. "While the dangers are real," Lynn Nelson warns, "the 'noble lie' [that politics can be kept out of science] is far more dangerous." "Science legitimates itself by linking its discoveries to power," Stanley Aronowitz tells us, "a connection which *determines* (not merely influences) what counts as reliable knowledge." Steve Fuller explains, in fluent Newspeak, that "although critics of prolescience typically read it as a veiled form of antiscience, it would be more instructive to regard prole-science as an implicit challenge to many of the elitist assumptions of plebi-science"; and boasts, "I don't see any difference between 'good scholarship' and 'political relevance.' Both will vary, depending on who you are trying to court in your work."[12]

What the New Cynics offer in place of argument or evidence for their startling epistemological claims is an astonishing farrago of confusion, non sequitur, rhetoric—accompanied by an astonishing outbreak of sneer quotes. It is beyond my power, and your tolerance, to deal comprehensively with all this; but not, I hope, to discern some main strategies, and a key fallacy.

The basic strategy is to shift attention from the normative notion of *warrant* (of how good the evidence is for this or that scientific claim) onto the descriptive notion of *acceptance* (the standing of a claim in the eyes of the relevant community). Some play down warrant and accentuate accep-tance, insisting that social values are inseparable from evidential ones; some ignore warrant altogether and acknowledge only acceptance, con-ceiving of scientific knowledge as nothing more than the upshot of pro-cesses of social negotiation; some engage in a kind of conceptual kidnap-ping, replacing the notion of warrant by a sociopolitical ersatz—thus, for example, "democratic epistemology."

Why the shift? In part, perhaps, because, coming from sociology, an-thropology, literary theory, or feminist philosophy, many New Cynics are predisposed to focus on the social or the rhetorical, and may not be well equipped to attend to the often formidable technicalities involved in ques-tions about the warrant of scientific claims. In part also, perhaps, because, inadvertently or otherwise, some New Cynics have run together legitimate social and political questions about, e.g., the uses of technology or government funding of scientific projects, with epistemological issues.[13]

More interestingly, some may have been led to the conclusion that scientific knowledge is nothing but a social construction by a faulty inference from the true premise that the scientific knowledge we now possess has been the work of a whole, inter-generational, community of inquirers. Some, again, may have been led to the conclusion that reality is socially constructed by a faulty inference from the true premise that (because of the ever-increasing interpenetration of theory and instrumentation), the objects of scientists' observations are often what one might call "laboratory phenomena"; or by the same faulty inference from the true premise that social institutions and categories (the objects of sociological theories) would not exist were it not for human activities. It obviously doesn't follow, and neither is it true, that reality, even that social or laboratory reality, is created by scientists' theorizing.

Most interestingly, many New Cynics disdain the notions of evidence and warrant because, as they are at pains to point out, what has passed for warranted theory, relevant evidence, known fact, objective truth, has often enough turned out to be no such thing. This is true; but the conclusion that the notions of warrant, evidence, truth, fact, reality, knowledge, are ideological humbug manifestly doesn't follow. So ubiquitous has this manifestly invalid form of inference become of late, however, that it deserves a name; I call it "the 'passes for' fallacy."

Applied, as the New Cynics apply it, to the concepts of evidence, warrant, etc., the "passes for" fallacy is not only fallacious but self-undermining; if the notions of evidence, fact, truth, etc., *were* ideological humbug, the "investigations" which supposedly established this could not, as advertised, have found evidence indicating the truth of the social-constructivist thesis, but could themselves be no more than socially negotiated myth-making. If you think this point too obvious to be worth making, listen to Stephen Cole: "Given that facts can easily become errors, what sense does it make to see what is at time 1 a 'fact' and at Time 2 an 'error' as being determined by nature?"; and then, a few pages later, "the most important evidence in favor of my position is the fact that . . ."[14] Feminists who maintain that the underdetermination of theories by data means that political values may legitimately take up the slack in deciding what theories to accept, and yet assume that we can know what theories would conduce to women's interests, likewise, are sawing through the branch on which they sit.[15]

The shallow rhetoric and the self-defeating arguments of contemporary cynics deserve, indeed, the treatment appropriate to dead oxymorons; and so, holding my nose and stepping delicately around these obstacles, I shall try, in what follows, to sketch an approach which might avoid the real difficulties of the Old Deferentialism without surrendering to the factitious despair of the New Cynics.

FROM THE FACT that what has passed in science for objective evidence, established truth, etc., has sometimes been nothing of the kind, it doesn't follow that there are no objective epistemic standards, nor that there is nothing epistemologically special about science. And these cynical ideas are not only unproven, they are false: there *are* objective epistemic standards, and there *is* something epistemologically special about science. The Old Deferentialist picture rightly acknowledges this, but in the wrong way—indeed, by conceiving of science as the source of our epistemic standards, in a way that gives aid and comfort to the "passes for" fallacy. A better way sees science, not as *privileged,* but as *distinguished* epistemically; as deserving, if you will, *respect* rather than *deference.* Science is neither sacred nor a confidence trick.

Our standards of what constitutes good, honest, thorough inquiry and what constitutes good, strong, supportive evidence are not internal to science. In judging where science has succeeded and where it has failed, in what areas and at what times it has done better and in what worse, we are appealing to the standards by which we judge the solidity of empirical beliefs, or the rigor and thoroughness of empirical inquiry, generally. (Nor, of course, is science the *only* source of knowledge.)[16]

It is important to distinguish two questions often run together in contemporary epistemology and philosophy of science: how to assess the worth of evidence for a proposition, and: how to conduct inquiry. The former kind of question, though hard enough, is a bit more tractable than the latter. The goal of inquiry is to discover significant, substantial truths; and since there is a certain tension between the two aspects of the goal— it is a lot easier to get truths if you don't mind the truths you get being trivial—there can be, at best, guidelines, not rules, for the conduct of inquiry. Criteria for appraisal of the worth of evidence, on the other hand, are focused on only one aspect of the goal, on truth-indicativeness.

Not all scientific theories are well confirmed by objective evidence; most are, at some stages of their career at least, no more than tenuously supported speculations; and some may get accepted, even entrenched, on flimsy evidence. Nevertheless, science has succeeded extraordinarily well, by and large, by our standards of empirical evidence.

The best model of those standards is not, as much recent epistemology has assumed, a mathematical proof, but a crossword puzzle. The clues are the analogue of experiential evidence, already-completed entries the analogue of background information. How reasonable an entry in a crossword is depends upon how well it is supported by the clue and any other already-completed intersecting entries; how reasonable, independently of the entry in question, those other entries are; and how much of the crossword has been completed. An empirical proposition is more or less warranted depending on how well it is supported by experiential evidence and background beliefs; how secure the relevant background beliefs are, independently of the proposition in question; and how much of the relevant evidence the evidence includes. How well evidence supports a proposition depends on how much the addition of the proposition in question improves its explanatory integration. There is such a thing as supportive-but-less-than-conclusive evidence, even if there is no formalizable inductive logic.[17]

Science has come up with deep, broad, and explanatory theories which are well anchored in experiential evidence and which interlock surprisingly with each other. And nothing succeeds like success; having, as it were, plausibly filled in long, central entries greatly improves the prospects for completing other parts of the puzzle.

The crossword analogy suggests a way to come to terms with some Kuhnian themes usually perceived as a threat to the idea of objective evidential support. Normal science can be thought of on the analogy of working on smaller, non-central entries while taking the correctness of intersecting, already-completed, long, central entries for granted. A crisis situation in which anomalies start to pile up for a paradigm can be thought of on the analogy of the smaller, non-central entries becoming more and more strained, as the constraints imposed by the already-completed central entries make it harder and harder to fill them in a way that really fits the clues. A scientific revolution can be thought of on the analogy of finding oneself obliged to revise several long, central entries and, as a result, having to rub out a whole slew of other entries, since they are no longer compatible with the revised ones. (I can't resist adding that fallibilism can be construed as the analogue of the principle: if you must use ink, make sure it's washable!)

The sting is taken out of the supposed paradigm-dependence of observations, things looking different after a paradigm shift, when it is thought of on the analogy of the way a crossword entry depends, not only on the clue, but also on intersecting entries. The thing observed doesn't change, nor the observer's perceptual state, but the judgment he makes of what he sees changes, because of his changed background beliefs.[18]

The sting is also taken out of the supposed paradigm-relativity of epistemic standards, which is not real incommensurability, but deep-seated disagreement in background beliefs. Suppose you and I are working on the same crossword. You think, given your solution to 7 across, that the fact that a solution to 2 down ends in an "E" is evidence in its favor; I, given my solution to 7 across, that the fact that it ends in an "S" is evidence in its favor. In a weak sense, we might be said to differ about "what counts as evidence"; but we are both seeking to fit the entry to its clue and to other relevant entries. In the sense that matters, there is no relativity of standards. Compare the case where you and I are both on an appointments committee; you argue that this candidate should be ruled out on the grounds that his handwriting indicates that he is not to be trusted, I think graphology is bunk and scoff at your supposed evidence. Once again, what we have is disagreement in background beliefs, not real incommensurability of epistemic standards; and the same goes, though on a much larger scale, for disagreements between proponents of rival paradigms.

Epistemic distinction, not privilege: when we turn to the question of method, of the conduct of inquiry, the same kind of curtailment of the Old Deferentialists' conception is called for. In the narrow sense in which the phrase supposedly refers to a set of rules which can be followed mechanically and which are guaranteed to produce true, or probably true, or progressively more nearly true, or, etc., results, there is no scientific method. No mechanical procedure can avoid the need for discretion—as is revealed by the Popperian shift from: make a bold conjecture, test it as severely as possible, and as soon as counterevidence is found, abandon it and start again, to: make a bold conjecture, test it as severely as possible, and if counterevidence is found, don't give up too easily, but don't hang on to it too long. In a broader, vaguer sense, in which the phrase refers to making conjectures, developing them, testing them, assessing the likelihood that they are true, of course there is such a thing; but not only scientists, but also historians, detectives, investigative journalists, and the rest of us, use "the method of science" in this sense.[19]

Nevertheless, there is something distinctive about inquiry in the sciences—or rather, a lot of things: systematic effort to isolate one variable at a time; systematic commitment to criticism and testing; experimental contrivance of every kind; instruments of observation from the microscope to the questionnaire; all the complex apparatus of statistical evaluation and mathematical modeling; and the engagement, cooperative and competitive, of many persons, within and across generations, in the enterprise of scientific inquiry.[20] All of us, in figuring out how things are, use, in Peirce's phrase, "the method of experience and reasoning"; but science has, by all the means just listed, enormously deepened and extended the range of experience and the sophistication of reasoning of which it avails itself. Once again, as one considers, for example, how theoretical advances enable new instrumentation, the phrase that comes to mind is, "nothing succeeds like success."

An adequate epistemology of science will not, as some Old Deferentialists expected, be exclusively logical, but will have a social dimension. Unlike the New Cynicism, however, it will not see the fact that science is a social enterprise as illegitimating its epistemic pretensions, but as an important factor contributing to its epistemic distinction; not as a reason for favoring the notion of acceptance and neglecting warrant, but as an important factor helping to keep warrant and acceptance appropriately correlated.

The ideal would be a scientific community of creative and careful inquirers, with adequate resources of equipment and time, all sincerely seeking the truth and unaffected by prejudice, and each making his work freely available to the scrutiny of others, who would thereby be enabled to build on what is solid and to correct what is not. For that would be a community in which creativity in hypothesis and care in seeking out and assessing the worth of evidence—the twin desiderata imposed by the dual goal of inquiry—were maximized.

Idealistic as this is, it already indicates why freedom of thought and information is vital to the scientific enterprise, and thus why pressure for "politically adequate research and scholarship," whether made by totalitarian governments or by feminist philosophers of science like Sandra Harding (whose no-doubt-unintentionally chilling words I just quoted),[21] is epistemologically as well as politically objectionable.

Making the model more realistic by acknowledging that any actual scientific community consists of real, imperfect human beings, reveals how individual idiosyncrasies or weaknesses may compensate for each other. I doubt that the Old Deferentialist aspiration to specify rules for when a theory should be accepted and when rejected is realizable. But in a community of inquirers, some will be more conservative in temperament, inclined to try adapting an old theory to new evidence, others more radical, readier to look for a new approach.[22] I doubt that real scientists are ever quite single-mindedly devoted to the truth; all, I expect, are motivated to some extent by the hope of fame or fortune, or to some degree in the grip of prejudice or partisanship. But to the extent that science is organized so as to maximize the likelihood that fame and fortune come to those who make real discoveries, or that partisans of one approach seek out the weaknesses which partisans of another are motivated to neglect, a real community of imperfect inquirers can be a tolerable ersatz of an ideal community.[23]

Everything I have said so far presupposes that talk of "science" is shorthand for referring to a complex congeries of disciplines and subdisciplines, the boundaries of which are more than a little fuzzy, and the different parts and stages of which are more than a little uneven in theoretical stability, methodological sophistication, and, yes, reliability. It is to be expected that the influence of prejudice and partisanship will be more of a hurdle in those areas of science where research bears most directly on politically contested issues, i.e., primarily, in the human and social sciences.

This prompts the further thought that the environment in which scientific work is done may be more *or less* conducive to good, honest, thorough, scrupulous inquiry. Among potential hindrances are: the necessity to spend large amounts of time and energy on obtaining resources, and to impress whatever body provides the funds, in due course, with one's success; dependence for resources on bodies with an interest in the research coming out this way or that, or in rivals being denied access to the results;[24] pressure to solve problems which are perceived as socially urgent, rather than freedom to pursue those most susceptible of solution in the present state of knowledge. It is no longer possible to do important scientific work with a candle and a piece of string—ever more sophisticated equipment is needed to obtain ever more recherché observations; so it is not surprising that my list of potential hindrances focuses on issues about resources. But other issues are also apropos: among them, a volume of publications so large as to impede rather than to assist communication; not to mention the influence of the New Cynicism in discouraging some who might otherwise become, if not practicing scientists, members of that vital concomitant of a healthy scientific community, an educated public sufficiently literate scientifically "to distinguish genuine science from fantasy and superstition."[25] It would be less than candid not to acknowledge that this list of potential hindrances by no means encourages complacency about the present condition of science.

Of late, sociology of science has been closely associated with the New

Cynicism; so closely associated, indeed, that not a few philosophers of science, and scientists too, have come to regard the whole enterprise of the sociological study of science with suspicion. This is unfortunate. For, as I said earlier, "an adequate epistemology of science will not . . . be exclusively logical, but will have a social dimension"; and good, sober sociology of science can throw welcome light on what aspects of the internal organization of science, and of its external environment, encourage, and what discourage, well-conducted, creative, honest inquiry.

Briefly and roughly, the good kind of sociology of science recognizes, and the bad kind ignores or denies, the fact that science is not *simply* a social institution like banking or the fashion industry, but a social institution *engaged in inquiry*, attempting to discover how the world is, to devise explanatory theories that stand up in the face of evidence. A little more precisely: the good, sober style of sociology of science accommodates considerations of warrant as well as acceptance; the bad, intoxicated style refuses questions of warrant, or transmutes them into purely sociological considerations. (Perhaps I need to add that there can of course be *bad* good sociology of science, i.e., sociology of science of the right kind, but poorly conducted.)

The bad style of sociology of science, ignoring or denigrating the relevance of evidential considerations, is invariably *debunking* in tendency. But, though proponents of the other kind like to suggest otherwise, good sociology of science is not invariably or inevitably *legitimating* in tendency. Acceptance and warrant may or may not be appropriately correlated; and a sober sociology of science will ask, not only what the mechanisms are by which they are appropriately correlated, but what goes wrong when they are not.

Because it is invariably debunking, bad sociology of science is invariably self-undermining. Claiming or suggesting that the real explanation of the currency of a scientific theory is always something about the historical or social circumstances of its origin, never a matter of its having been recognized that there is good evidence for it, bad sociology of science undermines its own pretensions to supply warranted explanations of the currency of this or that theory. But, to repeat, the problem is not with sociology of science as such, but with sociology of science conducted (as, unhappily, some recent sociology of science has been conducted) under the influence of amnesia or skepticism about the role of evidence in scientific inquiry.

As for the question of the progress of science, on which the Old Deferentialism tends, as usual, to excessive optimism, and the New Cynicism to excessive pessimism, again we need a nuanced answer. At any time, some parts of science may be advancing, some stagnating, and others, quite possibly, regressing. Where there is progress, this may be a matter of accumulation of truths, or of replacement of discredited theories by better ones; and in the latter case, the new theory may entail that the old was correct in a limited domain, or may be incompatible with it, or may partially overlap it, and/or may introduce a new scheme of categories and concepts that can be translated into the older vocabulary only by clumsy circumlocution.

I have sketched an epistemology of science which is realistic in the ordinary sense, neither too optimistic nor too pessimistic, and realistic also in some of the technical senses most directly tied to questions about objectivity. A scientific claim is either true or else false; true or false objectively, i.e., independently of what an*y*body believes. The evidence for a scientific claim is strong or weak; strong or weak objectively, i.e., independently of how anybody judges it. There is no guarantee that every scientist is fully objective, i.e., is an absolutely disinterested truth-seeker. Nor is there any guarantee that, as science proceeds, it invariably adds to its accumulation of truths, or replaces false theories by true, or gets nearer the truth. But though there are no grounds for complacency, though like all human enterprises, science is far from perfect, it has been (if we don't blow it, it can continue to be) the most impressively successful of human cognitive enterprises. And—I conclude as I began, by quoting Charles Peirce, himself a working scientist as well as the greatest of American philosophers— "a man must be downright crazy to doubt that science has made many true discoveries."[26] Or a woman.

NOTES

1. *Collected Papers,* ed. Charles Hartshorne, Paul Weiss, and Arthur Burks, Harvard University Press, Cambridge, MA, 1931–58, 7.49. (See essay 3, "As for that phrase 'studying in a literary spirit' . . . ," on Peirce's use of "science.")

2. *Addition aux pensées philosophiques* (c. 1762); my source is *The Oxford Book of Aphorisms,* ed. John Gross, Oxford University Press, Oxford, 1983, pp. 24–25.

3. Sheldon Lee Glashow, "The Death of Science!?" in *The End of Science,* ed. Richard Q. Elvee, University Press of America, Lanham, MD, 1992, 23–31; the quotation is from p. 25.

4. I quote from the letter of invitation to the conference on "The End of Sci-

ence," held at Gustavus Adolphus College in 1989—the letter about which Glashow is expostulating above. My source is Larry Laudan, who quotes from the letter in the Preface to *Science and Relativism,* University of Chicago Press, Chicago, 1990, p. ix.

5. My concern here will be exclusively with epistemological issues. But I don't deny the legitimacy or the importance of moral and political issues about priorities in scientific research, or the paucity of female physicists or black biochemists, etc. I have had something to say about some of these issues in "Science 'From a Feminist Perspective,'" *Philosophy,* 67, 1992, 5–18, reprinted in Peter Halfpenny and Peter McMylor, eds., *Positivist Sociology and Its Critics,* Edward Elgar Press, Aldershot, Hants, 1994, vol. 3, 99–112.

6. This is often referred to as "the Duhem-Quine thesis," but the attribution to Duhem is not accurate; his thesis, that scientific claims are often not testable in isolation but only in conjunction with a bunch of other claims involved in reliance on instruments, is significantly more modest. Even Quine's commitment to the thesis is not unwavering; in "Empirical Content" (*Theories and Things,* Belknap Press of Harvard University Press, Cambridge and London, 1981, 24–30) he suggests that what he formerly described as empirically equivalent but incompatible theories would really be verbal variants of one theory (pp. 29–30).

7. Norwood Russell Hanson, *Patterns of Discovery,* Cambridge University Press, Cambridge, 1958. The thesis that observation *statements* are theory-dependent is already found in Karl Popper, *The Logic of Scientific Discovery* (1934), Hutchinson, London, 1959.

8. Nelson Goodman, "The New Riddle of Induction" (1953), in *Fact, Fiction, and Forecast,* Harvard University Press, Cambridge, 1955, 59–83.

9. See Thomas S. Kuhn, "Postscript–1969" in the second edition of *The Structure of Scientific Revolutions,* University of Chicago Press, Chicago, 1970; "Logic of Discovery or Psychology of Research?" and "Reflections on my Critics," in I. Lakatos and A. Musgrave, eds., *Criticism and the Growth of Knowledge,* Cambridge University Press, Cambridge, 1970, 1–24 and 231–78; "Second Thoughts on Paradigms," in F. Suppe, ed., *The Structure of Scientific Theories,* University of Illinois Press, Urbana, 1970, 458–517; *The Essential Tension,* University of Chicago Press, Chicago, 1977; "Commensurability, Comparability, Communicability," in Peter D. Asquith and Thomas Nickles, eds., *PSA 1982,* Philosophy of Science Association, East Lansing, MI, 1983, volume 2, 669–88; "Afterwords," in *World Changes,* ed. Paul Horwich, Bradford Books, MIT Press, Cambridge, MA, 1993, 311–41.

10. Paul K. Feyerabend, *Against Method,* New Left Books, London, 1975.

11. Kenneth Gergen, "Feminist Critique of Science and the Challenge of Social Epistemology," in *Feminist Thought and the Structure of Knowledge,* ed. Mary M. Gergen, New York University Press, New York, 1988, 27–48, p. 37; Harry Collins, "Stages in the Empirical Programme of Relativism," *Social Studies of Science,* 11, 1981, p. 3; Bruno Latour and Steve Woolgar, *Laboratory Life: The Social Construction of Scientific Facts,* Sage Library of Social Research, Beverly Hills, CA, and London,

1979, p. 82; Sandra Harding, "After the Neutrality Ideal: Science, Politics, and 'Strong Objectivity,'" *Social Research*, 59.3, 1992, 567–87, p. 575 and note 12.

12. Bruno Latour, *Science in Action*, Harvard University Press, Cambridge, MA, p. 205; Lynn Hankinson Nelson, *Who Knows? From Quine to a Feminist Empiricism*, Temple University Press, Philadelphia, 1990, p. 102; Stanley Aronowitz, *Science as Power: Discourse and Ideology in Modern Society*, University of Minnesota Press, Minneapolis, 1988, p. 204; Steve Fuller, *Philosophy, Rhetoric, and the End of Knowledge*, University of Wisconsin Press, Madison, 1993, p. xviii, and E-mail posting, 5.4.94.

13. I don't mean to imply that no Old Deferentialists have ever been guilty of the same confusion.

14. *Making Science: Between Nature and Society*, Harvard University Press, Cambridge, MA, and London, 1992, pp. 12, 21. Cole is, by the way, regarded as a dangerous moderate among hard-line social constructivists, since he allows that the world *does*, after all, play some role in science; see the review of his book by the egregious Steve Fuller, *American Scientist*, June 1994, 295–96.

15. For example, "Nineteenth-century biologists and chemists claimed that women's brains were smaller than men's and women's ovaries and uteruses required much energy and rest in order to function properly. . . . Feminist scholars have analyzed these self-serving theories and documented the absurdity of the claims. . . . Feminist science . . . must insist on the political nature and content of scientific work. . . ." (Ruth Hubbard, "Some Thoughts about the Masculinity of the Natural Sciences," in Mary M. Gergen, ed., *Feminist Thought and the Structure of Knowledge*, 1–15, pp. 7, 13). See also Ruth Bleier, "*Science* and the Construction of Meanings in the Neurosciences," in Sue V. Rosser, ed., *Feminism within the Science and Health Care Professions: Overcoming Resistance*, Pergamon Press, Oxford and New York, 1988, 91–116, discussed in detail in "Science as Social?—Yes and No," essay 6 in this volume.

16. It may be prudent to add that all I mean by this remark is that historians, detectives, investigative journalists, and the rest of us all have perfectly good empirical knowledge; not that there are mysterious "ways of knowing" beyond experience and reasoning. On the relation of science, literature, and philosophy, see "As for that phrase 'studying in a literary spirit' . . . ," essay 3 in this volume.

17. The simplified account sketched here is developed in detail in my *Evidence and Inquiry: Towards Reconstruction in Epistemology*, Blackwell, Oxford, 1993, chapter 4, and in "The Foundherentist Theory of Empirical Justification," in *Theory of Knowledge*, ed. Louis Pojman, second edition, Wadsworth, Belmont, CA, 1998.

18. It is clear that Kuhn's view is that the subject's perceptual experience changes; see, particularly, "Second Thoughts," in Suppe, *The Structure of Scientific Theories*. Mine, by contrast, is that the perceptual judgment, always dependent on background beliefs as well as one's perceptual experience, changes as the background beliefs change, but the experience itself does not.

19. Perhaps Feyerabend's radical-sounding claim that there is no scientific

Science as Social?—Yes and No

Ours is an age in which partial truths are tirelessly transformed into total falsehoods and then acclaimed as revolutionary revelations. THOMAS SZASZ[1]

Some feminist philosophers of science claim the insight that science is social.

It is true that the cooperative and competitive engagement of many people, within and across generations, in the enterprise of scientific inquiry contributes to its success. It is false that social values are inseparable from scientific inquiry; false that the purpose of science is the achievement of social goals; false that knowledge is nothing but the product of negotiation among members of the scientific community; false that knowledge, facts, reality are nothing more than social constructions; false that science should be more democratic; false that the physical sciences are subordinate to the social sciences.

Of course, that was a position statement, not an argument! In what follows, I shall first offer an account of what is epistemologically distinctive about scientific inquiry in which the proposition that science is social, in its true interpretation, plays a significant part. Next, I shall argue that in its other interpretations—the inevitability or desirability of politicized inquiry, social constructivism, "democratic epistemology," and the rest—the proposition that science is social is false. And then, turning to the question, what, if anything, all this has to do with feminism, I shall argue that "science as social" is either a genuine insight, but not a feminist one, or else is no insight at all; and, in conclusion, that feminism has taken a wrong direction in pursuing the project of a feminist epistemology of science—a project that is neither sound epistemology nor sound feminism.

method, that "anything goes," is based in part on the correct perception that there are many scientific *techniques,* but no exclusive *method.* But this is no encouragement to epistemological anarchism.

20. "Cooperative and competitive" is intended as shorthand to indicate that, unlike some fuzzy feminists, I conceive of the relevant interactions, not simply as manifestations of "trust," but as involving expertise, authority, institutionalized mutual criticism, and so on. David Hull, *Science as Process,* University of Chicago Press, Chicago, 1988, is a good source on these matters.

21. Sandra Harding, *Whose Science? Whose Knowledge?* Cornell University Press, Ithaca, NY, 1991, p. 280.

22. Kuhn says something not dissimilar in "Postscript—1969" to the second edition of *The Structure of Scientific Revolutions,* p. 199.

23. See also Michael Polanyi, "The Republic of Science," in *Knowing and Being,* ed. Marjorie Greene, University of Chicago Press, Chicago, 1969, 49–62.

24. Cynthia Crossen, *Tainted Truth,* Simon and Schuster, New York, 1994, illustrates the kinds of danger I have in mind.

25. Paul R. Gross and Norman Levitt, "The Natural Sciences: Trouble Ahead? Yes," *Academic Questions,* 7.2, 1994, 13–29, p. 27.

26. *Collected Papers,* 5.172.

The . . . causes of the triumph of modern science, the considerable numbers of workers and the singleness of heart with which—(we may forget that there are a few selfseekers . . . ; they are so few)—they cast their whole life in the service of science lead, of course, to their unreserved discussion with one another, with each being fully informed about the work of his neighbour, and availing himself of that neighbour's results; and thus in storming the stronghold of truth one mounts upon the shoulders of another who has to ordinary apprehension failed, but has in truth succeeded in virtue of his failure.[2]

A LONG TRADITION has taken science to enjoy a peculiar epistemic authority because of its uniquely rational and objective method of inquiry; a long history of failed attempts to articulate what that uniquely rational and objective method is suggests a need for some rethinking of the presuppositions of this Old Deferentialist approach.

Radical critics of the Old Deferentialist picture—the New Cynics—conclude that there *are no* objective epistemic standards and that there is *nothing* epistemologically special about science. My view of the matter is much less exciting. There are objective standards of better and worse evidence and of better- and worse-conducted inquiry. These are the standards by which we judge the worth of empirical evidence, and the rigor and thoroughness of empirical inquiry, generally. They are not set by, not internal to, the sciences (though doubtless they are influenced by them). But, by these standards, the natural sciences, at least, have succeeded strikingly well. They are not epistemically privileged; but they have earned a certain epistemic distinction.[3]

Standards of better and worse evidence and standards of better- and worse-conducted inquiry are often confused. But they are as different as criteria of nutritiousness are from guidelines for menu planning; or as criteria for judging roses are from instructions for growing them (unlike the former, the latter would, for example, inevitably mention horse manure). Standards of evidential quality are, in a sense, prior; for well-conducted inquiry requires thoroughness, honesty, and good judgment in seeking out evidence and assessing it. Questions about the criteria of evidential quality are also, in a sense, more tractable. What evidence has to be to be good is truth-indicative. But the goal of inquiry is dual: to discover truths, yes, but not just any truths—substantial, significant truths.[4] And because of the potential for tension between the two aspects of the goal—it's a lot easier to get truths if you don't mind the truths you get being trivial—there can't be rules for the conduct of inquiry, only guidelines requiring discretion in their application.

The main focus in what follows will be on questions about the conduct of inquiry. What I have to say about this will, however, presuppose my model of the structure of evidence as analogous to a crossword puzzle, according to which an empirical proposition is more or less warranted depending on how well it is supported by experiential evidence and background beliefs (analogue: how well a crossword entry is supported by its clue and other completed entries); how secure the relevant background beliefs are, independently of the proposition in question (analogue: how reasonable those other entries are, independent of this one); and how much of the relevant evidence the evidence includes (analogue: how much of the crossword has been completed). How well evidence supports a proposition depends on how much the addition of the proposition in question improves its explanatory integration.[5]

When I say that the natural sciences have succeeded well, by and large, by our evidential standards, I don't mean to deny that most scientific theories are, at some stages of their career, no more than tenuously supported speculations; nor that some get accepted, even entrenched, on flimsy evidence. But it seems to me undeniable that, through a long, ragged, fumbling, and always-fallible process, the natural sciences have come up with deep, broad, and explanatory theories well anchored in experiential evidence and interlocking surprisingly with one another. And just as plausibly filling in long, much-intersected crossword entries greatly improves the prospects for completing other parts of the puzzle, so the natural sciences have tackled new problems with the help of solutions to old.[6]

How have they done this? I don't believe it is because they use a uniquely rational method of inquiry unavailable to historians, detectives, or the rest of us. It is rather that they have found ways to extend their evidential reach and stiffen respect for evidence, to strengthen, deepen, and extend the method all of us use when we seriously try to figure out some empirical question.

Old Deferentialists sought "the logic of science," the inferential patterns which could be shown to produce true, or probably true, or progressively more nearly true, or progressively more instrumentally successful, or, etc., results. But no mechanical procedure can avoid the need for discretion, good judgment. In a broad, vague sense, in which it refers to making conjectures, developing them, testing them, assessing the likelihood that they are true, certainly there is such a thing as "the method of science"; but so construed, it is neither distinctive of the sciences nor guaranteed to make progress.

Does this mean there is nothing distinctive about natural-scientific inquiry? No. Such inquiry has many striking features. Among them: a systematic commitment to criticism and testing; experimental contrivance of every kind; systematic effort to isolate one variable at a time; elaborate and constantly developing instrumentation; all the complex apparatus of statistical evaluation and mathematical modeling; *and*—the engagement, cooperative and competitive, of many persons, within and across generations, in the enterprise of scientific inquiry. The fact that science is, in this sense, a social enterprise, has been an important factor contributing to its epistemological distinction.

There are all kinds of tasks that get done better if many people are involved. But scientific work isn't much like shelling an enormous quantity of peas (which will get done quicker the more people are helping);[7] nor much like carrying a very heavy log (which can be done by several people but not by a single person). It is—of course!—more like working on an enormously complicated crossword puzzle. And the epistemological significance of the social character of science is, correspondingly, quite complex and subtle—no simple case of "many hands make light work." It depends, not purely and simply on the involvement of many people, but on the internal organization of science, as well as on its external environment.

Scientific inquiry is forwarded by division of labor. Members of various subcommunities and sub-subcommunities of what philosophers of science sometimes refer to, by a considerable abstraction, as "the" scientific community, work on different problems. Members of each subcommunity, in turn, work on different aspects of "their" problem. It is as if different subgroups, and different persons within them, worked on different parts of a crossword puzzle. The result?—the benefits not only of specialization but also, provided each individual and each subgroup has access, as needed, to the work of the others, of saving duplication of work in checking the consistency of their entries with other, distant but still obliquely interconnected, areas of the puzzle. Then again, some inquirers are better suited by taste and temperament for deep or broad theoretical speculation, some for precise and patient observation, some for devising complex instrumentation, some for elaborate statistical evaluation, and so forth (rather as if we had whizzes at anagrams, specialists in Shakespearean allusions, devotees of exotic place-names, and so on, working together on part of a crossword).

The social character of science can also help to compensate for individuals' weaknesses and idiosyncrasies. I doubt that criteria of better and worse evidence will yield a linear ordering, and I am sure that no mechanical decision-procedure for theory-choice is to be anticipated. But a community of inquirers will usually, and usefully, include some who are quick to start speculating toward a new theory when the evidence begins to disfavor the old one, and others who are more inclined patiently to try to modify the old. And though real, imperfect inquirers are seldom, if ever, altogether free of prejudice and partisanship, a community of inquirers will usually, and usefully, include partisans of one approach keen to seek out and expose the weaknesses which partisans of a rival approach are motivated to neglect.

Implicit in all this has been an important distinction between *warrant* and *acceptance*. Warrant is a normative notion; the warrant-status of a proposition is a matter of how good or bad the evidence with respect to that proposition is.[8] Acceptance is a descriptive notion; the acceptance-status of a proposition is a matter of the standing of the claim in the eyes of the scientific community or relevant subcommunity: rejected as definitely false; regarded as a possible maybe worthy of further investigation; as a reasonable candidate among several rivals; as probable but not yet acceptable as definitely true; as established unless and until something unexpected turns up; and so on. Ideally, the acceptance-status of a claim will vary concomitantly with its warrant-status. What was suggested rather vaguely earlier may now be restated a bit more precisely: though individual scientists will likely fall short of the ideal of proportioning their belief to the degree of evidence, in a community of scientists with various prejudices and preconceptions and varying tendencies to over-belief and to under-belief,[9] acceptance and warrant may nevertheless come to be, more or less and by and large and in the long run, appropriately correlated.

Also implicit above, and also worth making explicit, is the thought that science is not only cooperative but also competitive—in virtue of competition between partisans of rival approaches or theories, and of competition between rival individuals or research teams hoping to be the first to solve this or that problem. And here is as good a place as any to mention how, besides combining cooperation with competition, science combines division of labor with overlap of competencies sufficient to permit justified mutual confidence, and the institutionalized authority of well-warranted results with institutionalized critical scrutiny.

Up to now I have focused, in a Pollyannish way, on how the social character of science contributes to its success. But I don't mean to deny that both the internal organization of science and the external environment in which scientific work is conducted could be such as to hamper progress, to discourage good, honest, thorough, scrupulous inquiry, to encourage fraud or fakery or pointless busywork.

The disaster in Soviet biology under Stalin[10] is a dramatic illustration of the dangers of the politicization of science, of putting scientists under pressure to find evidence favoring a politically desired conclusion instead of honestly investigating what hypothesis is best warranted. But there are plenty of other potential hindrances, less dramatic but far from negligible: all those potential obstacles listed in the previous essay—political pressure to tackle this problem rather than that, dependence on funding bodies with their own agendas, an explosion of publications making it harder to find the relevant, and nontrivial, stuff,[11] and so forth and so on.

As science proceeds, as ever more elaborate and sophisticated equipment is required to make ever more recherché observations, scientific work tends to get more expensive. When only governments and large industrial concerns can afford to support science, the danger of some of the potential hindrances on my list grows greater. And of others, too, as some scientists are tempted to go prematurely to the press, some find it possible to make fortunes from their work, the expert-witness business booms. There are no grounds for complacency.

Scientists are fallible human beings, rarely if ever entirely free of prejudice and partisanship. One may incline to favor a certain approach because it was initiated by his mentor; another may incline to resist that approach because it is favored by his rival. In the social and human sciences, the sciences to which it falls to investigate human biology, psychology, and society, prejudice and preconception may be of a political as well as professional character. And this makes those sciences especially vulnerable to some of the potential hindrances I have been discussing.

I must confess that I belong to that class of scallawags who purpose . . . to look the truth in the face, whether doing so be conducive to the interests of society or not. Moreover, if I should ever tackle that excessively difficult question, "What is for the true interest of society?" I should feel that I stood in need of a great deal of help from the science of legitimate inference.[12]

MOST OF THE PHILOSOPHERS who have recently insisted on the importance of the social character of science give the claim that science is social one or another (or several) of various interpretations much more radical than the one I have been exploring, seeing the social character of science as significantly undermining its epistemic pretensions. For them "science as social" is a key step on the way from the Old Deferentialism to the New Cynicism: to the conclusion that science is not a uniquely rational cognitive enterprise with a special claim to epistemic authority, nor even, as I believe, an imperfect but thus-far remarkably successful cognitive enterprise deserving of epistemic respect, but a politics-permeated social institution in urgent need of transformation by an infusion of progressive values.

The fundamental difference between the conception of "science as social" which I think correct, and the radical conceptions which have recently become fashionable, is that whereas mine sees the social character of science as one of the—as I have been stressing, the very fallible and imperfect—factors which help to *keep acceptance appropriately correlated with warrant,* they insist on "science as social" as a way of focusing on *acceptance at the expense of warrant.* In fact, quite a good way to get a grip on these various radical interpretations is to classify them according as they play down warrant and accentuate acceptance; ignore warrant altogether and acknowledge only acceptance; or attempt to replace the notion of warrant by some sociopolitical ersatz.

Those who play down warrant and accentuate acceptance insist on the underdetermination of theory by evidence and the inextricability of nonevidential factors in theory-choice. Hence the first of the radical interpretations of "science as social" I want to consider: that social values are inseparable from scientific inquiry.

What makes this seem plausible may be the following thought: evidence never obliges us to accept this claim rather than that, and we have to accept something, so acceptance is always affected by something besides the evidence,[13] which had better be good, progressive values rather than bad, regressive ones. But we *don't* "have to accept something"; if the evidence is inadequate, why not just acknowledge that we don't know? Not all scientific claims are either accepted as definitely true or rejected as definitely false, nor should they be; evidence may be better or worse, warrant stronger or weaker, and the acceptance status of a claim can, and should, vary accordingly.

Some may object that I have missed the force of the underdetermination thesis. "The point," they will say, "is not that, in practice, we don't always have enough evidence to decide whether a theory is true, but that, in principle, even all possible evidence is insufficient to decide, that there is always an incompatible, but empirically equivalent, theory." One might reasonably feel that, considering how much weight they are asking it to bear, those who appeal in this context to Quine's thesis of underdetermination-in-principle owe us something more than an appeal to authority—especially as Quine himself has never suggested that his thesis tends to encourage the politicization of science; but set that aside. If the thesis is true, then, for those propositions theoretical enough to fall within its scope, no amount of observational evidence could enable us to tell whether p_1 or empirically-equivalent-but-incompatible p_2 is true. In that case, the most we could learn by inquiry is that either p_1 or p_2. It doesn't follow, and neither is it true, that we should decide which disjunct to accept by asking which would be politically preferable. Indeed, given that the thesis presumably applies only to the in-principle unobservable, it is not clear even how political values could have a bearing (is quark theory or kwark theory politically more progressive?—the question makes no sense).

But now, perhaps, it will be objected that I have missed the force of the insistence that "we have to accept something." "The point," it may be said, "is that we have to act, and so we have to accept some theory as the basis on which to act." This objection is best answered by distinguishing between accepting a theory as true (which is the sense relevant to my argument), and deciding, without committing oneself to its truth, to act as if the theory were true (which is the sense in which it is sometimes true that "we have to accept something").[14] Besides answering the objection before us, this distinction bears on questions of prudence in policy; when we are obliged to act, and decide to proceed as if such-and-such were true although we can't be sure it is, it is wise to take whatever precautions are feasible against its turning out to have been false after all.

But perhaps it is a mistake to focus too exclusively on the argument(s) from underdetermination. Perhaps we should think of the thesis that social values are inseparable from scientific inquiry as the terminus of a different line of thought: that not only what scientific questions are tackled, but also what solutions are envisaged, is constrained by social values. In the human and social sciences, at least, this is doubtless to some degree the case (that was the burden of the last paragraph of the previous section). But to reach any conclusion more radical than the modest interpretation of "science as social" I have defended, another step is needed, to show that social values are not distinct from, not an interference with, but are built into, standards for the worth of evidence.[15]

That further step looks easy if one supposes that degree of confirmation of a hypothesis is relative to the alternative hypotheses available. But the supposition is false. To be sure, *our judgment of* whether or to what degree this evidence supports this hypothesis will depend on whether, and to what degree, this hypothesis better explains the evidence than others we can think of; but it doesn't follow, and neither is it true, that whether or to what degree this evidence *actually does* support this hypothesis depends on what alternative hypotheses have occurred to us.

A closely related interpretation of the theme of "science as social" is that the goal of science is the improvement of society.[16] There is a temptation to respond by pointing to the *OED*'s: "**research**—endeavour to discover facts"; but this would miss the point, which is, I take it, that the goal of science *ought to be* the improvement of society. This has a weaker and a stronger interpretation.

Even taken in a weaker interpretation, as proposing only that science focus its attention on socially urgent problems, it is open to question. Knowledge is interconnected in unpredictable ways, so it is hard to be sure what research will bring social benefits; and focusing scientific effort artificially on problems perceived as socially urgent can mean wasted resources, for the problems which we most want solved are not always those most susceptible to solution in the current state of knowledge. This doesn't mean that such focus is always a bad idea; but we need to be aware that it carries a price.

Taken in a stronger interpretation, as proposing that those scientific theories should be accepted, the acceptance of which conduces to the interests of society, the thesis that the goal of science is the improvement of society is simply a variant formulation of the interpretation of "science as social" just considered, that what scientific theories are accepted should be determined by social values; and is, likewise, untrue.

I turn next to the second kind of radical interpretation of the theme of "science as social," the kind favored by those who, ignoring warrant altogether, acknowledge only acceptance.

The favored phrase is that scientific knowledge is "socially constructed"; but this exploits an ambiguity. In one sense, it is true that scientific knowledge is socially constructed. Science has been the work of many persons, within and across generations; the scientific knowledge we now possess has been achieved, in part, through institutionalized mutual checking and criticism.

But what is at issue is a much more radical interpretation: that scientific knowledge is nothing more than the product of processes of social negotiation.[17] This is doubly false. First, the processes through which scientific knowledge is achieved are not *merely* a matter of social negotiation; they are processes of seeking out, checking, and assessing the weight of *evidence*. Second, not everything that has thus far survived those processes is knowledge; what survives those processes is what *counts as* knowledge, what is *accepted as* knowledge—but not all of it *is*, necessarily, knowledge. Some may, despite surviving those processes, not be warranted; some may turn out to be false.

Some hold not only that knowledge, but also that reality, is socially constructed, thus committing the same kinds of confusion twice over. Scientific theories are devised, articulated, developed, by scientists; theoretical concepts like **electron, gene, force,** and so forth, are, if you like, their construction. And the entities posited in true scientific theories are real. But it doesn't follow, and neither is it true, that electrons, genes, forces, etc., are constructed by the intellectual activity of the scientists who create the theories which posit them.

True, as science proceeds, instrumentation and theory get more and more inextricably intertwined, and one increasingly encounters claims which refer, not to natural, but to what one might call laboratory phenomena. But that such phenomena are created in the laboratory does not mean that they are made real by scientists' theorizing.

True, again, social institutions (marriage, say, or banking) and social categories (gender, say, as distinct from sex) are, in a sense, socially constructed; if there weren't human societies, there would be no such things. These are the objects of sociological theories—not so incidentally, the kinds of theory with which social constructivists are most familiar. But, again, they are not made real by scientists' theorizing.

The third kind of radical interpretation of "science as social" engages in a kind of conceptual kidnapping, replacing the concept of warrant by an ersatz of a purely politicosociological character.[18] This is the strategy of those who urge the merits of "democratic epistemology." Democracy is a political value, and would be apropos if theory-choice in science were a matter of "social negotiation" pure and simple. But it isn't; it is a matter of seeking out, checking, and assessing the worth of evidence. Unless you are befogged by the emotional appeal of the word "democratic," it is clear that the idea is ludicrous that the question, say, what theory of subatomic particles should be accepted, should be put to a vote. Respect for evidence is required by well-conducted inquiry of any kind; but, where many scientific claims are concerned, only those with appropriate expertise are competent to judge the worth of the evidence.

True, freedom of thought and speech are important conditions for scientific inquiry to flourish; and it may be that some who favor "democratic epistemology" have confused the concept of democracy with the concept of freedom of thought. If so, the only reply needed is that these are distinct concepts.

True, if we are sociologists or anthropologists trying to understand the institution of polygamy in this society, or of slavery in that, then talking to wives *and* husbands, or to slaves *and* masters, would indeed be desirable

as part of our evidence-gathering. But this is just one aspect of the requirement of comprehensiveness of evidence. It has not the slightest tendency
to support the idea that democracy could replace warrant—support-
iveness, independent security, and comprehensiveness of evidence—as epistemic values.

But perhaps, when it is said that science ought to be "more democratic,"
the point intended is only that no one should be excluded from a scientific
career on the basis of irrelevant considerations such as race, sex, or eye
color. This seems right, both morally (it *is* a bad thing if, for irrelevant
reasons, people are excluded or discouraged from work for which they
have talent), and epistemologically (other things being equal, scientific
work *will* get done better, the more open to talent scientific careers are).
But this is a claim entirely compatible with the understanding of the thesis
of "science as social" defended earlier; and surely rather meritocratic than
democratic in its thrust.

Or, possibly, calls for a more democratic epistemology should be interpreted as protests about the role of authority in science. But the institutionalized authority of well-warranted results is essential to the progress of
scientific inquiry; unless the entries inked in by earlier generations can be
taken for granted, each scientist would have to start the whole crossword
anew and alone—which is not to deny that even experts are fallible, or that
even the best-warranted results might turn out to be in need of revision.

What, finally, of the thesis that the physical sciences are subordinate to
the social sciences? This would be a consequence of the claim that reality
is socially constructed; if physical science were, as that claim has it, a kind
of myth-making, then, indeed, anthropology would achieve a certain priority over physics. But it is a consequence so grossly implausible as to
amount to a reductio ad absurdum—albeit a redundant one—of social
constructivism.[19]

As the caveat heard from time to time in the first section of this essay,
"in the natural sciences, at least," none too subtly hinted, the fact is that
it is hard to think of analogues, in the social sciences, of the discoveries which, in the natural sciences, have plausibly filled in long, much-
intersected entries of the crossword and enabled further successes. In any
event, I shan't linger over the "physics as subordinate to sociology" thesis,
since it now appears for what I believe it is: a desperate last-ditch effort to
save one or another of the radical interpretations of "science as social" by
focusing attention on complications which, if not examined too closely,
can give the false impression that in those radical interpretations it is true
of the social sciences.

When we began theorizing our experience . . . we knew our task would be a difficult though exciting one. But I doubt that in our wildest dreams we ever imagined we would have to reinvent both science and theorizing itself to make sense of women's social experience.[20]

WHAT HAS "science as social" to do with feminism? Nothing. It is either a genuine insight but not a feminist one, or else is no insight at all.

Since self-styled feminist philosophers of science have generally not explicitly distinguished the various possible interpretations of "science as social" as I have done, they sometimes convey the impression that acknowledging "social epistemology," or recognizing that science is the work of a community, is in itself feminist (and even that taking an interest in the logical or the personal dimensions of scientific work betrays hostility to women's interests). But this is completely wrong-headed.

In the modest sense spelled out in the first section of this essay, it is true, and epistemologically significant, that science is social. But there is nothing particularly feminist about this. Peirce, Polanyi, Quine, Popper, come immediately to mind as philosophers neither female nor feminist who have acknowledged, with varying degrees of detail and subtlety, something along those lines.[21]

Some feminist philosophers have apparently been attracted to the idea that science is cooperative, and that scientists must trust each others' work, because they think it suggests the importance of the supposedly feminine virtues of trust and cooperation.[22] But this is triply mistaken. First, it rests on an old, sentimental stereotype of masculine and feminine qualities: a stereotype which is, incidentally, undermined by the fact that science, which has thus far been conducted largely by men, is, inter alia, a cooperative enterprise. Second, it ignores the fact that science is competitive as well as cooperative, and that a realistic account of the social character of science will acknowledge the role of expertise, authority, justified confidence in others' competence, rather than, simply, "trust." And, third, it evades the question, why a theory of scientific knowledge stressing supposedly feminine qualities should be supposed to be a better—truer, more adequate— theory of scientific knowledge.

Most feminist philosophers of science, however, have been attracted to the theme of "science as social" in one and/or another of the radical interpretations discussed in my second section. Though here, again, it is not difficult to think of philosophers neither female nor feminist who have subscribed to the thesis of "science as social" in those radical interpretations, it is possible to make a connection, albeit a fairly loose one, with feminism. For all these radical interpretations suggest, in one way or another, the inevitability or desirability of a role for social and political values in the epistemology of science. "Doing science as a feminist," the thought is, requires one to ensure that it is feminist values that inform one's work; and not just with respect to applications of scientific results, or the treatment of test subjects, or even what questions one chooses to tackle, but with respect to what theories one accepts.

Longino and Nelson are committed to the thesis that social values are inextricable from the epistemology of science, both urging that the under-determination of theories by data leaves "slack" to be taken up by political considerations.[23] But, in the relevant interpretation, the thesis that science is social is false.

Harding is apparently committed to the thesis that "strong objectivity" is achieved by a democratic incorporation of "multiple standpoints," writes approvingly of the social constructivism of Latour et al., and maintains that physics is subordinate to sociology—in all of which interpretations, the thesis that science is social is false. To make matters even more confusing, in Harding the connection with feminism is not achieved by any of these claims, but only by another, which appears, furthermore, to be incompatible with the democratic thrust of the emphasis on multiple standpoints; some standpoints, those of oppressed and disadvantaged classes, women among them, turn out to be, supposedly, epistemologically better. Distinguishing standpoints from perspectives, Harding tells us that what this means is that scientific work is best begun by "thinking from women's lives"—leaving me, I'm afraid, simply baffled by how work on quantum physics, say, *could* be undertaken as she recommends—let alone by why it *should* be. Of course, if physics were, as Harding claims, subordinate to sociology, this might have some plausibility. But her recommendation looks, again, more like a reductio of the priority-of-sociology thesis than a plausible consequence of it.[24]

I think feminism has taken altogether the wrong path here. The problem started when feminist criticisms of sexism in scientific theorizing grew, as the quotation from Harding boasts, into something enormously more ambitious. Some of those criticisms, I think, were (are) correct. In the social and human sciences, theories about women's capacities, or incapacities, *have* sometimes come to be accepted by the relevant scientific sub-community when they were not well warranted; and the explanation of how this came about *would*, probably, refer to the prejudices and stereotypes common among scientists as well as in the larger society. But this kind of detailed criticism of specific scientific work—which is, I should add, quite difficult, requiring competence in the relevant scientific specialty sufficient to judge the worth of evidence—has now been extrapolated in two exciting-seeming, but illegitimate, directions.

The claim began to be heard (significantly, mainly from feminist philosophers, sociologists, and literary theorists, not from feminist physicists and chemists) that sexism infects *all* the sciences, the physical sciences included. This idea depends in part on simple exaggeration about the supposed ubiquity of sexist metaphors in the writing of scientists and philosophers of science. It also relies, much more interestingly, on misunderstandings of the cognitive role of metaphor. It is true that metaphors are not always just decorative, but can be cognitively important. It is true, also, that some cognitively significant metaphors implicitly compare natural with social phenomena—the chaperone molecule, say, or reproduction "investment." But whether a cognitively important metaphor is fruitful, whether it makes us look in the right or in the wrong direction, *is independent of* the desirability or otherwise of the social phenomenon on which it calls.

But I shan't pursue these issues, which deserve a paper to themselves.[25] It is the second illegitimate extrapolation that concerns me here: the fallacious inference from the true premise what has passed for relevant evidence, known fact, objective truth, and so forth, sometimes turns out to be no such thing, to the false conclusion that the notions of relevant evidence, known fact, established truth, etc., are revealed to be ideological humbug.

The ubiquity of this fallacious inference—"the 'passes for' fallacy"—is closely related to the astonishing outbreak of sneer quotes one finds in the literature of feminist philosophy of science ("knowledge," "truth," "reality," "objectivity," etc.), as well as with the pull toward accounts which accentuate acceptance, i.e., what at a given time *passes for* scientific knowledge, over warrant, or which confuse what we *take as* confirmation with what really confirms a hypothesis.

The "passes for" fallacy is ubiquitous; but I want to focus for a while on one characteristic instance. It occurs in a paper in the first half of which Ruth Bleier explains why she believes that the claim that there are differences in brain structure and function between the sexes which explain the (as she adds, the presumed) gender-related differences in cognitive ability, is not well warranted by the evidence. She complains of the "sloppy methods, inconclusive findings and unwarranted interpretations," and the "unacknowledged ideological commitments" on which this supposed knowledge is based. She may be right; I don't know.[26] But then, in the second part of the paper, what conclusion does she draw? Not that we need better investigation using rigorous methods, seeking more conclusive findings, based on warranted interpretations and free of ideological commitments—but that bias is everywhere, that objectivity is impossible, that the "social production of knowledge" is inextricably conditioned by "gender, class, race, and ethnicity, and consequently, a set of values, beliefs, viewpoints, needs, and goals."[27]

I shan't pause to protest the egregious assumption that one thinks with one's skin or one's sex organs. The point I want to stress here is that this form of argument, when applied to the concepts of evidence, truth, etc., is not only fallacious; it is also pragmatically self-undermining. For if the conclusion were true, the premise could only be—as it alleges that the research it criticizes is—an expression of prejudice, as the conclusion takes all "inquiry" to be (here we really need the scare quotes; if you aren't trying to get the truth, you aren't really inquiring).

Furthermore, if the conclusion were true, it would also undermine the possibility of a science informed by feminist values, in which evidential slack was taken up by reference to women's interests. For if there were no genuine inquiry, no objective evidence, we couldn't know what theories are such that their being accepted would conduce to women's interests, nor what women's interests are.

At this point, I suppose, some might be tempted to argue that, since I grant that some feminist criticisms of sexism in scientific theorizing are correct, whether I like it or not my own position is in fact a form of "feminist empiricism." I set aside problems about the meaning of "empiricism," except to note that the term has of late sometimes been associated with a kind of neo-instrumentalism to which I certainly do not subscribe. Assuming that "empiricism" is being taken in its older, much broader and vaguer sense, don't I fall, after all, under Harding's characterization of a feminist empiricist as one who holds that sexism in scientific theorizing is simply bad science, and curable, therefore, by better adherence to the norms of science? I do, indeed, think that sexism in scientific theorizing is often bad science; and that it is curable by seeking out more, or paying closer attention to, evidence.[28] But I resist the assimilation; and not only because, since I don't think epistemic standards are internal to science, I don't think it appropriate to describe the cure simply as "better adherence to the norms of science." More importantly, the reason I think sexism in scientific theorizing is often bad science is not that it is contrary to women's interests, but that it is not good, honest, thorough inquiry; so it is not appropriate to describe my epistemological position as "feminist" *anything*. The problem is, as Longino points out,[29] that Harding's characterization is tendentiously designed as a foil to the feminist standpoint theory she favors. No position deserves the name "feminist empiricism" unless, like Longino's and unlike mine, it makes some serious conceptual connection between the feminism and the epistemology.

The point isn't that I don't think sexism in scientific theorizing is often bad science; I do. It isn't that I don't care about justice for women; I do. It isn't that I don't think there are legitimate feminist questions about science—ethical and political questions—about access to scientific careers, about funding priorities, about applications of scientific discoveries; I do.[30] It is, rather, that I see the aspiration to a feminist epistemology of science—to an epistemology which embodies some specifically feminist insight, that is, rather than simply having the label stuck on adventitiously—as encouraging the politicization of inquiry; which, by my lights, whether in the interests of good political values or bad, is always epistemologically unsound.

And it is no more sound feminism than it is sound epistemology. It would take another paper to spell out in detail why, in my opinion, what is presently conceived as "feminist philosophy of science" is contrary to women's interests; here I can offer only a few sketchy sentences. For generations, talented girls were discouraged from science because of ill-founded ideas about women's (in)abilities. Now there is a danger that talented girls will be discouraged by ill-founded ideas about the masculine or masculinist values with which science is allegedly imbued.[31] And there is a danger of a new kind of sexist science, this time a science supposedly informed by feminist values, which will reinforce the old stereotypes: the sexist science of such works as (heaven help us!) *Women's Ways of Knowing*.[32] Not to mention—but I feel I must—the waste of talent and energy if those who are interested in the epistemology of science, and also care about justice for women, come to fear that they must restrict themselves to approaches certified as "feminist,"[33] or be guilty of complicity with sexism.

NEITHER SOUND EPISTEMOLOGY nor sound feminism requires us to "reinvent science and theorizing," as Harding's preposterous[34] announcement informed us; on the contrary, both require us to be on our guard against such "total falsehoods . . . acclaimed as revolutionary revelations."

NOTES

1. *The Second Sin,* Anchor Books, Doubleday, Garden City, NY, 1974, pp. 26–27.

2. C. S. Peirce, *Collected Papers,* ed. Charles Hartshorne, Paul Weiss, and Arthur Burks, Harvard University Press, Cambridge, MA, 1931–58, 7.51.

3. See my *Evidence and Inquiry: Towards Reconstruction in Epistemology,* Blackwell, Oxford, 1993, chapters 6, 7, and 8; "Puzzling Out Science," essay 5 in this volume; "The Puzzle of 'Scientific Method,'" *Revue internationale de philosophie,* 4/1997, 495–505.

4. "Substantial," here, should not be interpreted as meaning, simply, "synthetic." There are, in the sense intended, substantial mathematical truths and trivial empirical ones. In this I follow Peirce; see *Collected Papers* 4.91: "those who [like myself] maintain that arithmetical truths are logically necessary" are "not *eo ipso* saying that they are verbal in their nature."

5. See also my *Evidence and Inquiry,* chapter 4; and "A Foundherentist Theory of Empirical Justification," in *The Theory of Knowledge,* ed. Louis Pojman, Wadsworth, Belmont, CA, 2nd edition, 1998.

6. I owe this way of putting it to W. V. O. Quine, *From Stimulus to Science,* Harvard University Press, Cambridge, MA, 1995, p. 16.

7. The analogy is due to Michael Polanyi, "The Republic of Science," in *Knowing and Being,* ed. Marjorie Grene, University of Chicago Press, Chicago, 1969, 49–62.

8. At the time of writing *Evidence and Inquiry* I pointed out some difficulties of extrapolating the explication there offered of "A is more/less justified in believing that p" to the impersonal locution, "p is justified." In my "Reply to Thayer," *Philosophy and Phenomenological Research,* 56.3, 1996, 641–43, I suggested how this task might be approached. In the present chapter I have chosen "warrant" instead of "justification" to mark the difference between the concepts.

9. A point explored in more detail in my "'The Ethics of Belief' Reconsidered," in Lewis Hahn, ed., *The Philosophy of Roderick M. Chisholm,* Open Court, La Salle, IL, 1997, 129–44.

10. See Valery N. Soyfer, *Lysenko and the Tragedy of Soviet Science,* Rutgers University Press, Newark, NJ, 1994.

11. See also "Preposterism and Its Consequences," essay 11 in this volume.

12. Peirce, *Collected Papers,* 8.143.

13. These steps of this argument are made very explicitly by Mary Hesse in "How to be a Post-Modernist without Being a Feminist," *The Monist,* 77.4, October 1994, 445–61.

14. This relates to a line of thought with which, like Dewey and Popper, I sympathize: that, since we can seldom be sure what the consequences will be, gradualism is the best strategy in social and political change.

15. On the distinctness of ethical and epistemic values, see again "'The Ethics of Belief' Reconsidered" (note 9 above).

16. This is the position of Karl Pearson, whose *The Grammar of Science*, Adams and Black, London, 2nd edition, 1900, Peirce is criticizing in the passage quoted at the head of this section.

17. See, for example, Bruno Latour, *Science in Action*, Harvard University Press, Cambridge, MA, 1987; Steve Fuller, *Social Epistemology*, Indiana University Press, Bloomington, 1988.

18. The strategy is illustrated in a particularly striking way by the terms in which, in *Whose Science? Whose Knowledge?* (Cornell University Press, Ithaca, NY, 1991) Sandra Harding discusses how to "justify" her theory, which unmistakably reveal that she has identified this with the question, how to *sell* her theory to this or that audience.

19. Putting me in mind of C. I .Lewis's shrewd description of the method "which the bigot unconsciously applies": "he simply doesn't believe any evidence which is unfavorable to his bigoted conclusion; and if any such is put forward, he will argue it away by using this same method over again" (*The Ground and Nature of the Right*, Columbia University Press, New York, NY), p. 32.

20. Sandra Harding, *The Science Question in Feminism*, Cornell University Press, Ithaca, NY, 1986, p. 251.

21. So in a way did J. S. Mill, who qualifies as a feminist if any male philosopher does. But this obviously does not establish the required connection.

22. See, for example, Lorraine Code, *Epistemic Responsibility*, University Press of New England, Hanover, NH, and London, 1987 (but note that, though she stresses "trust," and recognizes the co-operative character of science, she is disposed to play down scientific knowledge in favor of the literary). See also my critical notice of this book, *Canadian Journal of Philosophy*, 1990, 91–107.

23. Helen Longino, "Can There Be a Feminist Science?" (1987), in Ann Garry and Marilyn Pearsall, eds., *Women, Knowledge, and Reality*, Allen Hyman, Boston, 1989, 203–16, and *Science as Social Knowledge*, Princeton University Press, Princeton, NJ, 1990; Lynn Hankinson Nelson, *Who Knows? From Quine to a Feminist Empiricism*, Temple University Press, Philadelphia, 1990. "Slack" is a term of which Nelson is fond; "doing science as a feminist" is a phrase Longino likes. I note that Longino tends to stress underdetermination *in practice*, whereas Nelson tends to take the Quinean line of underdetermination even *in principle*.

24. Sandra Harding, *Whose Science? Whose Knowledge?*; "After the Neutrality Ideal: Science, Politics, and 'Strong Objectivity,'" *Social Research*, 59.3, 1992, 567–87.

25. On the general issue of the role of metaphor in inquiry, see essay 4, this volume. On feminist criticisms of supposedly sexist metaphors in Bacon, see Alan Soble, "In Defense of Bacon," *Philosophy of the Social Sciences*, 25.2, 1995, 192–215; and Iddo Landau, "Feminist Criticisms of Metaphors in Bacon's Philosophy of Science," *Philosophy*, 70, no. 283, 1998, 47–61.

26. Carole Tavris, whose good sense I respect, suggests that she is; see *The Mismeasure of Woman*, Touchstone, Simon and Schuster, New York, 1992, 49–51.

27. "*Science* and the Construction of Meanings in the Neurosciences," in Sue V.

Rosser, ed., *Feminism within the Science and Health Care Professions: Overcoming Resistance,* Pergamon Press, Oxford and New York, 1988, 91–104; the quotations below are from pp. 92 and 100.

28. "Often," not "always," because I am using the term "sexist" to apply only to claims which are *false* as well as such that their being accepted is contrary to women's interests; and because theories which are false may sometimes be sufficiently well warranted that one would hesitate to say that their coming to be accepted is bad science. In my usage, that a claim is offensive to some women is neither necessary nor sufficient for its counting as sexist.

29. *The Science Question in Feminism,* chapter 6. I note that Nelson is not a feminist empiricist in Harding's sense, either; her position, like Longino's, is too radical to qualify. See Longino's "Science, Objectivity, and Feminist Values," *Feminist Studies,* 14.3, 1988, 561–74, p. 571.

30. See section 1 of my "Science 'From a Feminist Perspective'" (*Philosophy,* 67, 1992, 5–18; also in Peter Halfpenny and Peter McMylor, eds., *Positivist Sociology and Its Critics,* vol. 3, Edward Elgar Press, Aldershot, Hants, 1994, 99–112); but note that the "legitimate feminist questions about science" there discussed are all of a social, political, ethical cast—*not* epistemological.

31. As Noretta Koertge, "Are Feminists Alienating Women from the Sciences?" *Chronicle of Higher Education,* 9.14.94, A80, observes, "What young women really need is special encouragement and equal opportunity to learn science, not a feminist rationalization for failure."

32. Mary Field Belenky, Blythe McVicker Clinchy, Nancy Rule Goldberger, and Jill Mattuck Tarule, *Women's Ways of Knowing,* Basic Books, New York, 1986. As antidotes, I recommend Carol Tavris, *The Mismeasure of Woman,* especially chapter 2; and Martha T. Mednick, "On the Politics of Psychological Constructs: Stop the Bandwagon, I Want to Get Off," *American Psychologist,* 44, 1118–23.

33. Harriet Baber, "The Market for Feminist Epistemology," *The Monist,* 77.4, October 1994, 403–23, is good on this.

34. I use the word in the sense explained in "Preposterism and Its Consequences," essay 11 in this volume.

Knowledge and Propaganda: Reflections of an Old Feminist

The New Feminism emphasises the importance of the "woman's point of view," the Old Feminism believes in the primary importance of the human being. . . . Personally I am an Old Feminist. WINIFRED HOLTBY[1]

I have been a feminist since the age of twelve, when I got the top grade in my first chemistry exam, and the boy who got the next-highest grade protested indignantly that it wasn't *fair,* "everyone knows girls can't do chemistry." And since I have been working in epistemology for more than a decade now, I think I qualify as an epistemologist. So I must be a feminist epistemologist, right? Wrong; on the contrary, I don't believe there is any such connection between feminism and epistemology as the rubric "feminist epistemology" requires.

Perhaps you think that only someone of extreme right-wing political views could possibly be less than enthusiastic about feminist epistemology. If so, you are mistaken; both because the only thing extreme about my political views is my dislike of extremes, and because my reasons for thinking the project of a feminist epistemology misconceived are, in any case, not political but epistemological.

The last twenty years or so have seen a major shift within feminist philosophy, from a modest style which stressed the common humanity of women and men, focused on justice and opportunity, and was concerned primarily with issues in social and political theory, to an ambitious, imperialist feminism which stresses the "woman's point of view" and claims revolutionary significance for all areas of philosophy, epistemology included.

So, yes, the pun in my title is intentional; my feminism is of the older-fashioned, more modest stripe. But I am taking issue here only with the imperialist ambitions of the new feminism with respect to epistemology specifically.

The rubric "feminist epistemology" is incongruous on its face, in somewhat the way of, say, "Republican epistemology." And the puzzlement this prompts is rather aggravated than mitigated by the bewildering variety of epistemological ideas described as "feminist." Among self-styled feminist epistemologists one finds quasi-foundationalists, coherentists, contextualists; proponents of epistemic naturalism, and unabashed relativists; some who stress connectedness, community, the social aspects of knowledge, and some who stress emotion, presumably subjective and personal; some who stress concepts of epistemic virtue, some who want the "androcentric" norms of the epistemological tradition to be replaced by "gynocentric" norms, and some who advocate a descriptivist approach; etc., etc.[2] Even where there is apparent agreement, e.g., that feminist epistemology will stress the social aspects of knowledge, it often masks significant *dis*agreement about what this means: that inquirers are pervasively dependent on one another; that cooperative inquiry is better than individual inquiry; that epistemic justification is community-relative; that only a social group, not an individual, can properly be said to inquire or to know; that reality is socially constructed, and so forth. As Louise Antony observes, "there simply is no substantive consensus position among feminists working in epistemology."[3]

It is all very confusing. Alcoff and Potter tell us that feminist epistemology is "a research program moving . . . to reframe the problematic of knowledge . . . internally heterogeneous and irreducible to any uniform set of theses," and that, since feminist epistemology "should not be taken as involving a commitment to gender as the primary axis of oppression," the term "feminist" identifies only "the historical trajectory of current work," i.e., its origin.[4] Sandra Harding tells us that it is to be expected that feminist epistemology will "contain contradictions," that it is "multiple and contradictory knowledge" out of which we are "to learn and think."[5] This isn't very reassuring.

The puzzlement is aggravated by the reflection that neither all, nor only, women, or feminists, favor all, or indeed any, of the ideas offered under the rubric "feminist epistemology." Peirce, for example, is critical of what he calls the "vicious individualism" of Descartes's criterion of truth, and has a subtle appreciation of the social aspects of inquiry; yet he was neither female nor (to judge by his use of "masculine intellect" equivalently to "tough, powerful mind") feminist.[6] I won't even *mention* Ayn Rand![7]

So: what is feminist about feminist epistemology?

Some of those who describe themselves as "feminist epistemologists" do so only because they are picking up some theme described elsewhere as "feminist"; and some, perhaps, for no better reason than that, since they are feminists, or female, and doing epistemology, what they are doing must be feminist epistemology. Some, possibly, are more or less conscious that the label "feminist" may help ensure that their work receives a sympathetic hearing in some, and may serve to divert criticism from other, quarters.[8]

But there seem to be two routes by which feminism and epistemology are taken to be connected, corresponding to two interpretations of the phrase, "the woman's point of view": as "the way women see things," or as "serving the interests of women."

Sometimes we are told that feminist epistemology represents "women's ways of knowing." This reversion to the notion of "thinking like a woman" is disquietingly reminiscent of old, sexist stereotypes—as, for example, Andrea Nye's "feminist critique" of logic[9] disquietingly echoes those old complaints that women are "so illogical." Still, there *are* disquieting truths, so this doesn't settle the matter.

I'm not convinced, however, that there *are* any distinctively female "ways of knowing." Such facts (if they are facts)[10] as that girls score better than boys, on average, in tests of verbal ability, and boys better than girls in tests of mathematical ability, have no tendency to show that women and men have different ways of knowing. Appeals to Object Relations theory, fashionable in the early days of feminist epistemology,[11] seem to have gone out of favor, perhaps because it has been recognized how very speculative and vague the theory is, and how tenuous its relevance to the claim that women have different ways of knowing than men. Perhaps the most influential effort is Belenky and co.'s *Women's Ways of Knowing*, a book which, riding on the coattails of Carol Gilligan's *In a Different Voice*, purports to offer empirical evidence of those other "ways of knowing." But the authors say at the outset that they *presupposed* that there is "a masculine bias at the heart of most academic disciplines, methodologies and theories," a claim supposedly already "convincingly argued" by feminist academics. And so they *told their subjects ahead of time* that the interviews in which they were participating were for the purpose of studying their special "women's ways of knowing"; making it impossible to be sure that their responses weren't biased by suggestion.[12]

All *any* human being has to go on, in figuring out how things are, is his or her sensory and introspective experience, and the explanatory theorizing he or she devises to accommodate it; and differences in cognitive style, like differences in handwriting, seem more individual than gender-determined.

The profusion of incompatible themes proposed as "feminist epistemology" itself speaks against the idea of a distinctively female cognitive style. But even if there were such a thing, the case for feminist epistemology would require further argument to show that women's "ways of knowing" (scare quotes because the term is tendentious, since "knows" is a success-word) represent better procedures of inquiry or subtler standards of justification than the male. And, sure enough, we are told that insights into the theory of knowledge are available to women which are not available, or not easily available, to men.

In all honesty, I can't see how the evidence to date could be thought to speak in favor of this bold claim; what my experience suggests is rather that the questions of the epistemological tradition are *hard,* very hard, for anyone, of whatever sex (or gender), to answer or even significantly to clarify. After all, the capacity for original, creative philosophical thought is quite a rare and unusual talent. Peirce once observed: "there is a kink in my damned brain that prevents me from thinking as other people think";[13] and it is just such kinks, just such individual idiosyncrasies—not the "groupthink" apparently admired by some feminists—that philosophical (and scientific, artistic, etc.) innovation requires.

It is often said that oppressed, disadvantaged, and marginalized people are epistemically privileged in virtue of their oppression and disadvantage.[14] If this were true, it would suggest that the *truly* epistemically privileged are not the affluent, well-educated, white, Western women who (mostly) rest their claim to special insight upon it, but the most oppressed, the most disadvantaged—some of whom are men. Sure enough, some feminist epistemologists, seeing that the "privilege of disadvantage" thesis suggests *greater* privilege for the *more* disadvantaged, claim special epistemological privilege for lesbians.[15]

But is there any good reason to think it true that oppression confers epistemic privilege? Kuhn observed that revolutionary scientific innovations are often made by persons who are at the margin of a discipline; but women, as a class, are not "marginal" in *this* sense. And one of the ways in which oppressed people *are* oppressed is, surely, that their oppressors control the information that reaches them. This argues, if anything, an epistemic *dis*advantage for "oppressed, disadvantaged, marginalized" people.

No such connection between feminism and epistemology as the rubric "feminist epistemology" requires is to be found under the first interpretation of "the woman's point of view" as "the way women see things."

Under the second interpretation, "serving the interests of women," the connection is supposed to be made, rather, by way of feminist criticisms of sexism in scientific theorizing.[16] The two routes supposedly connecting feminism and epistemology would merge on the assumption—which, of course, I don't accept—that sexism in scientific theorizing is the result of the exclusion of female "ways of knowing." A very faint trace of the first would be detectable along the second on the assumption—which, with the caveat that it would be naive to suppose that only men subscribe to sexist stereotypes, I am inclined to grant—that women are a bit more likely than men to notice such sexism.

In the social and human sciences, sometimes also in primatology, etc., claims which are not well supported by the evidence have sometimes come to be accepted by scientists, most often male scientists, because they have taken stereotypical ideas of male and female behavior uncritically for granted. Of course, each feminist critique of alleged sexism in this or that bit of scientific theorizing has to be considered individually, on its own merits.[17] In many instances, it will be difficult for someone outside the field to determine what those merits are (a commitment to feminism is not a sufficient qualification for this kind of work, and an excessive sensitivity to suspected whiffs of sexism could prove a handicap). And efforts to extend feminist critique of sexism in scientific theorizing to all areas of science, including physics, chemistry, etc., seem far-fetched.

But the key step comes with the claim that the discovery of sexism in scientific theorizing obliges us to acknowledge political considerations as legitimate ways to decide between theories. On the face of it, however, criticisms of sexism in scientific theorizing suggest exactly the opposite conclusion: that the ideal is for acceptance to be appropriately correlated with warrant, with quality of evidence—and that politics should be kept out of science.[18]

I can make sense of how things got so startlingly transmuted only by looking at feminist epistemology, not just as part of a larger development in feminism, but also as part of a larger development in philosophy of science. Here the last thirty years or so have seen a major shift: from the Old Deferentialist view, which took science to deserve a kind of epistemic authority in virtue of its peculiarly rational and objective method of inquiry, to the New Cynicism, which sees science as a value-permeated social institution, stresses the importance of politics, prejudice, and propaganda, rather than the weight of the evidence, in determining what theories are accepted, and sometimes goes so far as to suggest that reality is constructed by us, and "truth" a word not to be used without the precaution of scare quotes.[19]

My diagnosis is that the New Cynicism in philosophy of science has fed the ambition of the new, imperialist feminism to colonize epistemology. The values with which science is permeated, it is argued, have up to now been androcentric, sexist, inhospitable to the interests of women. Feminist criticisms of sexism in scientific theorizing, the argument continues, can't be seen merely as criticisms of bad science; the moral to be drawn is that we must abandon the quixotic quest for a science that is value-free, in favor of the achievable goal of a science informed by feminist values. There would be a genuinely feminist epistemology if the idea could be legitimated *that feminist values should determine what theories are accepted.*

The arguments offered to motivate the shift from feminist criticisms of sexism in scientific theorizing to feminist epistemology are of precisely the kind this diagnosis would predict. I can consider here only the two most important lines of argument, each of which focuses on a notion dear to the hearts of the New Cynics: underdetermination and value-ladenness.

The first appeals to the underdetermination of theories by data, claiming that, since there is unavoidable slack with respect to what theories are accepted, it is appropriate to allow political preferences to determine theory choice.[20] Suppose, first, that the appeal to underdetermination is intended only to point to the fact that sometimes the available evidence is not sufficient to decide between rival theories, and that in some cases (e.g., with respect to theories about the remote past, "man the hunter" and all that) additional evidence may be, in practice, unobtainable. The proper response is that, unless and until more evidence is available, scientists had better suspend judgment—and that the lay public, philosophers included, should not be too uncritically deferential to scientists' sometimes unwarrantedly confident claims about what they have discovered. Underdetermination, in this sense, hasn't the slightest tendency to show that we may legitimately choose to believe whatever theory suits our political purposes.

Suppose, next, that the appeal to underdetermination is intended, rather, to rest on the Quinean thesis that there can be incompatible theories with the same observational consequences, theories, therefore, between which not even all possible evidence could decide. I am not sure this thesis is true; and neither, apparently, is Quine, who sometimes seems to suggest that what he elsewhere describes as empirically equivalent but incompatible theories might really be verbal variants of one theory.[21] If, however, the thesis *is* true, it is presumably be true only of the genuinely theoretical (in the sense of "unobservable"); irrelevant, therefore, to such questions as whether men's hunting or women's gathering mainly sustained prehistoric communities. And if it *were* relevant to such questions, the feminists' appeals to it would be self-defeating, since in that case it would undermine their presumption that we can know what theories conduce to the interests of women, or what those interests are.

The second line of argument urges the necessity of "rubbing out the boundary between science and values,"[22] and hence, again, the appropriateness of allowing feminist values to determine theory choice. In one version, the argument seems to be that the idea that feminist values couldn't constitute evidence with respect to this or that theory rests on an untenable distinction of descriptive versus normative. This argument is only as good as the reasons for thinking the required distinction untenable. What is at issue is not whether moral or political criticisms of priorities within science, or of uses of the findings of science, are ever appropriate; not whether an evolutionary account of moral values is defensible; not whether simplicity, e.g., might have a more than pragmatic role; not whether some epistemic norms may turn out to be covertly of a descriptive, means-end character; but *whether it is possible to derive an "is" from an "ought."*[23] I can find no argument in the literature that even purports to show this, and neither can I think of one. That it is false is manifest as soon as you express it plainly: that propositions about what states of affairs are *desirable* or *deplorable* could be evidence that things *are*, or *are not*, so.

In another version, the argument seems to rest on the claim that it is impossible entirely to exclude "contextual" (i.e., external, social, and political) values from science. In this version, the argument is a non sequitur. Perhaps it is true that scientists are never entirely without prejudice; perhaps it is impossible that they should entirely put their prejudices out of sight when judging the evidence for a theory; it doesn't follow that it is proper to allow prejudice to determine theory choice. From the fact that it isn't possible to make science perfect, it doesn't follow that we shouldn't try to make it better.

The failure of these arguments is symptomatic of the false presupposition on which the second attempt to connect feminism and epistemology depends: that since the Old Deferentialist picture is not defensible, there is no option but the New Cynicism. But these are not the only options; the truth, as so often, lies in between. The Old Deferentialism over-stresses the virtues, the New Cynicism the vices, of science; the Old Deferentialism focuses too exclusively on the logical, the New Cynicism too exclusively on the sociological, factors that an adequate philosophy of science should combine. The natural sciences have been the most successful of human cognitive endeavors, but they are fallible and imperfect—not entirely immune to partiality and politics, fad and fashion.

Implicit here is a conception of the epistemological role of sociology of science which is worth making explicit, since it challenges an assumption which, it seems, both some Old Deferentialists and some New Cynics take for granted: that the sociology of knowledge constitutes a threat to traditional epistemological concerns. It is manifest as soon as it is stated plainly that no sociological investigation or theory could be sufficient by itself to show that the idea of theories' being better or worse supported by evidence is untenable. But to say this is not to deny that sociology of knowledge has any possible relevance to epistemology.

Sometimes scientists are scrupulous in seeking out and assessing relevant evidence; sometimes not. Presumably there is always some explanation of why they behave as they do, sometimes an explanation appealing to the individual psychology of the scientists concerned, sometimes an explanation appealing to considerations of a more sociological kind (political pressures led these scientists to ignore or gloss over the relevance of such-and-such easily available evidence; the knowledge that their work would come under the critical scrutiny of a rival team also aspiring to the Nobel Prize ensured that those scientists left no stone unturned, and so on). The value of such sociological investigations to epistemology is that they may suggest what ways of organizing science are apt to encourage, and what to discourage, scrupulous attention to the evidence.[24]

If my diagnosis is correct, though it is not inevitable that all the themes offered under the rubric "feminist epistemology" are false, it *is* inevitable that only those themes can be true which fail in their cynical intent. It is true, e.g., that inquirers are profoundly and pervasively dependent on each other; it is true that sometimes scientists may perceive relevant evidence *as* relevant only when persuaded, perhaps by political pressure, out of previous prejudices. But such truths have no radical consequences; it doesn't follow, e.g., that reality is however some epistemic community determines it to be, or that what evidence *is* relevant is not an objective matter.

And the epistemological significance of feminist criticisms of sexism in scientific theorizing, though real enough, is undramatic and by no means revolutionary. One traditional project of epistemology is to give rules, or, better, guidelines, for the conduct of inquiry; another is to articulate standards of better and worse evidence, of better or worse justified belief. One sub-task of the "conduct of inquiry" project is to figure out what environments are supportive of, and what hostile to, successful inquiry. One sub-task of this sub-task is to figure out how to minimize the effect of unquestioned and unjustifiable preconceptions in encouraging the acceptance of theories which are not well supported by evidence. Sober feminist studies of sexist science, like studies of the disasters of Nazi or Soviet science, could be a useful resource in this sub-sub-task of the "conduct of inquiry" project. But this is a role that requires the conception of theories as better or worse supported by the evidence, and the distinction of evidential and non-evidential considerations, traditionally investigated in the "standards of evidence" project.

Still, you may ask, given that I haven't denied that some themes presented under the rubric "feminist epistemology" are true; given that I acknowledge that some feminist criticisms of sexist science seem well founded and could have a minor but bona fide epistemological role; and given that I am quite willing to grant that a true theory of the determinants of evidential quality and of well-conducted inquiry might be of use to feminists seeking to understand the concepts of bias, objectivity, etc.;[25] why am I so troubled by the label?

Well, since the idea that there is an epistemology properly called "feminist" rests on false presuppositions, the label is at best sloppy. But there is more at stake than dislike of sloppiness; more than offense at the implication that those of us who don't think it appropriate to describe our epistemological work as "feminist" don't care about justice or opportunity for women; more than unease at sweeping generalizations about women and embarrassment at the suggestion that women have special epistemological insight. What is most troubling is that the label is designed to convey the idea that *inquiry should be politicized*. And *that* is not only mistaken, but dangerously so.

It is dangerously mistaken from an epistemological point of view, because the presupposition on which it rests—that genuine, honest inquiry is neither possible nor desirable—is, in Bacon's shrewd phrase, a "factitious despair" which, as he says, tends to "cut the sinews and spur of industry."[26] Serious intellectual work is hard, painful, frustrating; suggesting that it is legitimate to succumb to the temptation to cut corners can only block the way of inquiry.[27]

I would say that inquiry really is best advanced by people with a genuine desire to find out how things are, who will be more persistent, less dogmatic, and more candid than sham reasoners seeking only to make a case for some foregone conclusion; except that, since it is a tautology that inquiry aims at the truth, the sham reasoner is not really engaged in inquiry at all.[28] This should remind us that those who despair of honest inquiry cannot be in the truth-seeking business (as they should say, "the 'truth' racket"); they are in the propaganda business.

For obvious reasons, it is only relatively rarely that this is quite openly acknowledged. Sandra Harding hints at it when she announces that "the truth—whatever that is!—cannot set us free"; and Linda Alcoff when she tells us that "epistemologies . . . are discursive interventions in specific discursive and political spaces."[29] But Elizabeth Gross doesn't pull any punches: "feminist theory . . . is not a true discourse . . . It could be appropriately seen, rather, as a *strategy*, . . . [an] intervention with definite political . . . aims . . . *intellectual guerilla warfare*" (second italics mine).[30]

This makes it apparent why the idea that inquiry should be politicized is not just a misconception, but a politically dangerous misconception, because of the potential for tyranny of calls for "politically adequate research and scholarship." Harding announces that "the model for good science should be research programs directed by liberatory political goals," and that "the authority to say what is theoretically and politically adequate research and scholarship must remain [*sic*] in the hands of the marginalized."[31] And what, then, would "politically *in*adequate research" be? Research informed by what some feminists deem "regressive" political ideas—and research not informed by political ideas at all, i.e., honest inquiry.

Have we forgotten already that in *Nineteen Eighty-Four* it was **thought-crime** to believe that two plus two is four if the Party ruled otherwise?[32] This is no trivial verbal quibble, but a matter, epistemologically, of the integrity of inquiry and, politically, of freedom of thought. Needlessly sacrificing these ideals would not help women; it would hurt humanity.

NOTES

1. She continues, "because I dislike everything that feminism implies. I desire an end to the whole business, the demands for equality . . . But while . . . opportunity [is] denied, I shall have to be a feminist . . ." (cited in the "Afterword," by Rosalind Delmar, to Vera Brittain's *Testament of Friendship* (1945), Virago, London, 1980, p. 450). It ought to be said that fewer opportunities are now denied, that the "end to the whole business" is, hopefully, closer than it was in 1926.

2. For example, Lorraine Code, *Epistemic Responsibility,* University Press of New England, Hanover, NH, and London, 1987, proposes an "empirico-realism" said to

be akin to foundationalism, but also hints, not very specifically, that the foundationalism/coherentism dichotomy is misconceived; and later, in "Taking Subjectivity into Account," in Linda Alcoff and Elizabeth Potter, eds., *Feminist Epistemologies*, Routledge, London, 1993, 15–48, proposes a feminist relativism. Lynn Hankinson Nelson, *Who Knows? From Quine to a Feminist Epistemology*, Temple University Press, Philadelphia, 1990, proposes a coherentist feminist epistemology derived from Quine—but acknowledges that Quine allows an important role for experience. Jane Duran, *Toward a Feminist Epistemology*, Rowman and Littlefield, Savage, MD, 1991, describes the female point of view as instinctively coherentist, but goes on to represent herself as a contextualist; and seems to hold both that feminist epistemology should be naturalistic in the sense of non-normative, and that it should replace androcentric by gynocentric norms. Alison Jaggar, "Love and Knowledge: Emotion in a Feminist Epistemology," in Ann Garry and Marilyn Pearsall, eds., *Women, Knowledge and Reality*, Unwin Hyman, Boston, 1989, 127–55, emphasizes the role of emotion. Etc., etc.

3. Louise Antony, "Quine as Feminist: The Radical Import of Naturalized Epistemology," in *A Mind of One's Own*, ed. Louise Antony and Charlotte Witt, Westview, Boulder, CO, 1993, 185–225, p. 186.

4. "Introduction: When Feminisms Intersect Epistemology," to *Feminist Epistemologies*, 1–14, pp. 3–4.

5. Sandra Harding, *Whose Science? Whose Knowledge?* Cornell University Press, Ithaca, NY, 1991, pp. 180, 285, 275.

6. C. S. Peirce, *Collected Papers*, ed. Charles Hartshorne, Paul Weiss, and Arthur Burks, Harvard University Press, Cambridge, 1931–58, e.g., 5.213–310 (critique of Cartesian epistemology), and 5.368–77 (social conception of inquiry). For Peirce's use of "masculine intellect" see 5.368; and his review of Lady Welby's *What Is Meaning?* 8.171 ("Lady Victoria Welby's book . . . is a feminine work, and a too masculine mind might think it painfully weak"). Other themes sometimes described as "feminist" are also to be found in Peirce (e.g., a triadic metaphysics which encourages the replacement of traditional dichotomies by trichotomies); and different supposedly feminist themes are to be found in the other pragmatists (e.g., William James's Will to Believe doctrine, allowing a legitimate cognitive role to "our passional nature"). But, for obvious reasons, I think it inappropriate to attempt to trace "anticipations of feminist/epistemology/metaphysics/philosophy of language/etc." in pragmatism, as in the symposium in *Transactions of the Charles S. Peirce Society*, 27.4, 1991.

7. Ayn Rand, *Objectivist Epistemology*, Mentor, New York, 1966.

8. See Harriet Baber, "The Market for Feminist Epistemology," *The Monist*, 77.4, 1994, 403–23.

9. Andrea Nye, *Words of Power*, Routledge, London, 1990. Ironically enough, where they are at all plausible Nye's criticisms of formal logic are familiar from the work of earlier male writers who stressed the inadequacy of symbolic logic to represent pragmatic aspects of reasoning: F. C. S. Schiller, *Formal Logic: A Scientific*

and Social Problem, MacMillan, London, 1912; P. F. Strawson, *Introduction to Logical Theory*, Methuen, London, 1952; Stephen Toulmin, *The Uses of Argument*, Cambridge University Press, Cambridge, 1958. The notion of "reading" which Nye wants to replace logic derives from the work of male writers such as Paul de Mann.

10. According to Carole Tavris, *The Mismeasure of Woman*, Touchstone, Simon and Schuster, New York, 1992, pp. 42–43 and 51–53, there is good evidence of a difference at the highest levels of mathematical ability, but the supposed evidence for difference in verbal abilities is more dubious.

11. Jane Flax, "Political Philosophy and the Patriarchal Unconscious: A Psychoanalytic Perspective on Epistemology and Metaphysics," in Merrill Hintikka and Sandra Harding, eds., *Discovering Reality: Feminist Perspectives on Epistemology, Metaphysics, Methodology, and Philosophy of Science*, Reidel, Dordrecht, the Netherlands, 1983, 245–82; Evelyn Fox Keller, *Reflections on Gender and Science*, Yale University Press, New Haven, CT 1985.

12. Carol Gilligan, *In a Different Voice*, Harvard University Press, Cambridge, 1982. Mary Field Belenky, Blythe McVicker Clinchy, Nancy Rule Goldberger, and Jill Mattuck Tarule, *Women's Ways of Knowing*, Basic Books, New York, 1986; the quotation is from p. 8.

13. See E. T. Bell, *The Development of Mathematics*, McGraw Hill, New York, 1949, p. 519.

14. See, e.g., Alison Jaggar, "Love and Knowledge: Emotion in a Feminist Epistemology," p. 146; Harding, *Whose Science? Whose Knowledge?* p. 271, Nelson, *Who Knows? From Quine to a Feminist Empiricism*, p. 40.

15. Marilyn Frye, "To See and Be Seen: The Politics of Reality," in *Women, Knowledge, and Reality*, 77–92, p. 77. See also Noretta Koertge and Daphne Patai, *Professing Feminism: Cautionary Tales from the Strange World of Women's Studies*, Basic Books, New York, 1994, chapter 3, on squabbles between lesbian and heterosexual, black and white feminists.

16. The issue is feminist criticisms focusing on the content of scientific theories, not feminist criticisms of the choice of problems on which scientists work, or of there being relatively few, and mostly relatively junior, women scientists.

17. For such criticisms see, e.g., Ruth Bleier in Bleier, ed., *Feminist Approaches to Science*, Pergamon Press, New York, 1986; Anne Fausto-Sterling, *Myths of Gender: Biological Theories about Women and Men*, Basic Books, New York, 1986; Helen Longino and Ruth Doell, "Body, Bias, and Behavior: A Comparative Analysis of Reasoning in Two Areas of Science" (1983), in Jean O'Barr and Sandra Harding, eds., *Sex and Scientific Inquiry*, University of Chicago Press, Chicago, 1989, 165–83. I have two cents' worth of my own to contribute here: the claim that male dominance is hormonally determined is confidently reiterated by critics of feminism such as Nicholas Davidson and Michael Levin, both of whom cite Steven Goldberg as their source; Goldberg cites a medical researcher called Money. Imagine my astonishment, then, on tracking down Money's work, to find that he says specifi-

cally that questions about dominance *were not addressed* in his study of genetic females exposed before birth to high levels of male hormones! For details see my review of Davidson and Levin, *International Studies in Philosophy*, 23.1, 1991, 107–9.

18. On the use of the term "feminist empiricism," which has created considerable confusion, see "Science as Social?—Yes and No," essay 6 in this volume.

19. See "Puzzling Out Science," essay 5 in this volume.

20. Helen Longino, "Can There Be a Feminist Science?" in Garry and Pearsall, eds., *Women, Knowledge, and Reality*, p. 206; Nelson, *Who Knows? From Quine to a Feminist Empiricism*, pp. 173–74, 187–88, 248.

21. W. V. O. Quine, "Empirically Equivalent Theories of the World," *Erkenntnis*, 9, 1975, 313–28, and "Empirical Content," in *Theories and Things* (Cambridge and London: Belknap Press of Harvard University Press, Cambridge, 1981), 24–30, especially pp. 29–30. My reservations begin with the fact that even to state the thesis apparently requires a sharply distinguished class of observational predicates, of which I am skeptical (as Quine is too, some of the time).

22. Nelson, *Who Knows? From Quine to a Feminist Empiricism*, p. 248. See also Longino, "Can There Be a Feminist Science?" and Harding, *Whose Science? Whose Knowledge?* pp. 57ff..

23. Or, more strictly speaking, whether that p ought [not] to be the case could be evidence that p is [not] the case.

24. After Peirce, Michael Polanyi seems to me to have best understood these issues, perhaps in part because of his having worked as a scientist, at different stages of his career, on both sides of the Iron Curtain—an experience which left him acutely aware of the dangers of politicizing science. See "The Republic of Science," in Marjorie Grene, ed., *Knowing and Being*, University of Chicago Press, Chicago, 1969, 49–62.

25. Antony's "Quine as Feminist," enlisting Quine's naturalized epistemology to the feminist cause, seems to depend on this idea. I agree with much of what Antony has to say about other feminist epistemologies. But, as I have argued elsewhere, though Quine's "Epistemology Naturalized" contains elements of truth, it rests on a series of equivocations (W. V. O. Quine, "Epistemology Naturalized," in *Ontological Relativity and Other Essays*, Columbia University Press, New York, 1969, 69–90; Haack, *Evidence and Inquiry*, chapter 6). Anyway, I am disinclined to call an epistemology "feminist" because, being true, it is potentially useful for feminist projects. (But I can't help wondering how many more friends and readers I might have had if I'd been willing to call my book, not *Evidence and Inquiry*, but *Feminist Foundherentism!*)

26. Francis Bacon, *The New Organon* (1620), Book 1, Aphorism 87.

27. "Do not block the way of inquiry" is, according to Peirce, a proposition that "deserves to be written on every wall of the city of philosophy" (*Collected Papers*, 1.135).

28. See "Confessions of an Old-Fashioned Prig," essay 1 in this volume.

29. Linda Alcoff, "How Is Epistemology Political?" in Roger S. Gottleib, ed.,

Radical Philosophy: Tradition, Counter-Tradition, Politics, Temple University Press, Philadelphia, 1993, 65–85, p. 66.

30. Elizabeth Gross [now Grosz], "What is Feminist Theory?" in *Feminist Challenges,* ed. Carole Pateman and Elizabeth Gross, Allen and Unwin, London, 1986, p. 177; cited in David Stove, "A Farewell to Arts," *Quadrant,* May 1986, 8–11, p. 9. Harding, *Whose Science? Whose Knowledge?* pp. xi, 58, 185.

31. Harding, *Whose Science? Whose Knowledge?* p. 98. Compare Duran, *Toward a Feminist Epistemology,* pp. 145–46: "would a model like the . . . computational model [of mind], be the result of politically incorrect theorizing that is, apart from being grossly androcentric, also the very sort of thing feminists have labeled oppressive to minorities, Third World points of view, and, indeed, to anyone who is not white, male and well-educated?"

32. George Orwell, *Nineteen Eighty-Four* (1949), Penguin Books, Harmondsworth, Middlesex, 1954, pp. 184, 198.

Multiculturalism and Objectivity

Truth is rarely pure and never simple. Modern life would be intolerable if it were either.
OSCAR WILDE[1]

Multiculturalism seems such an engaging idea; and yet, somehow, threatening. Why do I, like many people, feel so ambivalent about it? The explanation is not, after all, so hard to find: the term "multiculturalism" is multiply ambiguous.

Sometimes the word is used to refer to the kinds of society in which people from different cultural backgrounds live together, to characteristic problems that arise in such circumstances, and, sometimes, to the idea that the majority culture in such a society should not impose unnecessarily on the sensibilities of minority culture(s)—social multiculturalism.

Sometimes "multiculturalism" is used to refer to the idea that it is desirable for students to know about other cultures than their own (sometimes, that it is especially desirable in multicultural societies in the sense just explained, for students to know something about the cultures of others with whom they live)—pluralistic educational multiculturalism.

Sometimes, again, "multiculturalism" is used to refer to the idea that students (especially students from minority groups in multicultural societies) should be educated in their own culture—particularistic educational multiculturalism. This comes in a weaker and a stronger form, the stronger holding that students should be educated *exclusively* in their own culture.

And sometimes "multiculturalism" is used to refer to the idea that the dominant culture is not, or should not be, "privileged" (in the contemporary American context, this is often expressed as the claim that "Western culture" should not be privileged)—philosophical multiculturalism.

Since pluralistic educational multiculturalism is outright incompatible with the strong form of particularistic educational multiculturalism, we are faced not only with different, but with conflicting, uses. But it is impossible to avoid making matters even more complicated by identifying another dimension of ambiguity, this time in the term "culture."

Some of the ambiguities are familiar: think of Snow's distinction of the "two cultures," the scientific and the literary; of the difference between "British culture" construed as referring to Shakespeare, Handel, Eliot, and so on, or as referring to soccer, fish and chips, warm beer, perennial miners' strikes, and so forth. Recall that, despite our membership in the Common Market, we British still have some difficulty thinking of ourselves, as opposed to those foreigners across the Channel, as Europeans, but would agree with the French in finding the idea that American culture is European somewhat comical; and that "Europe" blurs together a great variety of languages, ways of life, religions—as "Africa" does, or "Asia."

And beyond these familiar kinds of fuzziness is the recent shift of meaning hinted at in my characterization of philosophical multiculturalism. Initially, the contrast seems to be between the majority culture in a multicultural society and minority culture(s)—as it might be, between the majority Hindu culture of India, and Muslim and Christian minorities; or, in this country, between the soi-disant "European" culture of the majority (actually itself pretty varied) and the many and varied not-even-distantly-European minority cultures. But of late "Western culture" has come to refer to anything associated with what is taken to be the dominant class of contemporary American society, and the theme is that *this* "culture" should not be privileged over the "cultures" of what are taken to be oppressed, marginalized, disadvantaged classes—classes identified in terms of race, sex, and sexual orientation. The scare quotes here are intended to signal that the term "culture" has now been stretched beyond anything its ordinary elasticity permits; for, so far from respecting the usual contrast of culture with nature, we are now to take "black" or "female" as designating cultures.

Diane Ravitch, distinguishing pluralistic and particularistic conceptions of multiculturalism, urges the value of the former and the dangers of the latter. Daniel Bonevac, distinguishing liberal and illiberal multiculturalism, complains of a "bait and switch" operation replacing the liberal by the illiberal. Richard Bernstein writes of a "*dérapage*," or slide, from a benign to an alarming kind of multiculturalism. Mary Lefkowitz distinguishes multiculturalism, of which she approves, from uniculturalism and anticulturalism, of which she does not.[2]

Lefkowitz's tripartite distinction reflects the need to accommodate both the difference between pluralism and particularism and the shift from an ordinary, vague, ambiguous, but maybe just-barely-serviceable notion of differing and overlapping cultures, to the more-than-debatable notion of cultures of the dominant and the oppressed, "cultures" identified by race, sex, etc.—from multiculturalism to counterculturalism, as I shall say.

The former difference is already included in my original fourfold distinction; accommodating the latter shift, we get eight distinguishable positions: besides particularistic educational multiculturalism, particularistic educational counterculturalism; besides philosophical multiculturalism, philosophical counterculturalism; and so on. In principle, that is; in practice it is often far from clear which of these is being proposed. It is part of the strong particularists' strategy to blur the distinction between their position and the pluralists'; and it is part of the counterculturalists' strategy to blur the difference between their use of "Western culture" and more ordinary uses. Bernstein's word is certainly a good one for this conceptually slippery situation.

I mention social multiculturalism only to put it aside. It raises very hard questions, even in the practically and morally more straightforward cases where a multicultural society is the result not of conquest or a territorial decision imposed from outside, but of immigration. That Muslim girls in British schools should not be obliged to wear gym uniforms which are, by their standards, immodest, is easy enough; but it is very far from obvious that the same tolerance should extend to, say, recognition of polygamous marriages, or to banning *The Satanic Verses*. But such questions, as well as questions about bilingualism, etc., important as they are, are beyond the scope of this essay.

The claim of pluralistic educational multiculturalism, that it is desirable for people to know about other cultures than their own, is true. (As I write this sentence, though, newly struck by that deceptively straightforward-sounding phrase, "their own," I am reminded of Dewey's observation that "the typical American is himself . . . international and interracial in his makeup.")[3] Pluralistic educational multiculturalism is desirable; but it is not easily achieved. A more-than-superficial knowledge of another culture is likely to require some fluency in another language; and it is not easily combined with ensuring that students acquire the other knowledge and skills they will need. Still, awareness that others do things differently and take different beliefs for granted helps you to discriminate the conventional from the non-conventional in your own practice and thinking, to avoid the "rightly are they called 'pigs'" syndrome. And, yes, knowledge of the customs of minority communities within a multicultural society surely can contribute to the accomplishment of a mutually tolerable, or, with good luck and good will, a mutually enriching, modus vivendi.

There is of course nothing objectionable, in fact much that is desirable, about efforts to keep the children of Americans of Lithuanian or Cuban or Chinese or Zulu, etc., descent in touch with Lithuanian/Cuban/Chinese/Zulu, etc., traditions. But the claim of the strong form of particularistic educational multiculturalism, which would have such children educated exclusively in Lithuanian/Cuban/Chinese/Zulu, etc., ways, is mistaken, and for some of the same reasons that make the pluralistic claim true. And, for some of the same reasons that pluralistic educational multiculturalism is likely to contribute to mutual tolerance, strong particularistic educational multiculturalism runs the risk of contributing to mutual *in*tolerance and resentment.

Sometimes strong particularistic educational multiculturalism is defended on the grounds that it will raise students' self-esteem. But this is wrong-headed not only in its presupposition that raising students' self-esteem is a proximal goal of education, but, more fundamentally, in its failure to acknowledge that a sense of self-worth is likely to be better founded on mastery of some difficult discipline than on ethnic boosterism, and that students can be inspired to achievement by the example of people of very different backgrounds from their own—as, for example, W. E. B. Du Bois testifies that he was by his education in the classics of European literature.

Sometimes, again, particularistic educational multiculturalism is defended on the grounds that students are unfairly disadvantaged unless they are educated in "their" cultural traditions. At the purely pragmatic level, this calls for a candid acknowledgment that children of immigrant parents are, on the contrary, likely to find themselves disadvantaged if their education doesn't make them familiar with the customs and practices of their new country. It also calls for a plain statement that it is simply untrue that only persons of Chinese descent can really master Confucius, or only persons of Greek descent, Homer, or only persons of French descent, Balzac, and so forth. I don't think I understand or appreciate Peirce any the less, for instance, because, unlike myself, he was American; nor Bacon any the more because, like myself, he was English.

Turning now to philosophical multiculturalism, I note that part of what is at stake may be the thought that when, as pluralistic educational multiculturalism reasonably urges, students are taught something of other cultures than their own, it should be *with respect*. It can be granted without further ado that all persons should be treated with respect; and that it is undesirable to encourage an attitude of suspicion or disrespect for what is unfamiliar merely because it is unfamiliar. But it doesn't follow, and neither is it true, that all opinions, practices, institutions, traditions, are equally deserving of respect. One of the benefits of knowing that others take for granted quite different opinions and practices than yourself is that it can help you see what is local and parochial in your own practice and belief: a benefit that would be sacrificed by an uncritical relativism that found *all* comparisons to be odious.

Let me try to find an example that won't touch on any local sensibilities. I find much to admire in the life of the Kalahari Bushmen: their closeness to the natural world, the vigor of their rock paintings, their delight in music and dancing, their taking for granted, in the extraordinary harshness of their conditions of life, that "if one eats, all eat."[4] And, thinking about the remarkable ingenuity of the triple-jointed poisoned arrows with which they hunt their game, I am set to wondering in a new way about what the social and intellectual conditions were that enabled the rise of modern science in seventeenth-century Europe. But it doesn't follow, and neither is it true, that Bushman myths about the origin of the world or the causes of the seasons, and so forth, are on a par with the best scientific theorizing.

Rather than consider all four forms of counterculturalism, allow me to turn my attention, now, directly to philosophical counterculturalism. Further disambiguation is still needed, since the "privilege" that is being denied may be ethical, aesthetic, epistemological, or all three. Of these, I shall consider only the third, epistemological counterculturalism.

"Western culture," the thought is, has been largely the work of white, heterosexual men, and consequently gives an undeserved authority to *their* ways of knowing or of seeing things, and serves *their* interests. The first phrase hints that there are black or female or homosexual "ways of knowing," an idea which seems to me not only false, but of the essence of racism or sexism; the second marks the connection with radical philosophies which deny the possibility of separating knowledge and power, inquiry and advocacy.

The point of epistemological counterculturalism is to contest the allegedly undeserved alleged epistemic privilege of white males. Thus, Wahneema Lubiano tells us that "strong multiculturalism" is "not about the liberal tolerance of difference, but about the contestation of differences"; Mike Cole urges that multiculturalism "must push against the forces of oppression, be they centered on race, class, gender or all three"; and Naomi Scheman suggests that "a useful umbrella under which to shelter diverse projects [of 'feminist epistemology'] would be that of 'anti-masculinism' by analogy with anti-racism," a link which, she continues, "points to the necessity for any feminist epistemology to be simultaneously committed to challenging the other sorts of bias that may be found within the dominant practices of acquiring, justifying, and accounting for knowledge."[5]

And now I can identify a main source of my uneasy feeling that there is something threatening as well as something engaging about multiculturalism: one of the many different and even competing ideas sheltered by the umbrella term "multiculturalism" is epistemological counterculturalism, which is one manifestation of the increasingly widespread and articulate irrationalism of our times.

"Rational" has a descriptive use, "having the capacity to reason," in which it is true of all normal humans, and a normative, "using that capacity well," in which it is true of only some of us, and of those only sometimes. And its normative use is multiform, encompassing inter alia: acting in a way which, given your beliefs, will likely achieve your goals; having goals which correspond appropriately to your needs; believing reasonably; going about inquiry appropriately. We humans have the capacity to reason, we are rational in the descriptive sense; but, far from always being rational in the normative senses, we are fallible, imperfect, often mentally lazy, careless, indifferent to the truth. And our capacity for reasoning brings with it the danger of thought turned pathological[6]—of grotesquely elaborate falsehood, of affected obscurity, of glossogonous nonsense.

Two main irrationalist strategies parallel the descriptive and the normative uses of "rational": a shift of emphasis to emotion, feeling, will, rather than thought, reasoning, cognition; and denigration of epistemic standards, standards of what makes evidence better or worse and of what makes inquiry well or ill conducted, as no more than local, conventional, and covertly political. There is useful work to be done identifying the sources of the first strategy—misconception of the emotions as brutally irrational,[7] for example, and confusion of the imaginative and the imaginary.[8] I shall focus here, however, on some recurrent themes in the counterculturalist assault on the objectivity of epistemic norms.

Epistemological counterculturalism rests on misconceptions about knowledge, society, power, and objectivity. These are, most importantly: first, that standards of good evidence, justified belief, bona fide knowledge, etc., are culture- or community-bound; and, second, that inquiry is inevitably disguisedly political. The first of these is dispiritingly skeptical in tendency, and the second is outright scary: if all inquiry really were political, there would be no difference between knowledge and propaganda, between inquiry and rhetorical bullying.[9] But the fact that a thesis is dispiriting or scary is not in itself a reason for supposing it false; so it is necessary to articulate why these misconceptions *are* misconceptions.

One source of the first misconception may have been the perception that neither of the traditionally rival theories of epistemic justification—foundationalism and coherentism—is acceptable, and the conviction that the only alternative is some kind of contextualism, according to which epistemic justification is context- or community-relative. Another source has been Kuhn's suggestion that, since proponents of rival scientific paradigms disagree even about what constitutes evidence, standards of better and worse evidence are paradigm-bound—which has encouraged the parallel conclusion, outside philosophy of science, that standards of better and worse evidence are culture-bound.

It is true that neither foundationalism nor coherentism will do. The trouble with foundationalism is that there are no such basic beliefs as it requires, no beliefs justified exclusively by the subject's experience and sufficient to serve as foundations for the rest of his justified beliefs. The trouble with coherentism is that it cannot consistently allow that a person's experience has any bearing whatsoever on the justification of his empirical beliefs. But contextualism, which makes justification context- or community-relative, is not the only, or the most plausible, alternative.

A theory intermediate between foundationalism and coherentism, which allows the relevance of experience to empirical justification without requiring any beliefs to be justified by experience alone, and which allows pervasive mutual support among beliefs without requiring that empirical justification be a matter exclusively of relations among beliefs, can avoid the difficulties of both foundationalism and coherentism.

In this intermediate theory (I call it, more accurately than euphoniously, "foundherentism"), the model for the structure of evidence is not, as much recent epistemology has supposed, a mathematical proof, but a crossword puzzle. I first thought of the crossword when casting around for a case where mutual support was clearly not viciously circular, and then noticed that the distinction between clues and completed entries paralleled that between experiential evidence and reasons.[10] In due course I realized that the analogy also suggests how deep-seated disagreement in background beliefs will give rise to disagreements about what evidence counts as relevant.

If you and I are working on the same crossword, and have filled in long, central entries differently, we will probably differ about whether the fact that this proposed solution to an intersecting entry ends in an "F" makes it more, or less, reasonable. Similarly, if you and I have significantly different background beliefs, we will probably disagree about what constitutes evidence in favor of, or against, related propositions. Nevertheless, in the case of the crossword you and I are both concerned with the fit of the entry in question with its clue and other completed entries (plus how independently reasonable those other entries are, and how much of the crossword has been completed); and in the epistemic case we are both concerned with the fit of the proposition in question with experiential evidence and background beliefs (plus how independently secure those background beliefs are, and how comprehensive the evidence is). There is no real relativity of standards of evidence; though disagreements in background beliefs, and consequential disagreements about evidential quality, can make it look as if there is.

However, though quality of evidence is an objective matter, our *judgments* of the quality of evidence are perspectival, since they can only be made from the perspective of our (fallible) background beliefs. For example: whether the way a candidate writes his "F"s is evidence relevant to his trustworthiness is an objective matter, depending on whether graphology is *true;* but whether I judge it to be relevant evidence depends on whether I *believe* graphology is true.

This, interestingly enough, not only identifies one mistake—confusing the perspectival character of judgments of evidential quality for relativity of standards of evidence—on which epistemological counterculturalism depends, but also begins to explain the truth that pluralistic educational multiculturalism accommodates. Awareness that others take different background beliefs for granted, and so make different judgements of the worth of this or that evidence, can prompt the realization that your own judgments of the worth of evidence depend on your background beliefs, and are only as good as those beliefs are secure.

The discussion thus far might suggest (as is often taken for granted) that all forms of epistemological counterculturalism are relativist. But this isn't quite right; rather, there is a persistent ambiguity in counterculturalists' talk of "privilege." All epistemological counterculturalists take for granted that epistemic standards differ from culture to culture. Some, the real relativists, explicitly or implicitly deny that the question, whether the standards of this or that culture are better, makes sense. But others, the tribalists, maintain that the standards of their culture are best. Epistemological counterculturalists of the former, relativist, stripe are committed to the claim that *no* standards, those of "Western culture" included, are privileged; those of the latter, tribalist, stripe are committed to the claim that *their,* non-"Western," standards are privileged.[11]

Arguments for the superiority of non-"Western" epistemic standards seem rather thin on the ground. But one theme that is sometimes heard is that they overcome the supposedly linear character of "Western" standards. If I am right, the structure of evidential support, like the structure of a crossword puzzle, is, indeed, non-linear. The irony, though, is that this has nothing to do with "Western" versus non-"Western" epistemic standards but, to the contrary, is part of the explanation of why the appearance of cultural divergence of epistemic standards is a kind of conceptual illusion. Looking at the right level of generality, at framework principles rather than specific judgments of relevance, and in the light of the multidimensional, crossword-like determinants of evidential quality, we will see that there is commonality underlying surface divergences. Tribesmen attributing lightning and thunder to the anger of the gods, like scientists attributing it to electrical discharges in the atmosphere and the sudden expansion of air in their path, are alike seeking explanatory stories to accommodate their experience.

Implicit in what has been said thus far, but needing to be made explicit, is the thought that an adequate epistemology will require a quasi-logical dimension (in its account of relations of evidential support); a personal dimension (in its recognition that you and I may believe the same thing, and yet I be justified and you unjustified, and that empirical justification depends ultimately on the individual subject's experience); and a dimension focused on human nature (in its recognition that our notion of the evidence of the senses presupposes that, for all normal humans, the senses are a source of information about the world).

One source of the second epistemological counterculturalist thesis, that knowledge is inherently political, has been the perception that inquiry is in some epistemologically important sense social. And in a sense, indeed, it is. Each of us, as a knowing subject, is pervasively dependent on others; and natural-scientific inquiry has been as successful as it has in part because of its social character, of the cooperative and competitive engagement of many persons, both within and across generations. So, yes, an adequate epistemology will also require a social dimension.

None of "black" or "female" or "homosexual," however, can plausibly be supposed to identify an epistemic community. And these observations about the epistemic interdependence of knowing subjects and the social character of scientific inquiry, rather than suggesting the conclusion that knowledge is inherently political, suggest, on the contrary, that one of the (of course, fallible and imperfect) mechanisms by means of which bias gets detected and corrected—in scientific theorizing, and, though less systematically, in inquiry generally—is by means of competition between supporters of rival theories or approaches.[12]

Another source of the idea that knowledge is inherently political has been the perception that racist, sexist, etc., ideas have sometimes come to be accepted, not because they were well supported by evidence, but because of unjustifiable prejudices and preconceptions. That is why epistemological counterculturalists generally refuse to use good plain terms like "truth," "knowledge," "evidence," etc., without hedging them with scare quotes; thus reducing "truth" to "so-called 'truth,'" "evidence" to "so-called 'evidence,'" etc.

Racist and sexist ideas have, indeed, sometimes passed for known fact or established theory; and sometimes, no doubt, at least part of the explanation of how this came about is that those ideas' being accepted served the interests of the more powerful race or sex. But it doesn't follow that there is no objective truth, knowledge, evidence, etc., or that the very notions of knowledge, fact, evidence, etc., are ideological humbug. Indeed, if the notions of knowledge, fact, relevant evidence, and so forth, were really no more than ideological humbug, then it couldn't be true (only "true"), it couldn't be known fact (only "known fact"), and it couldn't be established by strong evidence (only by "strong evidence"), that racist or sexist theories have sometimes been accepted on inadequate evidence (or "evidence"). The "passes for" fallacy[13] is self-defeating as well as fallacious.

It is perfectly possible to acknowledge the shortcomings of foundationalism and coherentism, human inquirers' pervasive epistemic dependence on one another, the social character of scientific inquiry, the complexity and fallibility of all human cognitive activity, the corruption of some claims to truth, without being obliged to grant either that epistemic standards are community- or culture-relative, or that inquiry is invariably political.

Genuine inquiry is so complex and difficult, and advocacy "research" has become so commonplace, that our grip on the concepts of truth and reason is being loosened—as the ubiquitous "passes for" fallacy and all those cynically dismissive scare quotes suggest. This is much to be regretted; and not least because honest, thorough inquiry—reasoned pursuit of the truth—is the best defense against racist and sexist stereotypes. (To the anticipated objection that reasoned pursuit of the truth is a "Western" ideal, I shall say only that, "Western" or not, it is an ideal of nearly incalculable value to humanity.)

The appropriate philosophical response—after, of course, patiently pointing out that one could not discover by honest inquiry that there is no such thing as honest inquiry, that it could not be really-and-truly true that "truth" is no more than ideological humbug, etc.—is to try to articulate the subtleties of the structure of evidence and the complexity, revisability, fallibility of inquiry. That, at any rate, is what I have tried to do.

NOTES

1. Actually, it was Algernon, in Oscar Wilde's *The Importance of Being Earnest.*

2. Diane Ravitch, "Multiculturalism: E Pluribus Plures," in *Are You Politically Correct? Debating America's Cultural Standards,* ed. Francis J. Beckwith and Michael E. Bauman, Prometheus Books, Buffalo, NY, 1993, 165–84; Daniel Bonevac, "Leviathan U," in *The Imperiled Academy,* ed. Howard Dickman, Transaction Publishers, New Brunswick, NJ, and London, 1993, 1–26; Richard Bernstein, *Dictatorship of Virtue,* Knopf, New York, 1994; Mary Lefkowitz, "Multiculturalism, Uniculturalism, or Anticulturalism?" *Partisan Review,* 1993.4, 590–97.

3. "Nationalizing Education," in *John Dewey: The Middle Works,* vol. 10, ed. Jo Ann Boydston, Southern Illinois University Press, Carbondale, 1988, p. 205.

4. See Elizabeth Marshall Thomas, *The Harmless People,* Vintage, New York, 1959.

5. Lubiano's remark is reported in Heather MacDonald, "Underdog and Pony Show: The Left Convenes at Hunter College," *The New Criterion,* June 1992, p. 88; Cole's is from "Teaching and Learning about Racism: A Critique of Multicultural Education in Britain," in Gajendra K. Verma, Sohan Mogdil, Celia Mogdil, and Kanka Mallick, *Multicultural Education: The Interminable Debate,* Falmer Press, London, 1986, 123–49, p. 142; Scheman's from "Feminist Epistemology," *Proceedings and Addresses of the American Philosophical Association,* 68.1, September 1994, 78–80, p. 79.

6. A phrase I have adapted from David Stove's brilliant and disturbing paper, "What Is Wrong With Our Thoughts?" in *The Plato Cult,* Blackwell, Oxford, 1991, 179–205, pp. 189, 193.

7. The fact that we speak of "irrational fears" is an indication that fears can be, in fact usually are, rational, appropriate given genuine danger.

8. See "As for that phrase 'studying in a literary spirit' ...," essay 3 in this volume.

9. See also "Knowledge and Propaganda: Reflections of an Old Feminist," essay 7 in this volume.

10. See Haack, *Evidence and Inquiry: Towards Reconstruction in Epistemology*, Blackwell, Oxford, 1993, chapter 4; "A Foundherentist Theory of Empirical Justification," in Louis Pojman, ed., *The Theory of Knowledge*, Wadsworth, Belmont, CA, 2nd edition, 1998; and "'Dry Truth and Real Knowledge': Epistemologies of Metaphor and Metaphors of Epistemology," essay 4 in this volume.

11. See also "Reflections on Relativism: From Momentous Tautology to Seductive Contradiction," essay 9 in this volume.

12. See also "Science as Social?—Yes and No," essay 6 in this volume.

13. See "Puzzling Out Science," essay 5 in this volume.

Reflections on Relativism: From Momentous Tautology to Seductive Contradiction

I would say of metaphysicians what Scaliger said of the Basques: they are supposed to understand each other, but I do not believe it. CHAMFORT[1]

"Relativism" refers, not to a single thesis, but to a whole family. Each resembles the others in claiming that something is relative to something else; each differs from the others in what it claims is relative to what. One might begin to make identikit pictures of various family members along the following lines:

... IS RELATIVE TO ...	
(1) meaning	(a) language
(2) reference	(b) conceptual shceme
(3) truth	(c) theory
(4) metaphysical commitment	(d) scientific paradigm
(5) ontology	(e) version, depiction, description
(6) reality	(f) culture
(7) epistemic values	(g) community
(8) moral values	(h) individual
(9) aesthetic values	
.	.
.	.
.	.

By including (h) on the right, I have classified the various forms of subjectivism as special cases of relativism.

While, obviously, not all the permutations this table allows represent real possibilities (that moral values are relative to scientific paradigm, for instance, is a non-starter), many seem to represent positions which have seriously been held. Various theses with more familiar noms de plume might be associated, at least conjecturally, with one or another item in my table:

—Quine's thesis of ontological relativity: (2)(c);

—Whorf's thesis of linguistic relativity: (4)(a);

—Putnam's thesis of conceptual relativity: (5)(b) or (5)(a);

—Feyerabend's meaning-variance thesis: (1)(c); Kuhn's variant: (1)(d);

—Goodman's pluralistic irrealism: (6)(e);

—(one common, though debatable, interpretation of) Kuhn's thesis of the incommensurability of scientific paradigms: (7)(d);

—epistemic contextualism, as defended by Annis, Field, and, sometimes, Rorty: (7)(f), (7)(g).

Several points implicit thus far need making explicit. The first concerns Quine's thesis of ontological relativity. Despite its name, Quine's thesis seems to relativize, not ontology, but the ontology of a language or theory, to analytical hypotheses; it might be better described as the thesis of referential than as the thesis of ontological relativity—hence, "the inscrutability [of late, Quine sometimes says 'indeterminacy'] of reference." There is an irony here: discussing a recent restatement in which Quine observes that "we could reinterpret 'Tabitha' as designating no longer the cat, but the whole cosmos minus the cat," Putnam remarks that he finds this so incredible as to constitute a reductio of any premises from which it follows. The irony is that his own thesis of conceptual relativity appears to be in one respect not less but more radical than Quine's of "ontological" relativity: if I understand it correctly, Putnam's thesis really *is* ontological.[2]

It is tempting to describe Quine's thesis as akin to Whorf's, which concerns, not how the world is, but how speakers of this or that language take the world to be. But though there is this affinity, there is also a significant difference, in the intended interpretation of "is relative to." Whorf, as I understand him, intends only to say that a person's metaphysical commitments *vary depending on* the grammatical structure of his native language. Quine, however, as I understand him, intends to say that questions of reference *make sense only relative to* analytical hypotheses; i.e., that "refers to . . ." is elliptical for "refers-relative-to-analytical-hypotheses-A to . . ."; thus, he writes that "it makes no sense to say what the objects of a theory are, beyond saying how to interpret or reinterpret that theory in another."[3] So Quine's thesis seems more deeply relativist than Whorf's, since it takes "is relative to" in a stronger sense.

This suggests a further distinction, between shallow relativism: to the effect that some item in the left column varies depending on some item in the right column, and deep: to the effect that some term in the left column makes sense only relative to some variable in the right column. This means that each permutation of items in my table potentially represents, not a single position, but a pair of positions—and that the conjectured assignment of noms de plume could use refinement, to specify which of each pair is intended.

With respect to (7), (8), and (9) in my table, the distinction between shallow and deep forms corresponds to the more familiar distinction between descriptive or anthropological epistemic, moral, etc., relativism (to the effect that different communities or cultures accept different epistemic, moral, or aesthetic values), and normative or philosophical epistemic, moral, etc., relativism (to the effect that talk of epistemic, moral, or aesthetic value makes sense only relative to some culture or community). I conjecture that shallow forms of relativism are sometimes taken to have more philosophical interest than they deserve because they are confused with, or wrongly taken to imply, the corresponding deep forms.

A related point worth making explicit concerns Rorty's position vis à vis epistemic relativism. Rorty seems to shift between two verbally similar but substantively different conceptions of epistemic justification: the contextualist, "A is justified in believing that p if and only if, with respect to his belief that p, A satisfies the criteria of *his* epistemic community," and the tribalist, "A is justified in believing that p if and only if, with respect to his belief that p, A satisfies the criteria of *our* epistemic community."[4] Both presuppose that epistemic standards vary from community to community. But only contextualism, which makes "A is justified in believing that p" elliptical for "A is justified-by-the-standards-of-community-C in believing that p," for *variable* C, is relativist in the deep sense. Tribalism, by contrast, makes "A is justified in believing that p" elliptical for "A is justified-by-the-standards-of-community-C in believing that p," for *constant* C.

My earlier hints that it is deep rather than shallow relativism that is of philosophical interest should not be understood to imply that I think that Rorty's epistemic tribalism is of anthropological interest only. But they should be understood to imply, what I believe is true, that what is philosophically interesting about epistemic tribalism is less its shallow relativism, the presupposition that epistemic standards vary from community to community, than an epistemic claim distinct from, and not implied by, that presupposition: the idea—incompatible with deep epistemic relativism—that some epistemic standards are objectively better than others.[5]

Rorty suggests that his position is also Quine's. Perhaps he has in mind that passage at the end of the first chapter of *Word and Object* where Quine seems to shift from what sounded like a deep relativist position: "Where it makes sense to apply 'true' is to a sentence couched in the terms of a given theory and seen from within the theory, complete with its posited reality," to what sounds like a form of tribalism: "Have we now so far lowered our sights as to settle for a relativist doctrine of truth, rating the statements of each theory as true for that theory . . . ? Not so. The saving consideration is that we continue to take seriously our own particular aggregate science. . . . Within our own total evolving doctrine, we can judge truth as . . . absolutely as can be. . . ." Quine himself, however, has of late indicated that he intended nothing so radical. The first claim, he tells us, is to be construed only as relativizing meaning, not truth, to theory; and in view of this the latter claim seems best interpreted as saying only that in our judgments of what is true, we rely on our background beliefs, rather than as suggesting a Rortyesque epistemic tribalism.[6]

One might mark subfamilies of kinds of relativism by reference to the term in the left-hand column: "moral relativism" for forms that relativize moral values to one or another of the variables on the right, "aesthetic relativism" for forms that relativize aesthetic values, "semantic relativism" for forms that relativize meaning, reference, or truth, "epistemic relativism" for forms that relativize epistemic values, "metaphysical relativism" for forms that relativize ontology or reality. Finer distinctions can be made by means of double-barreled expressions; extra- versus intra-scientific versions of epistemic relativism, for example, can be identified as "epistemic-cultural relativism" and "epistemic-paradigm relativism," respectively. Accommodating, additionally, the distinction of shallow versus deep relativism would call for triple-barreled expressions.

Even closely related family members may be very different in import. For example, the thesis that "true" is elliptical for "true-in-L" is an unalarming acknowledgment of the possibility that the same string of symbols may have different meanings in different languages,[7] while the thesis that "true" makes sense only relative to background theory is a substantial, and alarming, claim. Part of the explanation is that the former but not the latter can, without embarrassment, be taken to fall within its own scope.

Though I hope to have done something in these few pages to convey a sense of how complex a phenomenon relativism is, it is certainly beyond my powers, and probably beyond your tolerance, for me to undertake an exhaustive survey of all its varieties and their logical relations to each other, let alone to evaluate whether any may be defensible. With respect to this last question, though, it is worth making explicit a thought already suggested by the previous paragraph: the stock objection that relativism is self-undermining seems clearly enough apropos with respect to some forms of semantic, epistemic and metaphysical deep relativism, but not to all of those, much less to all forms of relativism indifferently. And, as you will see, my difficulties with the particular form of relativism on which I shall focus henceforth are not of this stock kind.

THE PARTICULAR FORM on which I shall concentrate is the thesis of "conceptual relativity," one component of the position which Putnam for some years saw as the way to avoid the excesses, on the one hand, of the metaphysical realism to which he earlier subscribed and, on the other, of both cultural relativism and Goodmanian irrealism. Putnam has recently changed his mind again, but allow me for now to concentrate on his earlier time-slice; or rather, since I shall not engage in detailed Putnam-exegesis, on a complex of ideas that I shall attribute to (the relevant time-slice of) Putnam, the author of *Renewing Philosophy*,[8] but subject to correction by scholars who might prefer that I speak of "Putnam*."

"Metaphysical realism," as Putnam uses it, refers to a complex congeries of intermeshing theses: that there is one real world, consisting of a fixed totality of mind-independent objects; that there is one true description of this one real world, a description couched in a privileged, "absolute," scientific vocabulary; and that its truth consists in its copying, or corresponding to, the world and the fixed totality of mind-independent objects therein.

Cultural relativism, as Putnam characterizes it, radically repudiates the metaphysical realist's conception of truth. It is the thesis that truth consists, not in any correspondence of description and world, but in a description's being accepted within a culture. (In the scheme offered earlier, this is the deep form of (3)(f), a brand of semantic-cultural deep relativism.) It follows that there is no one true description of the world, but many descriptions each true relative to some culture: D_1, true-in-community-C_1, D_2, true-in-community-C_2, and so on.

Goodmanian irrealism radically repudiates the metaphysical realist's conception of the world. It is the thesis that there is no one real world, only many "versions," the descriptions and depictions made by scientists, novelists, artists, and so on.

According to Putnam's thesis of conceptual relativity, there is (contra Goodman) one, real world; but this world does not (contra the metaphysical realist) consist of a fixed totality of mind-independent objects. The question, how many and what kinds of object there are, makes sense only relative to vocabulary, to conceptual scheme; there is no absolute, privileged, scientific vocabulary which describes the world as it is independent of our conceptual contribution. And truth is a matter neither (contra the metaphysical realist) of a description's copying or corresponding to the mind-independent objects in the world, nor (contra the cultural relativist) of its being accepted in this or that community. It is a matter, rather, of the description's being such that, in epistemically ideal circumstances, we would be justified in accepting it.[9] This has a verbal affinity with Peirce's definition of truth, but it is substantively different. For, as Putnam construes it, idealized justification is context-dependent; and this presumably precludes, what Peirce's definition requires, that there be one true description of the world, the final representation.

This last point, about the context-dependence of idealized justification and hence of truth, begins to suggest why some readers have wondered how much Putnam's view really differs from a cultural relativism about truth.[10] But I set that worry aside, because my present purpose is not to give a comprehensive critique, but to convey a sense of puzzlement.

The thesis Putnam calls "conceptual relativity" appears to be metaphysical-conceptual-deep relativism in my triple-barreled terminology. I say "appears," not "is," because my puzzlement begins right at the beginning. The thesis of conceptual relativity says that how many and what kinds of objects or properties there are is relative to conceptual scheme or vocabulary. But what could it *mean* to say, "relative to conceptual scheme C_1 there are rocks, but relative to conceptual scheme C_2 there are not"? It seems to waver unsteadily between the trivial: "you can't describe the world without describing it"—the momentous tautology of my subtitle—and the manifestly false: "incompatible descriptions of the world can be both true"—the seductive contradiction of my subtitle.

In one paragraph of *Renewing Philosophy*, after telling us that there are no descriptions of reality as independent of perspective, and that it is impossible to divide our language into two parts, a part that describes the world as it is anyway, and a part that describes our conceptual contribution, Putnam goes on to say that this "simply means that you can't describe the world without describing it" (p. 123). But that is our momentous tautology; so either conceptual relativity says more or Putnam is mistaken in supposing that "the phenomenon of conceptual relativity does have real philosophical importance" (p. 122).

Perhaps we are intended to interpret "there are no descriptions of reality as independent of perspective," not as the triviality that there are no descriptions of reality that don't use some vocabulary or other, but as the substantive claim that there is no vocabulary, and hence no description of reality, that doesn't refer, explicitly or implicitly, to some human perspective.[11] And perhaps we are intended to interpret "our language can't be divided into parts, one that describes the world as it is anyway, and one that describes our conceptual contribution," not as the tautology that there are no descriptions of reality that don't use some vocabulary or other, but as the substantive claim that there are no descriptions of reality that don't refer, explicitly or implicitly, to human beings' conceptual goings-on. So interpreted, however, these claims no longer seem plausible. Just as when, a few pages earlier, Putnam had observed that "you can't beat Goodman at his own game by naming some mind-independent stuff" (p. 113), the natural reaction was, "why not?—rocks, for instance," so, here, the natural reaction is, "why not?—why need a description of the rocks in the Kalahari, for instance, refer, explicitly or implicitly, to any perspective or human conceptual activity?" (Of course, it makes a difference if the rocks are being described as the site of Bushman paintings—but that's the point: it makes a difference. Of course, also, any description involves some conceptual activity on the part of the describer; but that is not the same as its referring to that conceptual activity of his.)

In other passages Putnam tells us that the number and kinds of objects/ properties there are can vary from one correct description of a situation to another, and "*either way . . . is equally 'true'*"; that there are many different "right versions" of the world; that there is no one uniquely true description of reality; that there are many true descriptions of the world in many different vocabularies, and one can't privilege any one as "absolute" (pp. 120, 109, 103). The first of these sounds suspiciously like the contradiction that incompatible statements can be both true—and that Putnam feels obliged to hedge "true" with scare quotes does little to lull one's suspicions. A few pages before, however, Putnam had acknowledged that of course incompatible statements *can't* be both true; leading one to wonder if his point could be only that different but compatible statements may be both true—once again, hardly a phenomenon of "real philosophical importance." But his real point, it seems, is that the usual way of looking at it asks too much of the notion of meaning; that there may be no determinate answer to the question, whether this and that description do or don't mean the same, nor, therefore, to the question, whether they are or aren't compatible (pp. 116–20). This leaves me wondering why we should suppose that there would, in that case, be an answer to the question, whether they were both true, and suspecting that those scare quotes ("either way is equally 'true'") may disguise Putnam's recognition that, indeed, there would not.

It is all very puzzling; and frustrating, too, for one who, like myself, sympathizes with Putnam's aspiration to avoid the lumbering machinery of metaphysical realism, on the one hand, and the excesses of cultural relativism or outright irrealism, on the other. This sets the task of the rest of the paper: to see how one might achieve that aspiration while avoiding the apparent instability of metaphysical-conceptual relativism, its shifting up and back between momentous tautology and seductive contradiction. I begin with a statement of what I call "innocent realism," a commonsense picture which is very plausible, but, or rather because, in various ways unspecific. I continue by exploring ways to make this innocent realist picture more specific without straying from the intermediate territory between cultural relativism/Goodmanian irrealism, on the left, and metaphysical realism, on the right.

In this exploration, my path and Putnam's will cross again; for he has of late moved away from the metaphysical-conceptual relativism of his Gifford lectures toward a position more realist than that, but less realist than metaphysical realism, so we have been exploring the same territory, and with the same purpose. And, in a sense, in the same spirit; for Putnam has of late been urging what he calls a "deliberate naïveté," which I think has some kinship with my Critical Common-sensism,[12] in our approach to these difficult issues. But in what follows (though occasional HP-sightings will be reported in footnotes) I shall not attempt to track the details of Putnam's recent explorations, only report my own.

HERE IS A PRELIMINARY STATEMENT of innocent realism.

The world—the one, real, world—is largely independent of us. Only "largely," not "completely," independent of us, because human beings intervene in the world in various ways, and because human beings and their physical and mental activities are themselves part of the world.

We humans describe the world, sometimes truly, sometimes falsely. Whether a (synthetic) description of the world is true depends on what it says, and on whether the world is as it says. What a description says depends on our linguistic conventions; but, given what it says, whether it is true or it is false depends on how the world is. True, some descriptions describe us, and some describe things in the world that we made; and whether such a description is true or is false depends on how we are, or on how the things we made are—for such descriptions, that *is* the relevant aspect of "how the world is." But whether even such a description is true or is false does not depend on how you or I or anybody *thinks* the world is.

We can describe how the world would be, or would have been, if there were, or had been, no human beings. To be sure, before there were human beings or human languages, the English sentence "there are rocks" did not exist; and so, if sentences are bearers of truth and falsity, it is not the case that "there are rocks" was true before there were people, or that "there are rocks" would have been true even if there had never been people. Nevertheless, there were rocks before there were people, and there would have been rocks even if there had never been people; and *that* is a (partial) description of how the world would be or would have been if there were, or had been, no human beings.[13]

There are many different vocabularies, and many different true descriptions of the world. Two descriptions in different vocabularies may say the same thing about how (some part or aspect of) the world is, or different things. If they say the same thing, they are of course compatible with each other; if they say different things, they may be compatible *or* incompatible with each other. Compatible descriptions may be combined in a longer, conjunctive description, which will be true just in case its conjuncts are; incompatible descriptions, however, cannot be jointly true.

Innocent realism obviously precludes Goodmanian irrealism, since my statement began, "the world—the one real world. . . ." And it equally obviously precludes cultural relativism, since my statement continued, "given what [a description of the world] says, whether it is true or false depends on how the world is." In fact, innocent realism is obviously enough not a relativist position of any kind.

The hard part is to see whether innocent realism can be articulated more specifically without collapsing—or, better, without inflating—into metaphysical realism, without appeal to that "fixed totality of mind-independent objects," the correspondence of descriptions to those objects, an assumed comparison of our descriptions with unconceptualized reality; and in a way that acknowledges the significance of our conceptual contribution, of conceptual change, of conceptual pluralism. I start with the question of that "fixed totality of mind-independent objects," which requires attention both to "mind-independent" and to "fixed totality of objects."

Of course, the world changes, objects come into and go out of existence; but the metaphysical realist does not deny this, and it is not what is at issue here. The "totality of mind-independent objects" that Putnam's metaphysical realist envisages is presumably supposed to be "fixed" *at a* time, not *over* time.

There was no reference in the statement of innocent realism to a "fixed totality of objects"; and the omission was deliberate. "Object," "thing"— these are the most hospitable of concepts. How many objects are there on my desk? The question has no determinate answer: should the count be five papers, or umpteen pages? one box of paper clips, or ninety-eight paper clips and one small cardboard box? one computer, or one central processing unit, one keyboard, one monitor, one printer? one pad of Post-it notes, or forty-seven Post-it notes and one backing sheet? . . .

There *was* an observation in the statement of innocent realism about the world's being largely independent of us; but this stands in need of a good deal of amplification, amplification which will inevitably entail some loss of innocence. Following Peirce, I shall distinguish the real, which is independent of how we think it to be, from the imaginary, fictions and figments. Still following Peirce, I distinguish, within the real, the external, which is not only independent of how anyone thinks it to be, but also independent of how we think, from the internal or mental, which is independent of how anyone thinks it to be, but not of how we think.[14] So "mind-independent" has a stronger interpretation ("real and external, independent of how we think") and a weaker ("real but internal, independent of how anyone thinks it to be"). Correspondingly, "mind-dependent" has a stronger interpretation ("a figment, dependent on how someone thinks it to be") and a weaker ("real but internal, dependent on how we think"). The weakly mind-dependent is also weakly mind-*in*dependent.

That there is a real world was the first thesis put forward in the name of innocent realism; and yes, what that means is that the world (the real world, not imaginary, fictional worlds) is independent of how anyone thinks it to be, mind-independent in the weaker sense. Many real things, those which are external, are also independent of how we think, mind-independent in the stronger sense. But some real things, the internal or mental ones, are not independent of how we think, and hence are not mind-independent in the stronger sense, but mind-dependent in the weaker sense.

These reflections begin to suggest why the example of which Putnam makes a big metaphysical deal—three Carnapian, physical objects, or seven Leśniewskian, mereological objects?[15]—is so confusing. It trades on the polymorphism of "object." In the situation Putnam describes, "here are three objects" and "here are seven objects" are indeed both true. But since "object" means "ordinary physical object" in the first, "mereological object" in the second, they are compatible. (Compare: a sofa and two armchairs, or a suite of furniture?) To make matters even more confusing, Putnam's example trades on the fact that mereological objects are—well, peculiar, to put it mildly. Mereological sums are wholes of which the parts may be spatially scattered, or even nonspatial; they cannot be cleanly classified either as concrete or as abstract. Counting the mereological sum of which the parts are Cleopatra's Needle and my nose as one thing, let alone counting an olfactory quale, a smell of coffee, say, and a time, as one thing, is thoroughly artificial—much more so than counting these stars as a constellation, let alone than as counting this dense heavenly body as a star.[16] I am inclined to think that what this calls for is a further distinction, of natural- versus artificial-object terms. But even if one were tempted to conclude that mereological sums are not mind-independent in the stronger sense, it wouldn't follow, and neither is it true, that rocks, stars, dogs, elephants, noses, monuments, etc., are not strongly mind-independent either.

The question, "is there or isn't there a fixed totality of mind-independent objects?" traps you in a metaphysical corner. Answer "yes," and you seem to be committed to something like a Logical Atomist picture, with its mysterious logically ultimate objects; answer "no," and you seem to be committed to the idea that our conceptual goings-on bring new objects into existence. The best strategy may be to refuse the question; and, in any case, to say plainly: there aren't logical atoms, but the world is not created by our conceptual goings-on.

I turn next (out of the frying pan into another frying pan!) to the issue of conceptual pluralism. Putnam refers us[17] to James's observations that we no longer think of the laws of mathematics or physics as authentically deciphering "the eternal thoughts of the Almighty," but recognize that "most, perhaps all, of our laws are only approximations," that any one of several rival theories "may from some point of view be useful," and that our descriptions of the world "tolerate much choice of expression and many dialects."[18] But there is nothing in these observations that innocent realism cannot accommodate.

Putnam's argument turns on those "many different true descriptions" from the possibility of which it is inferred that there is no one uniquely true description of the world. His argument relies, not on truth-as-idealized-justification, but on conceptual relativity. One version of this has already been dealt with. Though there are different true descriptions of Putnam's imagined situation ("there are three regular physical objects," "there are seven mereological objects"), it doesn't follow, and neither is it true, that there is no one true description ("there are three regular physical objects, but seven mereological objects"; or, better, "there are seven mereological objects, *of which* three are regular physical objects").

Sometimes, when Putnam observes that there are "many different true descriptions of the world," the difference being stressed is between the vocabulary of the sciences and other, non-scientific vocabularies.[19] Here, the premise of the argument is that there is no scientific vocabulary to which all other, or more inclusive, vocabularies can be reduced. I shan't challenge the premise. Though pieces of furniture, for instance, and human beings, are physical things, there is no guarantee that all our descriptions of tables and chairs will turn out to be reducible to descriptions in the vocabulary of physics, nor that all our descriptions of peoples' beliefs, hopes, fears, etc., will turn out to be reducible to descriptions in the language of physiology. But it doesn't follow, and neither is it true, that there is no one uniquely true description of the world. These different descriptions are compatible, and so, if true, may be conjoined in one true description of the world.

To the anticipated objection that the heterogeneous conjunction envisaged would not be a unified description, the reply is that, though indeed it would not be a description couched wholly in a privileged, scientific, vocabulary to which all other vocabularies were reducible (not "unified" in the Positivists' strong sense of that term), innocent realism doesn't require a unified description in that sense, and the lack of a unified description in that sense doesn't require any concession to metaphysical-conceptual relativism. For there to be one true description of the world requires only that the different true descriptions be compatible, not that there be one to which the others are reducible. A heterogeneous true description of the world is no less true for its heterogeneity; any more than a map which superimposes a depiction of the roads on a depiction of the contours of the relevant terrain, or a map which inserts a large-scale depiction of a major city in a corner of a small-scale depiction of a state, is less accurate for *its* heterogeneity.

Another, intra-scientific, version of the "many different descriptions" objection appeals to different "different descriptions" again, stressing that cognitive advance is not always a matter of new claims in an old vocabulary, but often a matter of conceptual innovations marked by new vocabulary, or by shifts in the meaning of old vocabulary. This is true, and epistemologically important; but it is not incompatible with innocent realism. From the fact that a term in one theory or paradigm does not have the same, or entirely the same, meaning as the same term in a different theory or paradigm, it doesn't follow that no sentence in the vocabulary of the one theory is translatable into any sentence (or clumsy paragraph) in the vocabulary of the other, only that no homophonic translation will do. There may or may not be failure of translatability.[20] For two theories to be incompatible, the negation of some sentence which is a theorem of the one must be a theorem of the other; and this requires that some sentence of the one be translatable in some fashion into the other. So if there is complete failure of translatability, there is compatibility. If, on the other hand, there is translatability, there may be compatibility or incompatibility.[21] If the different descriptions are incompatible, they cannot be both true, and the premise that there are different true descriptions fails. But if the different descriptions are compatible, though the premise holds, the conclusion does not follow, since, as before, the different true descriptions can be conjoined in a single (even if heterogeneous) true description.

I turn now to the issue of that "comparison of a description of the world with unconceptualized reality" which innocent realism may be accused of presupposing. The quick retort would be that innocent realism is a metaphysical position, not an epistemological one, and hence says nothing about *how we tell* which descriptions are true. But the epistemological issues at stake here are too important to sidestep.

That there is a kind of procedure in which we engage which, outside philosophical contexts, we would naturally describe as "comparing a description with reality"—when we look to see whether the suspect fits the witness's description, for example—does not settle the issue. Simply pointing to this philosophically artless usage evades the key claim which innocent realism may be suspected of precluding, that perception involves conceptualization. What the innocent realist must do, rather, is explain why, though he acknowledges that perception involves conceptualization, he does not grant that this acknowledgment obliges him to concede that reality is concept-relative.

Perception is interpretative; but it is also direct. Ordinarily, perceptual event and perceptual judgment are phenomenologically inseparable— I just look and see that there is a cardinal in the bird feeder; but nevertheless they are conceptually distinct. Our normally spontaneous judgments or descriptions of what we perceive involve interpretation, depending on background beliefs, expectation, set, as well as sensory input; but what we perceive, and sometimes misperceive, is not sense data or ideas, nor phenomenal as opposed to noumenal cardinal birds, but things and events around us—the cardinal alighting at the feeder, for example.[22]

The point is not that perception doesn't involve conceptualization, but that it also involves something else, something with the potential to surprise us. True, our perceptual judgments are conceptualized, interpretative; but what testifies that in perception we are in contact with something real, independent of our interpretations, of how anyone thinks it to be, is exactly that potential for surprise. (As Peirce once put it: "A man cannot startle himself by jumping up with an exclamation of 'Boo!'")[23]

I turn, finally, to the twin questions: to what does innocent realism commit us with regard to the definition of truth? and, more specifically: is innocent realism covertly committed to some kind of correspondence theory?

It doesn't follow from the fact that innocent realism precludes a cultural-relativist conception of truth that it is committed to some version of the correspondence theory. And in fact, so far from being committed to anything like the Logical Atomists' version of the correspondence theory, my development of innocent realism precludes it, since it does not acknowledge the logical atoms, ultimate objects, which that theory requires.

The situation is different with respect to Austin's version of the correspondence theory, in terms of a co-incidence of the demonstrative and descriptive conventions governing a statement, which doesn't require logical atoms or anything like them. Innocent realism is compatible with this theory, but not committed to it. The same holds, so far as I can see, with respect to Tarski's semantic theory, which construes truth as a relation of expressions to something non-linguistic, but, instead of requiring anything like the Logical Atomists' ontology, is neutral with respect to the character of the objects satisfaction of all sequences of which constitutes truth.

But, though it is compatible with accounts that construe truth as a relation of truth-bearer and something else, innocent realism does not require a relational account. It is equally compatible with Aristotle's "to say of what is, that it is, or of what is not, that it is not, is true", etc.; and with Ramsey's "a belief is true if it is a belief that p, and p."[24] These are, indeed, in a sense akin to mine in "innocent realism," metaphysically the most innocent of theories of truth.

Now let me turn to the question of the relation of innocent realism to Peirce's characterization of truth as concordance with the ultimate representation, the Final Opinion, compatible with all possible experiential evidence and the fullest logical scrutiny, which would be agreed by all who investigate were inquiry to continue indefinitely.[25] (It is almost, but perhaps not quite, too obvious to need saying that this is very different, not only from Putnam's construal of truth as idealized justification, but also from Rorty's disastrous transmutation of Peirce's account into an identification of truth with whatever can "survive all conversational objections."[26] *That*, of course, innocent realism obviously precludes.)

But isn't it equally obvious that the innocent realist idea that a statement is true just in case the world is as it says cannot be reconciled with the pragmaticist idea that a statement is true just in case it would belong to the hypothetical final opinion? Not quite. For Peirce's conception of reality has two aspects, of which, thus far, I have taken account of only one. The real, he holds, though independent of what you or I or anybody thinks it to be, is what is represented in the final opinion.[27] So a statement is true, on Peirce's account, just in case the world—the real world, *in his sense*—is as it says.

But it is hard to avoid a feeling that this "reconciliation" is only verbal; that something significant has been lost if "real," or "independent of how we think it to be," is interpreted as meaning no more than, "independent of how any actual person or persons think(s) it to be," and not implying, "independent of how any actual *or hypothetical* person or community thinks *or would think* it to be." Though Peirce's account avoids the cultural relativism, the tribalism, and the irrealism of some contemporary neo-pragmatists, it is certainly some way from an entirely innocent realism.[28]

What motivates Peirce's not-so-innocent conception of the real is the thought that talk of a reality beyond the reach of all possible cognition, of the "absolutely incognizable," is pragmatically meaningless, that "we have no conception" of it. His argument is that "what I think is of the nature of a cognition. . . . Consequently, the highest concept which can be reached by abstractions from judgments of experience—and therefore, the highest concept which can be reached at all—is the concept of something of the nature of a cognition. . . . *Not*, then, . . . is a concept of the cognizable. Hence, not-cognizable . . . is, at least, self-contradictory. . . . In short, *cognizability* (in its widest sense) and *being* are not merely metaphysically the same, but are synonymous terms."[29]

Now you begin to worry that Peirce may have succumbed to one of those momentous tautologies: that he is overimpressed by "you can't conceive something without conceiving it," as Putnam is by "you can't describe the world without describing it" (and as Berkeley is by "you can't think of a physical object without its being in your mind"). But it is a bit more complicated than that. "Conceive" and "cognize" are not quite equivalent; and Peirce's "we have no conception of the absolutely incognizable" is ambiguous between the tautology that it is impossible to conceive of something without conceiving of it, and something else: that it is impossible to make sense of any question to which we could not, however long inquiry continued, determine the answer. The ambiguity lubricates Peirce's shift from a repudiation of a world of unknowable things-in-themselves to a denial that there are questions about the world—*the* world—which we may not be able to answer.[30] Now one sees why the problem of buried secrets[31]—that his account of meaning, truth, reality has the counterintuitive consequence that now-undecidable propositions about the past must be deemed meaningless, neither true nor false—*is* a problem for Peirce.

It is no problem, however, if we reconstrue Peirce, not as giving us the meaning of "true," but as drawing attention to the fact that some statements, though linguistically meaningful, gramatically constructed from meaningful components, are nevertheless epistemically absolutely idle. This is a thought which innocent realism not only can but should accommodate, a thought which enables it to avoid that hopeless obsession with "the skeptical challenge" to which rigider realisms seem drawn.

THESE REFLECTIONS have meandered a little, as reflections are apt to do, so let me recall the main landmarks along the way: relativism is not a simple, single thesis, but a complex and confusing family of positions; insofar as Putnam's thesis of conceptual relativity seems plausible, it is because of an inherent instability; but there look to be more plausible, and stabler, positions in the logical space which it was intended to occupy—positions which, however, are not relativist.

This has been, obviously, nothing like a Refutation of Relativism; but I hope it has suggested how some of the considerations which have motivated certain forms of relativism might be accommodated in a nonrelativist way.

NOTES

1. *Maximes et pensées,* 1805; my source is J. Gross, ed. *The Oxford Book of Aphorisms,* Oxford University Press, Oxford, 1983, p. 234.

2. W. V. Quine, "Ontological Relativity," in *Ontological Relativity and Other Essays,* Columbia University Press, New York, 1969, 26–68, and *The Pursuit of Truth,* Harvard University Press, Cambridge, MA, 1990, 1992, where Quine writes (p. 51 of the first edition) that "kindly writers have sought a technical distinction between my phrases 'inscrutability of reference' and 'ontological relativity' that was never clear in my own mind." Hilary Putnam, *Words and Life,* Harvard University Press, Cambridge, MA, 1994, p. 280, referring to Quine's *Pursuit of Truth,* pp. 31–33; the quotation about Tabitha is from p. 33.

3. Quine, "Ontological Relativity," p. 50. Note Quine's phrase, "the objects *of a theory,"* which indicates a focus on ontological commitment rather than ontology.

4. Richard Rorty, *Philosophy and the Mirror of Nature,* Princeton University Press, Princeton, NJ, 1979, especially p. 175 (where Rorty suggests the contextualist view that to say that S knows that p is a remark "about the status of S's reports among his peers"), and p. 178 (where he offers the tribalist view that "truth and knowledge can only be judged by the standards of inquirers of our own day"). See

T E N

The best man for the job may be a woman . . . and other alien thoughts on affirmative action in the academy

That men should rush with violence from one extreme, without going more or less into the contrary extreme, is not to be expected from the weakness of human nature. THOMAS REID[1]

At first, as I wrestled with the topic before us, I thought my difficulties were—well, my difficulties. My philosophical work has been in logic, epistemology, philosophy of science, pragmatism; I had rarely ventured before even into ethical theory, and only once, decades ago, into applied ethics. And affirmative action is, besides, such a very American idea, perhaps not easily mastered by someone who thinks in an accent like mine.

Then later, reading book upon unsatisfying book, article upon unsatisfying article, uneasy lest my judgment be clouded as I found myself obliged to think about my own career in disturbing ways, I began to wonder if the problem might be (as Peirce suggested long ago) that to engage in philosophical argument about moral issues puts one in chronic danger of falling into "sham reasoning"—making a case for a conclusion to which one's commitment is already unbudgeably evidence- and argument-proof at the outset.

Eventually, though, I came to believe that what makes the topic seem so intractable is that we just haven't paid serious enough attention to the complexity and the difficulty of the issues surrounding affirmative action. We have succumbed to a kind of This-or-Nothingism, too eager to debate whether affirmative action is a Good Thing or a Bad Thing instead of asking what its benefits and drawbacks might be as a solution to this problem or to that perhaps quite different one, or compared to the benefits and drawbacks of this alternative approach or that.

To sort it all out, however (even supposing I could), would surely require not a few months and a modest-sized paper, but at least several years and a fat book. I shall confine myself for now to affirmative action in academia, beginning—since this is where my thinking began—with questions about women in my profession, and then asking whether the issues are essentially the same or relevantly different where race is concerned. Even within this quite narrow scope, as it turns out, the dangers of This-or-Nothingism soon become apparent.

I RECALL, about a quarter of a century ago now, a job interview at which the chairman opened the proceedings by assuring me he had nothing against the employment of married women, he thought they might be quite good for the women students. I told him—vamping it up just a little—that, actually, I hoped to be good for the men (too). And that, naturally, was that. Was I the best person for the job? I don't know. But I could tell you a dozen such stories; and I'm pretty sure that at least once, yes, I was.

Still, by the time my temporary position at a woman's college came to an end, I had landed a real, tenure-track job—in a recently founded university which as I recall then had about three hundred faculty, of whom eight (including me) were women. Why were we so few? Sometimes the best candidate didn't get hired because of that reluctance to hire women I had encountered earlier; but some talented women found the geography impossible given a husband's career plans; some got discouraged at the graduate school stage; some never got to that stage because of discouragement from teachers or parents or peers. Doubtless, also, some women got discouraged from, or in, graduate school because they suspected they would encounter that reluctance, and some of the reluctance resulted from the belief that a woman would leave if her husband found an opportunity elsewhere; etc. This was a pity; talented women were losing out, and universities were losing out too.

Is affirmative action a good solution to the kinds of problem I have described? The term seems to be used of a range of policies, from requiring that all reasonable steps are taken to ensure that positions are properly advertised, that women are not discouraged from applying, that fair procedures are followed, etc., to requiring, overtly or by implication, that some-

times a woman be preferred even though she is not judged the best applicant. Though probably there are mixed and borderline cases, one can mark
a key distinction by speaking of procedural-fairness policies, on the one
hand, and preferential hiring policies, on the other. I shall assume it is
unnecessary to argue the desirability of the former; it is the latter kind of
policy that generates all the excitement.

When, as perhaps happened once or twice to me, the best candidate
fails to get the job for no other reason than that she is a woman, that is,
certainly, a bad thing; as I was moved to argue in the pages of *Philosophy*,[2]
twenty years or so ago, in response to an article arguing (yes, really!) that
it is perfectly OK. But though I am sure discriminatory hiring is a bad
thing, I am not sure preferential hiring is the best solution.

In fact, if the reason it's a bad thing if the philosophy department at
Euphoric State[3] fails to hire the best candidate simply because she is a
woman, is—as I think it is—that her sex is irrelevant, it might look as if
there is a very straightforward argument that preferential hiring is a bad
thing. If what is bad is that an irrelevant consideration, the sex of the candidate, is influencing the process, how could it be any less bad to give preference to someone who is not the best candidate on the grounds that she
is a woman, which requires the same irrelevant consideration to influence
the outcome?

A common response is that sex *is* relevant after all: that appointing
women contributes to a desirable diversity in the academy; that women
are needed as role models; that women bring special philosophical insights.
The trouble with the first of these suggestions is that "diversity" has become one of those foam-rubber, public-relations words[4] which muffles the
otherwise obvious: that a philosophy department as varied as you like with
respect to sex, race, ethnicity, and all that, all of whom were students of
Professor Davidson's working on adverbs ending in "ingly" (or all of whom
were students of Professor Harding's tracking down rape and torture metaphors in Newton—or whatever) would not, for all its diversity in one
sense, be diverse in the sense that matters.

But perhaps *you* are imagining a philosophy department as intellectually diverse as you like, but all of whom are male Americans of Greek descent. Wouldn't there then be a case for hiring someone female, and/or not
of Greek descent? If the idea is that this is a way to improve intellectual
diversity, my reply is that there is a better way: read the candidates' work.
If the idea is that, since ex hypothesi we already have maximal intellectual
diversity, social diversity is the next priority, my reply is that the candidate's

ability to teach and do philosophy should be the first criterion. I mean, not to deny that a university may legitimately have other goals as well, but to affirm that the best possible teaching and intellectual work should be its first priorities (and to remind you, and myself, of the value to society of a genuinely excellent, genuinely meritocratic, educational system).

But now I see that if intellectual bent were significantly correlated with sex or ethnicity or etc., neither of the scenarios I just imagined would be possible anyway. So it is a relief to realize that the question of the relevance of sex doesn't need to be settled at this point. The argument considered above fails for reasons independent of the relevance or otherwise of sex; it relies on a confusion of "candidate who *is* the best" with "candidate who is *judged* the best."

Suppose the reason a woman doesn't get hired even when she's the best candidate is that women's abilities tend to be systematically undervalued; then a policy of preferring a female candidate even when she was not judged the best could result in the best candidate being hired after all. And, indeed, a pervasive disinclination, conscious or, more often, otherwise, to take women philosophers quite as seriously as men surely is part of the reason why a woman may not be judged the best even when she is. Furthermore, where junior appointments are concerned, merit is in considerable measure a matter of potential; and perhaps there is, still, enough subtle discouragement of young women to justify the thought that a given level of achievement at the new-Ph.D. stage might indicate more potential in a young woman than in a young man.

It is often taken for granted that rules ensuring formal, procedural equality—"equal-opportunity" or "antidiscrimination" policies, as we sometimes somewhat optimistically call them—would suffice, at least on the nontrivial assumption of an equal distribution of talent and commitment, for a representation of women equal to their representation in the applicant pool; with, perhaps, also some indirect effects on the causes of their underrepresentation in that pool. Perhaps sometimes it is also taken for granted that formal, procedural equality is now a matter of course. But positions which are advertised have sometimes already been decided; and ways are sometimes found to avoid even having to place a pro forma advertisement. Anyway, formal, procedural equality does *not* necessarily guarantee equality of opportunity in hiring, can*not* by itself ensure there is no covert disadvantage faced by women.

Now there looks to be a very simple argument that preferential hiring is a good solution: it's a way, albeit a backhanded way, of getting the best person appointed despite her sex. And if the man who is judged the best isn't the best, he is not really wronged when preferential hiring gives the job to a better, female, candidate.

But right away I start to worry about the price carried by the backhandedness. If it is known, even if it is falsely believed, that the policy is to prefer women even when they are not judged the best, many of those who are turned down will believe they have lost out to someone less capable than themselves. Doubtless the resentment is often unjustified—for every man who has failed to land an academic job because of preferential hiring, there must be scores, at least, who believe they have—but unfortunately it is real, and has real effects, nonetheless. (And, I might add, the idea is encouraged that when women fail to get jobs for which they apply, the reason is invariably, or at least often, prejudice on account of their sex; when, for every woman who has failed to land an academic job because of sex discrimination, there are probably tens, at least, who believe they have. The most usual reason—do I really need to say this?—is that there are so many candidates, so few jobs.)

When it is known that a policy of preferential hiring is in force, this encourages the belief—even when it is false—that when a woman is appointed, it is because she is a woman, not because she is the best candidate. If a weak or mediocre woman is hired, her shortcomings will be only too salient to many who—resentful of preferential hiring and not really convinced, in their hearts, about women's capacities—easily manage to overlook the shortcomings of the many weak and mediocre men around. And all this, besides tending to undermine women's confidence in themselves, encourages precisely that disinclination to take women academics quite fully seriously which sometimes prevents a woman being appointed when she is the best applicant.

Now I see why that role model argument worries me. It is of course false that only a woman can be a role model for women, or that women can be role models only for women. (I say "of course," but I am disturbed by how often I *still* hear that more women faculty are needed because "they might be quite good for the women students"; and troubled by male faculty who apparently hope to slough off their responsibilities to women students by appointing a female colleague to take care of that kind of thing, and female faculty who don't seem to feel they have the same obligation to the men as to the women among their students.) More to the present point, though, is the disturbing possibility that by adopting a policy of preferential hiring we will give young women, and young men, the impression that women aren't really worthy of academic positions. Even when it is false that this woman would not have been appointed had she not been a woman; even when it is true, but she was the best candidate anyway—her usefulness as role model is, not necessarily undermined, but potentially tainted.

This begins to suggest why attitudes to women in the academy now seem less thoughtlessly dismissive than they once were, more uneasily ambivalent: an edgy combination of the overtly indulgent and the covertly hostile. Perhaps it also begins to suggest why, these days, you sometimes encounter a correspondingly edgy combination of diffidence and resentfully defensive hypersensitivity to slights (now there's an interesting word!) among women academics.

While I have been worrying about bad indirect effects of preferential hiring, I have been assuming that it would often enough have the desirable direct effect of getting the best person appointed despite her sex. This looks obvious once you grant that there may be a systematic undervaluation of women's abilities; but now it is time to confess that I have a nasty suspicion that, all the same, it isn't true.

Thinking of a systematic undervaluation of women's abilities by, say, 10 percent, we feel assured that, under a policy of preferring a woman if she is judged to fall within 10 percent of the best, the best candidate would get the job even if she's a woman. Suppose for now that we could get the degree of preference just right. Even then the conclusion follows only on a further assumption: that the best woman would get the job. As she *would*, if what ordinarily happens were that a straightforward effort is made to appoint the best person, skewed only by that annoying tendency to underestimate the merit of women candidates. But this is by no means always what happens (a thought that brings to mind the senior member of the department where I earned my Ph.D. who, after I was hired for that tenure-track job, was heard to say of my new chairman: "poor X, forced to appoint on grounds of merit . . .").

Sometimes women don't get positions that they should; sometimes men don't, either. The problem isn't only (though it is partly) that when there are hundreds of applications, impossible to read them all, "contacts," those off-the-record phone calls, etc., are bound to be significant. Nor is it only (though it is partly) that philosophical ability is so subtle, so many-faceted, and the criteria used often so narrow and so crude, overvaluing the confident and the fluent and undervaluing the less flashy but deeper thinker, overvaluing the "productive," as we say, and undervaluing the slower but more rigorous or creative mind. Worse, the hiring process is too often less a straightforward if ill-informed and clumsily conducted effort to identify the best candidate than an unseemly struggle of greed and fear.

Greed: we want someone who will improve the standing of the department, who has contacts from which we might benefit, who will willingly do the teaching we'd rather not do, who will publish enough so the tenure process will go smoothly. Fear: we don't want someone so brilliant or energetic that they make the rest of us look bad, or compete too successfully for raises and summer money, or who will vote with our enemy on controversial issues. We look, in short, for someone who "fits in." (The foam-rubber PR term is "collegiality.")

Hence the faction fights; a candidate who excites the greed of some is quite likely to excite the fear of others. Hence the dismaying tendency—even when the market favors the buyer as much as it does now—to appoint more of the same, whether "the same" happens to be the grayly mediocre or the flashily self-confident. (If the word hadn't been ruined by its promotion to slogan, I would be tempted to speak of "diversity" myself at this point.) No one wants to admit, even to themselves, that they are moved by greed and fear rather than merit; so we tell ourselves, though of course we don't entirely succeed in believing it, that fitting in *is* merit. Hence the hypocrisy, double-talk, self-deception, and sheer confusion. (Not long ago I heard a chairman indignant about allegations of racism protest: "my department, racist? That's ridiculous! Why, they FORCED me to appoint a woman last year . . .")

I don't mean to deny that the relative importance of this or that ability, including the relative weight attached to research and to teaching, may quite properly differ depending on the kind of institution doing the hiring; the best person for this job may not be the best for that. I suspect, though, that the idea that a really good philosopher can't be expected to be a good teacher as well (and its converse, which has sometimes worked against women) is overdone; and that the greed of which I spoke earlier sometimes makes modest departments, hoping for sudden promotion to the ranks of the prestigious, vulnerable to the cheap allure of the confident, quick, and shallow. ("Prestige" is another of those foam-rubber words; perhaps if we remembered its etymological connections with "prestidigitation," we wouldn't forget that a department with unrealistic hopes of landing someone who can speak thirteen languages and walk on water is likely to end up hiring a fraud.)

Nor do I mean to deny that there may sometimes be more than one equally good candidate for a job; quite a likely upshot, in fact, given how complex and many-faceted the relevant talents are. So what about a minimal policy of preferring the woman if two candidates are judged equal-best? Since the candidate appointed would always have been judged at least equal-best, this should have no tendency to encourage the idea of women's unworthiness; though it would still, doubtless, create resentment among unsuccessful candidates. But unfortunately there is the same reason as before to wonder whether it would get the, or even a, best candidate appointed; and in practice what I'd expect is the same old shabby politics ensuring that a tie is, or that it isn't, reached—as procedural-fairness policies are sometimes circumvented by decorating shortlists with the names of women who have no real chance of being hired.

Plenty of male candidates, including sometimes the best person for the job, fail the fitting-in test (too specialized, too broad; too quiet, too glib; didn't go to the right school, is bound to move off when a more prestigious job comes along; etc.). But since, still, the majority of the profession, and more of the more senior ranks, is male, female candidates are apt to fit in, by and large and on the whole, less well than male; for trivial reasons (perhaps they have a hard time hiding how little discussions of football—in my case it was cricket—thrill them), and not-so-trivial (plenty of men are, still, more comfortable with women as secretaries, wives, students, than as colleagues). Small wonder, then, that "forced to appoint a woman," sometimes departments hire, not the best woman applicant, but the least threatening: the conventional, the conformist, the student of one's own mentor, or, failing that, the specialist in feminist philosophy, who, though not "one of us," needn't, in private anyway, be taken quite seriously—and might earn us points with the dean.

I suspect that departments under pressure to appoint a woman sometimes advertise for a specialist in feminist philosophy as code for "we have appoint a woman this time or the dean won't give us the money." (Possibly because, while a notice on the front page of *Jobs for Philosophers* requires that "no qualification for [a] position that will be given weight in making the appointment be concealed from . . . applicants," the "Instructions to Department Chairpersons Listing Vacancies" on the back page warn that "while notices will be accepted stating that an employer has a special interest in receiving applications from women or minority groups, no notice will be accepted which suggests that others will not also be considered . . ."; presumably, not even if it is true.)[5] This is unfortunate, not least for young women who happen to be talented in logic, metaphysics, medieval philosophy, or whatever, and disinclined to jump on the "feminist philosophy" bandwagon.

When I speak of a bandwagon I refer, of course, not to work on those good, hard, philosophical questions raised by feminism which may be, and have been, tackled by philosophers of both sexes, but to "feminist philoso-phy" in the now more usual sense: an enterprise for which being of the appropriate sex, or, as the jargon goes, "gender," seems usually to be quietly assumed a qualification.

Well, *are* there special insights which women, qua women, can bring to philosophy? In my experience, the intellectual differences among individu-als are far, far more significant than any supposed commonalities among women. (I think of all the women students I have taught, every one differ-ent; and of the Israeli philosopher with whom I corresponded for years without knowing his or her—actually, as I very recently discovered from a reference in a journal, his—sex.) To be sure, women who have been taught at an impressionable age that there are women's ways of philoso-phizing do manifest a certain uniformity of thought; it would be surprising if they didn't, but it is of no relevance that they do.[6]

It is discouraging, to put it mildly, when the special insights claimed for women—or is it perhaps only for WOMEN, those who are of the right gender as well as the right sex?—are, as they sometimes are, reminiscent of those old, sexist stereotypes of women as emotional, intuitive, and all that. It is disturbing, to put it mildly, when it is suggested, as it sometimes is, that anyone who believes that there is such a thing as truth, and that it is possible to discover the truth by investigation, thereby reveals their complicity with sexism. It is dispiriting, to put it mildly, when the claim is, as it sometimes is, that women have this supposed insight into the allegedly ideological character of the concepts of truth, evidence, etc., because they are oppressed—which (unless, unlike myself, one is convinced by the epistemological pronouncements of Marx or Foucault or etc.). is apt to prompt, besides the worry that it will promote a tendency to dwell exces-sively on our grievances, the protest that it neglects to mention the most important qualities talented women have to offer philosophy: logical acu-men, textual sensitivity, creative imagination, analytic rigor, conceptual subtlety and penetration, etc., etc. As I should have answered the very dis-tinguished male philosopher who told me that his women graduate stu-dents *had* brought special insights: they had pointed out Aristotle's and other philosophers' unenlightened attitudes to women—enough already: serious women philosophers deserve better than this![7] But these individu-alistic, old-fashioned-feminist thoughts, unlike the special-insight idea, may not be so congenial to those who formerly managed to confine women to the old ghetto of the permanently-temporary lecturer, and when "forced to appoint a woman," wouldn't altogether mind if the woman they are forced to appoint confines herself to what Harriet Baber has shrewdly identified as the new pink-collar ghetto of academia;[8] nor does it offer any relief to the cognitive dissonance of those who would like to think they're hiring on merit, but are under pressure to treat sex as relevant; nor any comfort to those, of both sexes, who still harbor a lingering suspicion that maybe women *can't* do philosophy, as traditionally conceived; nor the same opportunities for—well, for opportunism.[9]

Of course, academic hiring isn't driven *wholly* by greed and fear; of course, the wish to identify the best candidate plays *some* part. So shouldn't preferential hiring of women, even if it didn't reliably result in hiring the best candidate, at least have some tendency to result in hiring better candidates? And isn't it, after all, better to appoint a better person than a worse, even if neither is the best? Better *is* better than worse, certainly. But I find myself unpersuaded that preferential hiring *has*, overall, improved quality. Why hasn't it? Well, what actually happens is rarely much like the 10 percent boost to compensate for underestimation of women's abilities that I earlier imagined, more often a matter of, every now and then, "we have to hire a woman this time." The pressures to hire women have been accommodated disproportionately by humanities departments and departments of Women's Studies, not uniformly across the disciplines. Because preferential hiring has encouraged efforts to show the relevance of sex, those who are willing or anxious to be professionally-women philosophers have benefited, by and large and on the whole, more than philosophers who happen also to be women. And I fear that, by grafting preferential hiring onto an already-corrupt system, we have gradually allowed ourselves to become more confused, more ambivalent, and less focused on quality of mind.

I don't doubt that preferential hiring of women in my profession has done good, that it has, in some cases, led to the appointment of women who would not otherwise have been hired, and who are such good philosophers, and such straightforward people, that they have advanced our discipline and helped to ease their students and colleagues out of any disinclination, conscious or otherwise, to see women as full participants in the life of the mind. But I fear it may have done more harm than good, failing reliably to get the best, or at least better, people appointed, feeding men's reluctance to take women seriously and women's diffidence about their own abilities, diverting energy into efforts to show the relevance of sex, and undermining our already enfeebled sense that it *matters* whether the best person gets the job. No wonder it makes me so uncomfortable; it pulls both against taking philosophy seriously, and against taking serious women philosophers seriously.

THE QUESTION ABOUT preferential hiring of women is the point at which a whole tangle of issues about women in the labor market, not all of which have anything specifically to do with academia, intersects with a whole tangle of issues about the gross oversupply of Ph.D.'s and dubious hiring practices in the academy, not all of which have anything specifically to do with women. It was never realistic to hope to fix this mess of problems by a crude readjustment at a single, late stage; and never realistic, either, not to anticipate that such a crude readjustment as preferential hiring would introduce new distortions, new resentments, new hostilities. "Late" is important. That someone might have been a fine philosopher had she not suffered this disadvantage or discouragement as a child is a waste and a shame; but though we can try to prevent it happening in the future, we can't fix it now by treating her as if she *is* a fine philosopher—though we could, to be sure, be less inhospitable to those, of either sex, who qualify themselves and seek entry-level jobs in middle age.

Qua woman in my profession, I can't have much direct effect on the many interacting factors outside the academy that have held women back. I and women like me can, however, have some *in*direct effect: students who learn from our example that women *can* be full participants in the work of the intellect will later be parents, schoolteachers, employers. And there are things we can do to bring the goal of a profession genuinely open to talent a bit closer: the best work of which we are capable, of course; treating all our students, regardless of eye color, etc., as individuals; grading anonymously, and explaining to our colleagues why that matters; advising younger women about the realities of the job market, salary negotiation, dealing with editors and publishers, the tenure process—it shouldn't *have* to be women who do that for other women, but someone's got to do it, and if our male colleagues are falling down on the job . . . ; working on those obstacles of geography and timetable which particularly affect women. And, the most essential and the most difficult thing: figuring out how to make the hiring process less disgracefully corrupt.

That will require hard thinking and tough decisions. We—now, of course, I mean "all of us, of either sex, who care about cleaning up the hiring process"—would have to be candid about the oversupply of Ph.D.'s and to acknowledge that faculty who delegate the most burdensome undergraduate teaching to T.A.'s and teach nice, small, graduate classes themselves have a powerful interest in the proliferation and expansion of graduate programs. We would have to be candid with graduate students and potential graduate students about what the employment prospects really are (and not, as I have seen happen in more than one department, celebrate those Ph.D.'s who succeed in finding jobs in philosophy while conveniently forgetting those who fail). We would have to be candid, also, about how relatively privileged tenured and tenure-track faculty benefit from the availability of that army of ill-compensated, overworked, and insecure lecturers. We would have to acknowledge that the geographical mobility required by an academic career creates a real problem for academic couples, and that it is not easy to avoid nepotism without unfairly penalizing, most often but not always, wives. (Which reminds me of the friend who, convinced that preferential hiring had led, in her department, to the appointment of more than one barely competent girlfriend, wanted me to make that line about "greed and fear," "greed, fear, *and lust*"!)

We should also think about ways to make more of the hiring process anonymous (perhaps we should place less weight on interviews, often primarily a means of identifying those who "fit in," and more on a person's work); and consider the option of drawing lots in the event of a tie. Anonymity blocks information without which prejudice can't get a purchase; chance blocks space within which prejudice might operate.

You know by now that my point isn't that talented women haven't faced particular difficulties in my profession, nor that procedural-fairness rules alone are sufficient to solve them; but that, relying on preferential hiring as a quick and simple fix, we have come to take far too easily for granted that all the real problems focus specifically around sex (and race, but I will get to that later), and that all the problems faced by women in academia are the result of sexist prejudice; and we have allowed our attention to be distracted from other issues that need it no less urgently.

How much easier and quicker to rely on preferential hiring as a way of getting more women into the academy!—which has, in fact, become the goal for many contemporary feminists. ("What we need now is more women deans," I sometimes hear. What we need now, as always, is more deans with good sense, good judgment, and the strength of character to use them—qualities which are rare enough, but not the exclusive prerogative of either sex. Better a man with them than a woman without them.) To rely on preferential hiring as a way of getting more women in, it seems to me, really is to redouble the effort while forgetting the aim; or rather, to turn an honorable concern about wasted talent into a new, feminist tribalism no more defensible than the familiar tribalism of the Old Boy Network it so disturbingly resembles.

In a moment of remarkable candor, after acknowledging, rather to one's surprise, that, yes, there can be such a creature as a male feminist, Sandra Harding reveals her tribalist colors by explaining that men who want to be "in feminism," "can teach and write about women's thought, writings, accomplishments.... They can criticize their male colleagues. They can move material resources to women and feminists." Don't let that last phrase fool you; Harding can only mean that men who want to be in feminism are to promote women's work, criticize other men, and move resources to women and to men who promote women's work, criticize men, and move resources to women and to men who, etc.... !

But, after all, shouldn't a feminist *want* to advance women? Not per se, no; that is to miss an essential point. The legitimate feminist concern is that something bad tends systematically to happen more to women than to men; but that presupposes that whatever-it-is, in this case waste of talent, is bad whoever it happens to. The specifically feminist concern is, and must be, secondary to the underlying more general concern.

Of course, it behooves me to be no less candid than Harding, and to say plainly that I care more about the genuinely talented man who fails to land the job because he doesn't fit in than about the mediocre woman who loses out to an equally mediocre man. Why? Every time we appoint a less talented person than we could have, the students lose out; the unsuccessful candidate loses out as well, and his talents may be lost to the profession altogether. Am I saying, I am sometimes asked, that what bothers me is the unfairness to the better but unsuccessful candidate? This seems to me too crude a way of looking at it. The talented young man I have been imagining may have benefited from sexism, and the mediocre young woman I have been imagining may have suffered from it (though we shouldn't forget that he may have suffered other disadvantages that she hasn't); but then he has almost certainly benefited far less from sexism in the academy than all those men who have long been safely tenured, and she has almost certainly suffered far less from sexism in the academy than all those women who have long been trapped in permanently-temporary lecturer slots.

The kind of serious improvement I want to see will be difficult, to put it mildly; though I think we tend to underestimate the potential for large cumulative effects of small improvements. Still, I certainly wish I thought it were easier. Nevertheless, only genuine meritocracy will achieve what I want to see—what I hoped twenty-five years ago I would live to see: the best people getting the jobs *regardless of their sex or any irrelevant etceteras.*

RACE IS ANOTHER of those irrelevant etceteras. Does it follow that the issues are parallel where race is concerned? Not necessarily; in fact, I think it is a good deal more complicated than that.

Indeed, I have already committed an oversimplification by asking how similar the case of race is to that of sex. The official phrase is "women and minorities," and as soon as you think about which the target minorities are, and how their members are identified, complication piles on absurdity dizzyingly fast. "Hispanic," though it identifies one of the target minorities, certainly doesn't pick out a race. It isn't clear to me, for that matter, even that there is a viable sense in which "black" picks out a race. (I wish, reading on this topic, I weren't sometimes disturbingly reminded of the old South African classification of the Japanese as white, the Chinese as colored, not to mention the Nazi preoccupation with identifying those with even a trace of "Jewish blood.")

And I have been too diffident, too acutely aware of how hard it is for an outsider fully to grasp what race means to Americans, yet to have said plainly that the situation of black Americans seems to me in many ways quite unlike the situation of other minorities, or of recent immigrants, or of white women; it is peculiar, distinctive, and—on average, of course, and with the possible exception of American Indians—worse. It is also distinctively American, in a way the situation of women is not.

So I shall confine myself here to asking whether there are relevant differences between the issues raised by preferential hiring of women in my profession and by preferential hiring of blacks. (No, I haven't forgotten that not all women are white, nor all blacks men; I am just getting overwhelmed, grammatically as well as intellectually, by how complicated it all is.)

At first it might seem that the differences, though considerable, aren't relevant. Certainly, the factors outside the academy that have held white women back, and the factors that have held black men back, are different in many very significant ways; the factors that have held black women back likely include both. But I have the impression that, within the academy, black philosophers are liable to encounter much the same disinclination to take them quite fully seriously that women philosophers sometimes do; if anything, more so.

If so, there would be the same reasons as before for thinking that procedural-fairness policies are insufficient to ensure that no covert disadvantage faces black candidates; and the same reasons as before for thinking that, if hiring were genuinely meritocratic except for a tendency to underestimate blacks', as well as women's, abilities, then preferential hiring of blacks, like preferential hiring of women, could be a backhanded way to get the best person appointed despite the color of his or her skin.

But unfortunately there would also be the same reasons as before for fearing that, even if it did get the best person appointed, its backhandedness would have the unhappy side effect of encouraging precisely the disinclination to take black philosophers fully seriously that may prevent a black person being hired when he or she is the best candidate for a job. And unfortunately there would be the same reasons as before to doubt that it reliably would get the best, or at least better, people appointed. There would be the same worry as before that the value of black philosophers as role models would be, not necessarily undermined, but potentially tainted by the knowledge that preferential hiring was going on; and the same worry as before about diverting energy into efforts to show the relevance of race.

Perhaps needless to say, I am no more convinced that there are special insights that blacks, qua blacks, can bring to philosophy than I am that there are insights that women, qua women, can bring; in my experience, the intellectual differences among individuals are far, far more important than any supposed commonalities among blacks. (I think of all the black students I have taught—every one different; and of the blind student of mine who took the same classes with an American exchange student for an entire year without knowing he was black.) To be sure, a competent specialist in African philosophy—no, almost certainly that should be "philosophies," in the plural—could be expected to bring insights culled from the philosophers he or she studies; but except on the assumption of a black way of philosophizing, it is hard to see why skin color should constitute either a qualification or a disqualification for such a specialty—a gift for languages seems more to the point.

But all this, however true so far as it goes, misses a crucial difference. Though doubtless the ratio falls short of their proportion in the population at large, there are substantial numbers of white women in the applicant pool for jobs in philosophy; but, so far as I am aware, there are few blacks. (I don't like relying on my possibly unreliable impressions, but I have been unable to find any less squishy evidence.) And if so, it is not clear that any hiring policies would have what I take to be the desired effect, namely, ensuring that talent is not lost merely because its possessor is black.

If blacks are seriously underrepresented in the applicant pool, preferential hiring is liable to produce further distortions besides those I worried about earlier: to create strong competition for the services of a few highly visible well-qualified black philosophers, perhaps to encourage the hiring of blacks from outside the United States, perhaps to result in the hiring of the underqualified, very probably to result in the hiring of white women when affirmative-action goals must be met but there are no suitable black candidates. But if blacks are seriously underrepresented in the applicant pool, then the strictly meritocratic hiring which (next after a healthier job market, of course) would do most to prevent loss of white women's talent couldn't realistically be expected to do much to prevent loss of black talent. More meritocratic hiring, after all, can help only the talented who make it to the applicant pool to begin with.

Now perhaps I begin to understand the anger some black philosophers seem to feel because after decades of supposedly preferential treatment there are still so few blacks in our profession. But the conclusion I am inclined to draw is not that, since preferential hiring has apparently had so little effect, racial prejudice in our profession must be especially severe and entrenched, but that we need to think again, in particular, about why there aren't more blacks in the applicant pool.

If the explanation were, simply, prejudice, overt or covert, in admissions to graduate programs, perhaps we could fix this by blinding graduate-school applications, blocking the information without which prejudice can't get a purchase. But I'm sure that prejudice in graduate admissions isn't all, and I'm not sure even that it is a very large part, of the explanation we are seeking.

Part of the explanation, surely, is that some intelligent young black people prefer, understandably enough, to pursue less chancy and better-remunerated career paths. Understandably, and perfectly reasonably; I for one feel ambivalent at best about efforts to encourage black students into graduate programs in philosophy. My ambivalence has nothing to do with race, however; in the current state of the job market—where, the last I heard, an open, tenure-track position may attract seven hundred or more applicants—I feel ambivalent about encouraging *anyone* to go to graduate school in philosophy. Not that I would discourage aspirants with real talent and real commitment; but I feel an obligation to do my best to give them a realistic picture of the prospects.

BUT NOW I SEE THAT ALL THIS, however true so far as it goes, still looks at things the wrong way; the light is at the other end of the tunnel! The underrepresentation of blacks in the applicant pool in philosophy, or in philosophy graduate programs, or for that matter among Ph.D.'s generally, is only a tiny part of a much larger picture of educational disadvantages, and of other, and interacting, disadvantages too. As far as I can tell, many young black people get sadly inferior educational opportunities from the beginning. Actually, as far as I can tell, nearly all young people get pretty poor primary and high school education; but by any measure, I believe, proportionately more black children are more seriously shortchanged.

This seems to me to call, first and foremost, for the most serious and urgent effort to improve schools, especially the worst of them. That doesn't mean throwing more money at a corrupt educational establishment; it means really trying honestly to figure out what works, whether in the schools or elsewhere, and actually doing it. To do what is really needed will require money, certainly (though it is hard to think of a better investment); but above all it will require intelligence, honesty, adaptability, willingness to acknowledge that not everything tried will succeed.

Preferences in college and university admissions and financial aid are no substitute for decent schools. It is far better to nourish talent from the beginning than to compensate later for not having done so earlier; it is far better that all children get decent schooling than that many don't but some get help later. Nevertheless, until that far better state is achieved, there seems to me a strong case for making second-chance opportunities later for those who get shortchanged earlier. College and university admissions and financial aid would be one, though by no means the only, place for making such opportunities. Since disproportionately many of the educationally shortchanged are black, many of those to whom it would be desirable to make such opportunities available would be black (it is a sign of how different the cases are that white women, as a class, are not comparably in need of educational second chances).

But to do it right, universities and colleges would have to invest intelligence and effort in identifying applicants who have native academic ability which has not been realized, and, when they are admitted, in really helping them to realize their potential. Universities and colleges would have to be—it's about time these words did some real work for a change!—genuinely discriminating, genuinely affirmative. My argument absolutely precludes the admission of students who have no chance of succeeding, perfunctory or dishonest remedial efforts, grade inflation or second-rate classes disguising failure as success, or focusing on—ugh, foam rubber again!—students' self-esteem instead of their education. To aim directly at fostering self-esteem is self-defeating; justifiable pride and self-confidence come from mastering something difficult, from overcoming previous limitations. My argument absolutely requires the most serious efforts to identify those with real academic potential despite disadvantage, the most serious efforts to help such students overcome earlier educational deficiencies, and the firmest commitment to holding them to high standards. Yes, that is hard, demanding, difficult, expensive in time, effort, imagination, integrity; but anything less cruelly shortchanges those young people yet again.

My impression is that, as things stand, too many *are* cheated yet again: that too many of those with real potential, instead of being helped to realize it, are either left to sink or swim more or less unaided, or else fobbed off with undemanding classes and/or inflated grades; that too many are admitted who don't have the potential to succeed in college (but who might, to make matters worse, have benefited had different kinds of second-chance opportunity been available to them). It is hardly surprising if many of the cheated-yet-again feel bitter resentment; they are amply justified.

Nor is it surprising, especially given that a college education is not only (sometimes, anyway) a good in itself, but also a positional good, i.e., it has value because not everyone has it, if, as things stand, many of those who believe they have been denied admission or financial aid in favor of others less qualified than themselves also feel bitter resentment. But the closer we could come to a situation where all those given special opportunities had real academic potential, and realized it, the less justified, and, one might reasonably hope, the less severe, such resentment would be.

EVEN WITHOUT thinking hard about other disciplines than philosophy, without asking about the role of black colleges and universities, without leaving the ivory tower for the real world,[10] without asking whether there are occupations where race or sex is a bona fide qualification, without considering those many occupations where there are likely to be large numbers of to-all-intents-and-purposes interchangeable applicants, without considering occupations where there is a shortage instead of an oversupply of qualified applicants, without raising questions about the scope and limits of public policy—the dangers of This-or-Nothingism are manifest.

But This-or-Nothingism is so entrenched that when I express reservations about preferential hiring in my profession, I am sometimes misconstrued as saying that there's no problem, the old system was fine. I didn't say that; and it *wasn't* fine. Unfortunately, the present system isn't fine either.

Even within the narrow sphere of my discussion, it is clear how unrealistic it is to imagine, as opponents of affirmative action sometimes seem to do, that laws against discrimination and rules ensuring procedural fairness are sufficient to guarantee that merit will rule in admissions and appointments and all problems will be solved; and it is hard to suppress the suspicion that some of those who have persuaded themselves otherwise may be motivated by the fear of losing the advantages that the old, corrupt system afforded them. But it is no less clear how unrealistic it is to imagine, as supporters of affirmative action sometimes seem to do, that all the problems can be solved by preferences based on sex or minority status; and it is hard to suppress the suspicion that some of those who have persuaded themselves otherwise may be motivated by the fear of losing the advantages that the new, corrupt system affords them. There are real, deep, and difficult problems; but what they need is not crude, quick, one-size-fits-all "solutions" with attendant distortions, resentments, and hostilities that can do more harm than good, but hard and discriminating thinking and genuine effort to achieve a less corrupt, and less wasteful, system.

Looking back, seeing how often I have said, in effect, "what we need is *real* change, *serious* improvement, not a crude readjustment," I begin to understand why the language in which the debate is conducted has become so debased and rubbery: This-or-Nothingism again. Words are fudged, stretched, distorted, stripped of essential content, or grow scare quotes as part of their normal spelling, as one party tries to mask the reality of the problems, and the other to mask the inadequacy of the only solution on the table. I have already complained to the point of tedium about the ruination of "diversity." Now I think of other words that have come to grief: "discrimination," for example, which has lost touch with its older, ameliorative sense and become almost irremediably pejorative; when not hiring the best candidate because you don't appreciate their abilities on account of their sex or their race is surely better described as a lack of discrimination in the good old sense than as discrimination in the bad new sense. The fate of the word "merit" is especially revealing: aware, or half-aware, that when opponents of affirmative action insist that admissions and appointments should be "merit-based," they disguise the possibility that judgments of merit may be prejudiced, some proponents of affirmative action now protest "the myth of merit," or refuse to use the word at all without the precaution of scare quotes.

I have come to think of the sad fate of the word "merit," abused by both sides, as a symbol of our present pass: of how well-intentioned but ill-conceived efforts to make colleges and universities better have weakened our sense that it matters much whether the most dedicated and imaginative teacher, the clearest and most creative thinker, gets hired; of how well-intentioned but ill-conceived efforts to make a person's race or sex matter less to our judgment of the quality of his or her mind have made us more acutely, more ambivalently, more anxiously aware of them; of how well-intentioned but ill-conceived efforts to welcome women and blacks as full participants in the life of the intellect have encouraged the bizarre—no, the tragic—idea that truth, evidence, reason, are tools of their oppression; of how well-intentioned but ill-conceived efforts to enrich universities and colleges with previously underused talent have encouraged the bizarre—no, the tragic—idea that "merit" is a myth, the quirks of the individual mind unimportant.

We need to do better than this. And than nothing.

NOTES

1. Thomas Reid, *Essays on the Intellectual Powers* (1785) II, 4, xvi.

2. "On the Moral Relevance of Sex," *Philosophy*, 49.187, 1974, 90–95. (I wouldn't write this article the same way today, but I still think the main point is right.)

3. I wish I'd thought of this; but I borrowed it from David Lodge, *Changing Places: A Tale of Two Campuses* (1975), Penguin Books, Harmondsworth, Middlesex, 1978.

4. I wish I'd thought of this, too; but I owe the phrase to Jacques Barzun, *A Stroll with William James* (1983), University of Chicago Press, Chicago, 1984, p. 223.

5. I suspect that it is quite common to shortlist candidates, female or male, who have no real chance of getting the job. A well-known specialist in practical ethics told me that, in the course of a recent search, his department had done exactly that. Clearly sincere in his belief that, since their goal was to hire a woman, they had done a Good Thing, he seemed not at all concerned about the waste of the other (in this case, the male) candidates' time, energy, and money.

6. Contemporary "feminist philosophy" manifests both a dreary uniformity and a confusing diversity: on the one hand, it is endlessly repeated that the feminist perspective will revolutionize this or that area of philosophy; on the other, a bewildering variety of epistemological, ethical, metaphysical, etc., ideas are proposed as "feminist." "Knowledge and Propaganda: Reflections of an Old Feminist," essay 7 in this volume, is pertinent to the issues raised in this and the following paragraph.

7. The same answer I should have given to the suggestion that we need women faculty so someone will be supportive of women students who get pregnant. (I was too busy thinking it was about time male faculty learned to be supportive of such students—and worrying whether being a parent, or divorced, or having had a nervous breakdown or a drug problem, etc., should be considered qualifications too.)

8. Harriet Baber, "The Market for Feminist Epistemology," *The Monist*, 77.4, 1994, 403–23.

9. See also "Preposterism and Its Consequences," essay 11 in this volume.

10. And without asking what universities might do to improve the pay and benefits of secretaries, janitorial staff, etc.—questions surprisingly rarely heard in discussions of sexism and racism in the academy.

Preposterism and Its Consequences

That is preposterous which puts the last first and the first last.... Valuing knowledge, we pre-posterize the idea and say ... everybody shall produce written research in order to live, and it shall be decreed a knowledge explosion. JACQUES BARZUN[1]

What I have to offer here are some thoughts about the "research ethic," and the ethics of research, in philosophy. There won't be any exciting stuff about the political wisdom or otherwise of research into racial differences in intelligence, or the ethics of scientists' treatment of laboratory animals, or moral issues concerning genetic engineering or nuclear technology, or anything of that kind. There will be only, besides some rather dry analysis of what constitutes genuine inquiry and how the real thing can come to be corrupted, some rather uncomfortable reflections about the present condition of philosophy, its causes and its consequences.

You are probably beginning to suspect already that I don't think philosophy is at present in a particularly desirable condition. You are correct; at any rate, when I read Peirce's wry complaints about philosophers "whom any discovery that brought quietus to a vexed question would evidently vex because it would end the fun of arguing around it and about it and over it," and his descriptions of metaphysics as "a puny, rickety and scrofulous science," and of philosophy as in "a lamentably crude condition,"[2] I don't feel moved to protest—yes, but that was then, whereas now . . .

My quotations from Peirce were not chosen only for vividness, nor are they incidental to what I shall have to say, which has much in common, epistemologically, with Peirce's diagnosis of the lamentable condition of philosophy in his day: as due in large part to the lack of the real love of truth, the "scientific attitude," as he sometimes called it, the "craving to know how things really [are]," the "Will to Learn."[3]

The chief reason why philosophy was *not* being undertaken with the scientific attitude, according to Peirce, was that it was largely in the hands of theologians, who were motivated less by a real love of truth than by the desire to devise a philosophical system to support theological principles their commitment to which was fixed and determined in advance of inquiry. Or rather, in advance of "inquiry"; for, according to Peirce, such people are not really engaged in genuine inquiry, but in sham reasoning.[4]

Peirce's observations about the importance of the motive with which intellectual work is undertaken are no less pertinent now than they were when he wrote them. But philosophy is no longer largely in the hands of theologians, so his account of the cause of the prevalence of sham reasoning in the philosophy of his time hasn't the same relevance. At least a significant part of the explanation of the present lamentable condition of philosophy is, rather, the "preposterism" of which Barzun complains, which has been an influence quite as "deplorably corrupt"[5] as Peirce thought the domination of philosophy by theologians had been.

I take it that philosophy is a kind of inquiry, i.e., that there are genuine philosophical questions to which there are true and false answers. I don't mean to deny that not a few of the questions with which philosophers have concerned themselves have turned out to be, and others may yet turn out to be, misconceived, e.g., to rest on false presuppositions; but I do mean to affirm that this is not in the nature of philosophical questions as such. (If this were false, if philosophy were not a kind of inquiry, then most of the questions I shall be discussing would themselves be misconceived.)

Let me begin, though, before turning my attention to philosophical inquiry specifically, with some reflections about inquiry generally.

INQUIRY AIMS at the truth. This is a tautology (*Webster's:* "**inquiry:** search for truth, information, or knowledge; research, investigation"). If you aren't trying to find out the truth about whatever-it-is, you aren't really inquiring. Genuine inquiry seeks the truth with respect to some question or topic; pseudo-inquiry seeks to make a case for the truth of some proposition or propositions determined in advance.

There two kinds of pseudo-inquirer. The sham reasoner is not primarily concerned to find out how things really are, but to make a case for some immovably held preconceived belief. The fake reasoner is not primarily concerned to find out how things really are, but to advance himself by making a case for some proposition to the truth-value of which he is indifferent.

Though the term "fake reasoning" is mine, Peirce's remarks about the corrupting effect of "vanity"[6] indicate that he was aware of the dangers of fake reasoning as well as of the sham—as does this biting comment on a contemporary of his: "real power ... is not *born* in a man; it has to be worked out; and the first condition is that the man's soul should be filled with the desire to make out the truth . . . ; but — is full of himself, and it stands immovably in the way of a thorough devotion to truth. He ought not to try to combine two aims so disparate and incompatible."[7]

Sham or fake inquiry is not genuine inquiry, true—tautologically so; but why do I refer to the "dangers" of sham and fake reasoning? Writing of "this first, and in one sense this sole, rule of reason, that in order to learn you must desire to learn,"[8] Peirce seems to suggest that the disinterested truth-seeking attitude is both necessary and sufficient for the discovery of truth. It is neither. All the same, Peirce exaggerates something true and important: that, in the long run and on the whole, disinterested truth-seeking tends to advance inquiry, sham and fake inquiry to impede it.

The sham inquirer tries to make a case for the truth of a proposition his commitment to which is evidence- and argument-proof. The fake inquirer tries to make a case for the truth of some proposition advancing which he believes will benefit himself, but to the truth-value of which he is indifferent. Both the fake and the sham reasoner, but especially the sham, are motivated to avoid looking too closely at any evidence which might go the wrong way, to play down its importance or minimize its relevance, to try to explain it away. Both, but especially the fake, are motivated to obfuscate, to indulge in that "affected obscurity" which Locke, whose phrase I just borrowed, rightly saw as a chief occupational hazard of philosophy.

Because a genuine inquirer wants to get to the truth of the matter that concerns him, he is motivated to seek out and assess the worth of evidence and arguments thoroughly—his work will manifest what Peirce once described, reflecting on his own intellectual strengths, as "peirceistence" and "peirceverance."[9] This doesn't just mean that he will be hardworking; it is a matter, rather, of willingness to rethink, to reappraise, to spend as long as it takes on the picky detail that just might be fatal, to give as much thought to the final 1 percent as to the rest. (I'm tempted to rephrase Edison: "genius is 1 percent inspiration and 99 percent peircepiration.") The genuine inquirer will be ready to acknowledge, to himself as well as to other people, where things aren't altogether clear, or the evidence quite unambiguous. He will be willing to go with the evidence even to unpopular conclusions. And, far from having a motive to obfuscate, he will try to see, and explain, things as clearly as he can.

Sham and fake reasoners may hit upon the truth, and, when they do, may come up with good evidence and arguments. After all, the commitment to a cause characteristic of the sham reasoner, and the desire for reputation characteristic of the fake reasoner, are powerful motives for hard work. But sham and fake reasoners are apt to waste their intelligence and ingenuity in suppressing unfavorable evidence or awkward arguments, or in devising impressively obscure formulations. Genuine inquirers may come to false conclusions or be led astray by misleading evidence or arguments. But an honest inquirer won't suppress unfavorable evidence or awkward arguments, nor try to hide behind affected obscurity when things go badly; so, even when he fails, he won't make others' work more difficult.

Of course, real human beings do not conform neatly to my three types; their motives are generally pretty mixed, and they are capable of every degree and kind of self-deception. The love of truth is, as A. E. Housman wrote, "the faintest passion,"[10] the bona fide Will to Learn both rare and fragile.

That is why it matters that the environment in which it is conducted may be more or less hospitable to good intellectual work. A good environment will encourage genuine inquiry and discourage the sham and the fake; and the worst damage of sham and fake inquiry will be mitigated, and the contributions to knowledge that sham and fake reasoners sometimes make despite their dubious motivation will get sifted from the dross, if the environment enables mutual scrutiny among workers in a field. Honest scrutiny is best; but scrutiny even by other sham or fake reasoners with different axes to grind may be effective as a way of exposing error, confusion, and obfuscation. A bad environment will encourage sham and fake inquiry, and/or impede mutual scrutiny.

The environment is hospitable to good intellectual work to the extent that incentives and rewards favor those who work on significant issues, and whose work is creative, careful, honest, and thorough; to the extent that journals, conferences, etc., make the best and most significant work in a field readily available to others working in the area; to the extent that channels of mutual scrutiny and criticism are open and successful building on others' work is encouraged. The environment is inhospitable to good intellectual work to the extent that incentives and rewards encourage people to choose trivial issues where results are more easily obtained, to disguise rather than tackle problems with their chosen approach, to go for the flashy, the fashionable, and the impressively obscure over the deep, the difficult, and the painfully clear; insofar as the effective availability of the best and most significant work is hindered rather than enabled by journals and conferences bloated with the trivial, the faddy, and the carelessly or deliberately unclear; insofar as mutual scrutiny is impeded by fad, fashion, obfuscation, and fear of offending the influential. Looking at that last clause, I recall that, centuries ago, Roger Bacon had characterized the main obstacles to honest inquiry:

> There are four chief obstacles to grasping truth, which hinder every man, however learned, and scarcely allow anyone to win a clear title to knowledge: namely, submission to faulty and unworthy authority, influence of custom, popular prejudice, and concealment of our own ignorance accompanied by ostentatious display of our knowledge.[11]

And looking again at my list, I don't see how the conclusion can be avoided that the environment in which academic work is presently conducted is an inhospitable one. I think this is true for all disciplines; but I shall focus, henceforth, primarily on philosophy.

"EVERYBODY SHALL PRODUCE written research in order to live"; Barzun exaggerates, but not much. Everybody aspiring to the tenure track, tenure, promotion, a raise, a better job, or, of course, academic stardom—increasingly, even everybody aspiring to a visiting position as a step on the way to the tenure track—had better produce written, published, research. "And it shall be decreed a knowledge explosion"; again, Barzun exaggerates, but, again, not much. It *is* pretty much taken for granted that this explosion of publications represents a significant contribution to knowledge.

Yet a good deal of what is published is, at best, trivial stuff, putting me in mind of that fine saying, "Rubbish is rubbish, but the history of rubbish is scholarship."[12] Seriously, though: few if any of us will have a truly original idea every few years, let alone every few months; genuinely important philosophical work usually takes years of frustration and failure, and a great philosopher may not produce his best work until middle age or later. Nevertheless, we not only half-pretend that this written research that everybody must produce in order to live is, nearly all of it, worthwhile; we breathe an atmosphere of puffery, of announcements in paper after paper, book after book, that all previous work in the area is hopelessly misconceived, and here is a radically new approach which will revolutionize the whole field. How did this atmosphere of preposterous exaggeration come about? Let me try to disentangle one strand of the explanation.

It is no longer possible to do important scientific work with a candle and a piece of string; ever more complex and sophisticated equipment is needed to make ever more complex and sophisticated observations. Research in the sciences has become very expensive; a culture of grants-and-research-projects has grown up; and science has become, inter alia, big business. The consequences for the sciences are not altogether healthy: think of the time spent "writing grants," not to mention attending seminars on grant writing, of the temptation to shade the truth about the success or importance of one's project, of the cost to the progress of science when a condition of this body's supporting the research is that the results be withheld from the rest of the scientific community, etc.[13] (Though "science is, upon the whole, at present in a very healthy condition," Peirce wrote in 1901, "it would not remain so if the motives of scientific men were lowered." And the worst threat, he continued, was that there were too many "whose chief interest in science is as means of gaining money.")[14]

When disciplines like philosophy, where serious work requires, not fancy equipment, but only (only!) time and peace of mind, mimic the organization of the sciences, when the whole apparatus of grants-and-research-projects becomes so ordinary that we scarcely notice how extraordinary it is, when we adapt to a business ethos, the consequences are still worse.

Why worse? In part because in philosophy the circumpressure of facts, of evidence, is less direct; in part because the kind of routine, competent, unexciting work that gets all the scientific details filled in has no real analogue in philosophy; in part because in philosophy the mechanisms of mutual scrutiny are perhaps more clogged and probably more corrupted.

How did this adaptation of philosophy to forms and organizational structures more appropriate to the sciences come about? In part because it is so intellectually impressive, in part because it is so useful, and in part, no doubt, because it is so expensive, science enjoys enormous prestige; prestige in which the rest of us would dearly like to share. Inevitably perhaps, in consequence of universities' having become such big businesses, many university administrators have become enamored of a business-management ethos which values "entrepreneurial skills," i.e., the ability to obtain large sums of money to undertake large research projects, above originality or depth, and which encourages conceptions of "efficiency" and "productivity" more appropriate to a manufacturing plant than to the pursuit of truth.

Headlines in the official Newsletter of the University of Warwick, I recall, announced "Major Research Success for Physics at Warwick"; the text told us, not of some breakthrough achieved by our physicists, but of their landing major research funding. The University of Miami's application form for stipends for summer research opens with a statement that preference will be given to "proposals that appear to best attract subsequent external funding," and on the next page advises that senior faculty "should emphasize career enhancement aspects of their project." I don't suppose either is atypical.

In disciplines like philosophy, feeling ourselves the poor relations in such a culture, we have adapted as best we could. At the extreme, this adaptation has encouraged such absurdities as the request for a letter of reference I not long ago received from a British university: though the job was described as a lectureship, it was made very clear that teaching ability wasn't important, that the main qualification for the position was that the person appointed should publish, during the three years of his or her appointment, a sufficient number of papers in sufficiently prestigious journals to raise the department's standing in the government's "research rankings"—so would I please be sure to say what papers my former student would publish in which journals over that period.

Though the brazenness of this request was unusual, the attitude it so brazenly revealed is not. Reporting on the state of the university, the president of the University of Miami mentions budget balancing, student numbers, faculty recruitment—and adds that our library's ranking in the Association for Research Libraries has gone up for "volumes added," for "serial subscriptions," for "materials expenditures," and that "our faculty is publishing at an unprecedented rate." No mention is made, in his twelve-page letter, of what anyone *found out*. I don't suppose this is atypical either.

Our adaptation to this culture has also encouraged a kind of philosophical entrepreneurship, which often diverts time and effort from real work, and is sometimes, to speak plainly, nothing more than philosophical hucksterism: centers for this and that, new journals for the legitimation and promotion of the latest fad, projects requiring secretaries, research assistants, or, better yet, more expensive and powerful computers or, best of all, a laboratory. At the extreme, this mimicking of forms more appropriate to the sciences has encouraged such absurdities as the blurb put out by the journal *Social Epistemology*, informing potential contributors that jointly written papers are as a matter of principle preferred over papers by only one author.[15] The model is the jointly authored scientific paper; and yet, how hard it is to think of any really major work of philosophy written jointly.[16]

Our adaptation to the culture of grants-and-research-projects has been a poor one, which has tended to lower the motive with which philosophical work is done; it has fostered an environment hospitable to sham and fake inquiry, inhospitable to the fragile intellectual integrity demanded by the genuine desire to find out. It is part of the meaning of the word "research" that *you don't know how things will turn out.* The culture of grants-and-research-projects, and the conception of productivity and efficiency that culture fosters, discourage candid acknowledgement that you may work for years at what turns out to be a dead end, and constitute standing encouragement to exaggeration, half-truth, and outright dishonesty about what you have achieved. In principle, you might fill out the application explaining what important breakthroughs your work is going to achieve, and fill out the report, later, explaining what important breakthroughs your work actually did achieve, without your private estimation of the worth of your work being affected. In practice, this is seldom exactly what happens; inevitably, intellectual honesty is eroded.

It has been a poor adaptation which significantly affects what kinds of work get done. True efficiency would have effort going into those questions most susceptible of solution at a given stage of inquiry; the present environment tends to channel effort into those questions most susceptible of attracting funding. In a philosophy department of which I was once a member, the argument was heard—and heeded—that we should "go into" postmodernism and literary theory, "because we can get Euro-money to do that." (I don't know whether any Euro-dollars were in fact forthcoming.) This attitude of "that's where the money is" is surely part of the explanation of the popularity of interdisciplinary work, especially work which allies philosophy with more prestigious disciplines such as cognitive psychology or artificial intelligence or medicine, etc.

Our adaptation to the culture of grants-and-research-projects can also significantly affect what kinds of conclusion are reached. Where effort is directed by the hope of large grants into, say, the border territory of epistemology with cognitive science, the probability rises significantly that the conclusion that will be reached is to the effect that long-standing epistemological questions can be quickly resolved or quickly dissolved by appeal to work in cognitive science. Where effort is directed by the hope of large grants into, say, the relevance of feminism to philosophy of science, the probability rises significantly that the conclusion that will be reached is to the effect that feminism requires us, as Sandra Harding preposterously puts it, to "reinvent science and theorizing."[17] (Challenged, nearly a decade later, by skeptics wanting to know what breakthroughs feminist science had achieved, Harding replied that, thanks to feminist scientists, we now know that menstruation, pregnancy, and menopause aren't diseases.[18] Gosh.) No one is so naive as to imagine that large grants might be forthcoming to show that cognitive science *has no* bearing on those long-standing epistemological questions, or even that its bearing is (as I believe) though real enough, oblique and undramatic;[19] or to show that (as I believe) feminism *has no* relevance to the theory of scientific knowledge.[20]

The psychological mechanisms involved are quite subtle. Simple dishonesty is the exception; some degree of *self*-deception is the rule. Conor Cruise O'Brien gets the psychological tone about right:

> Young scholars . . . are likely to believe that if they write with excessive candor about certain realities . . . doors will close to them; certain grants will be out of reach, participation in certain organized research programs denied, influential people alienated, the view propagated that the young man is unbalanced or unsound. These fears may be exaggerated . . . but they are not without foundation . . . Inevitably some . . . will adapt . . . with such concessions as they believe are necessary. And the scholars who adapt successfully are likely to be highly influential in their fields in the next generation.[21]

The adaptation of which O'Brien writes is likely, naturally, to leave a residue of ambivalence, such as one can hear in this plea for the psychologization of epistemology: "a return [to a psychologistic conception of epistemology] is especially timely now, when cognitive psychology has renewed prestige and promises to improve our understanding of cognitive processing."[22] The relevance or otherwise of psychology to epistemology is a hard meta-epistemological question: on which, needless to say, the prestige of cognitive psychology has no bearing.

Increasingly, supposedly academic decisions have turned into intensely politicized competition for resources; questions of curricular requirements, for example, are only too obviously really small skirmishes in larger turf wars.[23] Still, all the puffery, the attempts to promote oneself or one's area, approach, or line, all this academic boosterism, might be *only* a waste of time if, eventually, it came out in the wash of mutual scrutiny and criticism. But instead of efficient mechanisms of communication and mutual scrutiny, what we have is a mind-numbing clamor of publications, conferences, meetings, of "empty books and embarrassing assumptions,"[24] a clamor which makes it close to impossible to hear what is worthwhile.

The waste of time, talent, energy is significant; what real work might have been done by those who feel obliged, instead, to devote themselves to pointing out the absurdities of the latest fad? Neither is the fact—almost, but not quite, too indecent to mention—that some who can make a better career of criticizing these absurdities than they could of constructive work have an interest, consciously recognized or not, in the survival of what they criticize.

Occasionally someone is a bit candid about the situation. The director of Rutgers University Press writes that "we are . . . part of the university personnel system and . . . often publish books whose primary reason for existence is the author's academic advancement, not the advancement of knowledge."[25] The editor of the *American Philosophical Quarterly*, Gary Gutting, writes that publishing in the journals has become less a way to communicate significant ideas than a form of professional certification, and that being adequately informed in your field no longer requires that you actually *read* all that stuff.[26] Even more startling than the candor of his observations about the real role of the journals is the blandness of his assumption that publication-as-professional-certification is perfectly OK. But it *isn't* perfectly OK; it gets in the way of—what is more than ever urgently necessary in a culture that encourages sham and fake reasoning— the mutual scrutiny that might mitigate the worst damage and separate the worthwhile from the dross.

Between 1900 and 1960, about forty-five new philosophy journals were founded in the United States, Canada, and Britain, fifteen of them in the decade between 1950 and 1960; between 1960 and 1970, about forty-four, i.e., almost as many in a decade as in the previous sixty years; between 1970 and 1980, about sixty-five; between 1980 and 1990, about fifty-five.[27] Inevitably, it has become impossible, except by sheer luck, to find the good stuff; inevitably, championship of a simple, startling idea, even, or perhaps especially, an egregiously false or an impressively obscure idea, has become a good route to reputation and money—and the self-serving variation on a fashionable party line a safe route to tenure, promotion, raises. Inevitably, too, the task of finding referees with the necessary expertise, time, patience, and integrity has become harder, the power of editors to make or ruin careers has grown, and once-idealistic young philosophers begin to say to themselves, "they're bound to ask for revisions anyway, so there's no point polishing it first," or "they like controversy in their journal, so why bother spelling out all the qualifications?" etc.

And, of course, inevitably, as it becomes harder to make yourself heard in the journals, you have to publish a book; and, as that book-published-by-a-reputable-academic-press becomes a requisite for tenure, we face ever more bloated publishers' catalogs filled with ever more exaggerated descriptions and endorsements. And, inevitably, once again, it becomes impossible, except by sheer luck, to find the good stuff, and . . . But I won't bore you by writing the previous paragraph all over again!

It is not unheard of to find that a book of which a review has just appeared, having sold the few hundred copies which, these days, philosophy books typically sell,[28] is already, just a couple of years after publication, out of print. Better, then, from the point of view of sheer self-preservation, let alone of impressing deans, etc., with your "scholarly productivity," not to spend too long writing a book. How absurd, after all, to spend ten years writing a book which, if you are lucky, five hundred people might read, and the life of which, if you are lucky, might be four or five years.

It used to be an important role of the academic presses to publish significant books too specialized to be economic. Increasingly, however, as subsidies from their universities have shrunk, university presses are under pressure to publish books they believe will make money.[29] One effect seems to have been that referees' reports, though important for supplying those blurbs and for convincing the dean of the legitimacy of your publication record, no longer determine academic publishing decisions. This too is discouraging, to put it mildly, to the investment of effort in difficult problems. Better, from the point of view of making yourself heard, to write the kind of book that might interest a trade publisher, or at least the kind of book that will get reviewed in the nonacademic press. And this too, inevitably, favors the simple, startling idea, even, or perhaps especially, the startlingly false or impressively obscure idea . . . But I promised not to bore you by writing that paragraph all over again!

Like books and journals, conferences might be, and occasionally are, important channels of communication. But we are all familiar with the reality that your home institution will pay your expenses *if* you give a paper; with the conference announcements which discreetly let it be known that, so long as you pay the large registration fee, your paper will be accepted; with the stupefying programs of day after day of umpteen parallel sessions; with the twenty-minute, the twelve-minute, even, of late, the ten-minute presentation; with the extent to which conferences have become less a matter of communication than of "contacts," of "exposure," and, of course, of expenses-paid trips to agreeable places.

Here is William James declining an invitation to join the then newly formed American Philosophical Association: "I don't foresee much good from a philosophical society. Philosophy discussion proper only succeeds between intimates who have learned how to converse by months of weary trial and failure. The philosopher is a lone beast dwelling in his individual burrow. Count me *out!*"[30] He has, with his usual shrewdness, got something important exactly right. Philosophy is a lonely business. You may make progress as a result of that hard-earned, real discussion James describes, which, however, may be more profitably engaged with some philosopher long dead than with a contemporary. But we surely overrate the usefulness of what we like to call "stimulation," and underrate the need for time, peace of mind, mature reflection.[31]

A young philosopher of my acquaintance tells me that his friends on tenure track, accepting that for now they must concentrate on producing enough publishable stuff to get by, sometimes dream of a future in which they will be able to do some real work. But some of the tenured seem unable to *stop* producing that barely-publishable stuff; and plenty of others, at least once they've made it to full professor, seem unable to do much of anything at all. And then, because pondering over a new topic takes time, and will probably produce nothing publishable for a while, there is that excessively narrow specialization (not excluding narrow specialization in fashionable interdisciplinary niches) that preposterism encourages—again stunting real intellectual growth.

Now I am put in mind of Santayana's character sketch of Royce: an "overworked, standardised, academic engine, creaking and thumping on at the call of duty or of habit, with no thought of sparing itself or anyone else."[32] Preposterism can only too easily turn the best of us into just such overworked, standardized, academic engines—and can only too easily turn the worst of us into purveyors of philosophical snake oil.

THUS FAR it may seem that the perils of preposterism are much the same for philosophy as for other humanities disciplines. This is not quite so. For philosophy is the discipline to which it falls to inquire into inquiry itself, its proper conduct and its necessary presuppositions; and that responsibility exposes us to a particular peril. Recent philosophy manifests two tendencies which, though on the face of it radically opposed to each other, are both encouraged by our adaptation to a "research ethic" more appropriate to the sciences than to the humanities: scientism, i.e., linking philosophy too closely, or inappropriately, to the sciences; and radical critique of the sciences as no more than ideology masked by rhetorical bullying in the form of appeals to "rationality," "objectivity," and so forth. The former might be described as the effect of envy, the latter as the effect of resentment, of the success of the sciences.

Given my characterization, it is trivially true that scientism is mistaken, but a substantial question what views qualify as scientistic, as linking philosophy to science *too* closely, or in the *wrong* way. Unlike some, I see philosophy as a kind of inquiry, of truth seeking, and so in that sense like the sciences; and I see it also as aspiring, as the sciences do, to as much precision and rigor as possible.[33] But I don't believe that philosophical questions should be abandoned in favor of questions that the sciences can resolve; or that it is realistic to expect that philosophical questions can be handed over to the sciences to answer; or even that philosophical writing can or should be held to the same standards of mathematization and rigor as, say, theoretical physics. These are, by my lights, the three chief varieties of scientism.

The last is in a way the most superficial, but not, for all that, insignificant. Mathematical or logical pseudo-rigor is one kind of affected obscurity. My point isn't that recourse to the languages of mathematics or logic never helps to make a philosophical argument or thesis clearer; of course it does. ("In order to be deep it is requisite to be dull," Peirce observed, having in mind particularly the dry details of his logic of relatives, on which, inter alia, his critique of Kant's categories depended.)[34] My point is, rather, that recourse to the languages of mathematics or logic sometimes stands in the way of real clarity by disguising failure to think deeply or critically enough about the concepts being manipulated with impressive logical sophistication.

The application form for National Endowment for the Humanities summer stipends requires applicants to indicate what "methodology" they will be using; not, obviously, a question expecting the answer: "I shall think about . . . ," but a question calling for some acceptably technical answer, appropriate or not.

My point about the second kind of scientism is not that it hasn't sometimes happened that problems that used to be the province of philosophy gradually came to be formulated in a way that made them susceptible of investigation by the sciences; of course it has—"what is the world made of?" for example. Nor is my point that there aren't border questions in which both philosophers and scientists may take an interest—"is perception a direct relation to external objects or a process of inference from sense data?" for example.[35] My point is, rather, that appeals to the sciences are often made in a way that covertly changes the subject—e.g., from, "which predicates are such that inductions involving those predicates are correct?" to, "why do humans tend, by and large, to make the kinds of inductive inference that are correct?" or from, "what processes of belief-formation are reliable?" to, "in what circumstances do people tend to use reliable, and in what unreliable, processes?"[36]

The most ambitious style of scientism, which would abandon philosophical questions in favor of scientific ones, represents the purest and most bizarre form of "science envy." (Philosophers of this boldest scientistic stripe, one might say, don't so much want to be *like* scientists, as to *be* scientists.) My point about this revolutionary scientism isn't that it is impossible in principle that results from the sciences might show that this or that philosophical problem is misconceived; they might, by revealing some presupposition of the problem to be false. My point is, rather, that no amount of investigation in the sciences could reasonably be expected to answer such characteristically philosophical questions as: is science epistemologically special, and if so, why? is its yielding true predictions an indication of the truth of a theory, and if so, why? etc. And it is incomprehensible why, unless these were not only legitimate questions, but legitimate questions with less-than-skeptical answers, one could be justified in proposing to do science instead of philosophy.

Perhaps that is why the revolutionary scientism encountered in contemporary philosophy often manifests a peculiar affinity with the antiscientific attitudes which, as I conjecture, are prompted by resentment, as scientism is prompted by envy, of the sciences.[37] Paul Churchland, on the scientistic side, tells us that, since truth is not the primary aim of the ceaseless cognitive activity of the ganglia of the sea slug, it should maybe cease to be a primary aim of science, and even that talk of truth may make no sense; Richard Rorty, on the antiscience side, tells us that truth is just what can survive all conversational objections, and that the only sense in which science is exemplary is as a model of human solidarity. Patricia Churchland, on the scientistic side, observes that "truth, whatever that is, definitely takes the hindmost"; Sandra Harding, on the antiscience side, observes that "the truth—whatever that is!—will not set you free." Stephen Stich, on the scientistic side, announces that truth is neither intrinsically nor instrumentally valuable, and that a justified belief is one his holding which conduces to whatever the believer values; Steve Fuller, on the antiscience side, announces that he sees no distinction "between 'good scholarship' and 'political relevance.'"[38]

Here is Peirce on what will happen if sham reasoning becomes commonplace: "men come to look upon reasoning as mainly decorative. . . .

The result of this state of things is, of course, a rapid deterioration of intellectual vigor. . . . Man loses his conceptions of truth and of reason. If he
sees one man assert what another denies, he will, if he is concerned, choose
his side and set to work . . . to silence his adversaries. The truth for him is
that for which he fights."[39]

I can match neither Peirce's prescience nor his eloquence. But perhaps
I can add a little circumstantial detail to his diagnosis. Preposterism is a
direct encouragement to sham and fake reasoning. Where philosophy is
concerned, it is also an encouragement to envy of science, thus to scientism
and to a certain kind of irrationalism, and to resentment of science and to
an only-slightly-different kind of irrationalism. Within philosophy, furthermore, as the discipline to which the task of articulating the nature and
goals of inquiry falls, the ubiquity of sham and fake reasoning has induced
a factitious despair of the possibility of attaining truth by investigation—
the despair revealed in the great storms of scare quotes with which so much
recent philosophical writing expresses its distrust of "truth," "reality,"
"facts," "reason," "objectivity," etc.

But why is it to be expected, as Peirce maintained, that if pseudo-inquiry
becomes commonplace, man will "lose his conceptions of truth and of
reason"? When sham and fake reasoning are ubiquitous, people become
uncomfortably aware, or half-aware, that reputations are made, acclaim
achieved, as often by clever championship of the indefensible or the incomprehensible as by serious intellectual work, as often by mutual promotion among influential cliques as by merit. Knowing, or half-knowing, this,
they become increasingly skeptical of what they hear and read. Their confidence in what passes for true declines, and with it their willingness to use
the words "truth," "evidence," etc., without the precaution of scare quotes.
As those scare quotes become ubiquitous, so people's confidence in the
concepts of truth and reason falters. The "passes for" fallacy smooths the
way; the fact that much of what passes for truth is really not true at all, is
confusedly taken to reveal that the very idea of truth is humbug. And the
idea is encouraged that there is, after all, nothing wrong with sham or fake
reasoning . . . , and so on.

And so, too, the bizarre idea comes to be taken for granted that to hold
that there is such a thing as truth, and that it is possible to discover the
truth by investigation, must be to harbor regressive political tendencies.
(*Of course* it isn't; to hold that there is such a thing as truth, etc., is by
no means to hold that whatever has been accepted as true, *is* true.) I am
distressed to find that, along with those ubiquitous scare quotes and the

ubiquitous "passes for" fallacy, this is an idea frequently encountered in recent feminist scholarship.[40]

Sad to say, the vast recent literature of feminist approaches to ethics, epistemology, philosophy of science, philosophy of language, and lately even logic,[41] is a striking manifestation of some consequences of preposterism. Reading in this vast literature, you can hardly fail to notice how endlessly it is repeated that feminism has radical consequences for this or that area of philosophy,[42] and how frequently those radical consequences turn out to be trivial, or obviously derivative from some male philosopher, or manifestly false; by how determinedly practitioners avert their attention from serious criticisms, and how lavishly they praise the work of others of their own persuasion.[43] Pondering on how this came about, you can hardly fail to think how many reputations and careers, how many centers, programs, conferences, journals, depend on the legitimacy of appealing to the feminist perspective on this or that; or to recall Sandra Harding's no-nonsense instructions to the would-be male feminist: "advance the understandings produced by women feminists ... teach and write about women's thought, writings, accomplishments. ... criticize [your] male colleagues ... move material resources to women and feminists."[44]

I hope I haven't given the impression that my point is that the feminist-philosophy bandwagon is peculiarly awful. I do find it peculiarly distressing; but I don't know that it is peculiarly awful, and in any case it is two quite other points that interest me here. The first is that the perception among these radical feminist philosophers that their profession is profoundly corrupt is, at worst, exaggerated; their profession *is* rife with pseudo-inquiry, and publication, promotion, stardom, etc., *are* cut loose from merit. I emphatically do *not* share these feminists' view that the way to deal with this is to develop a shadow profession that is no less corrupt, but in which the corruption favors them.[45] But leave that aside. The second point is that it is this perception of the ubiquity of pseudo-inquiry which has induced despair of the possibility of honest inquiry, now an almost obligatory theme in feminist philosophy.

And in much other contemporary philosophy too; to repeat, the point is not to pick on the feminists, but to articulate how the epidemic of sham and fake reasoning encouraged by preposterism threatens to loosen our grip on the concepts of truth and inquiry. (Though, I confess, I am struck by the irony of Peirce's writing, "*man* loses his conceptions of truth and of reason," as of O'Brien's unself-conscious assumption that the "young scholars" of whom he writes are "young *men*"; for women, certainly, as contemporary feminist philosophy reveals, are no less susceptible to the consequences of preposterism.)

THUS FAR, though I have talked at length about the "research ethic" in philosophy, I have said nothing explicit about the ethics of research. Implicit in what I have been saying is the conviction that the "factitious despair" of the possibility of honest inquiry which has begun to be heard in so many quarters of contemporary philosophy will, as Francis Bacon so eloquently put it long ago, "cut the sinews and spurs of industry"[46]—i.e., impede real work. More strictly ethical is a thought which follows on the heels of this: that there is something indecent about making your living as an academic if you do not—as those who despair of the possibility of honest inquiry *cannot*—acknowledge that "tacit professional oath never to subordinate the motive of objective truth-seeking to any subjective preference or inclination or any expediency or opportunistic consideration."[47]

SINCE THIS HAS BEEN in the nature of a lay sermon—and since I am, after all, one of those supposedly naive philosophers whom Rorty likes to dismiss as "lovably old-fashioned prigs"—perhaps it is appropriate to end, as sermons do, with a text. Mine is the motto of chapter 11 of George Eliot's *Felix Holt the Radical:*

> Truth is the precious harvest of the earth.
> But once, when harvest waved upon a land,
> The noisome cankerworm and caterpillar,
> Locusts, and all the swarming foul-born broods,
> Fastened upon it with swift, greedy jaws,
> And turned the harvest into pestilence,
> Until men said, What profits it to sow?

NOTES

1. Jacques Barzun, *The American University*, Harper and Row, New York, 1968, p. 221.

2. C. S. Peirce, *Collected Papers*, ed. Charles Hartshorne, Paul Weiss, and Arthur Burks, Harvard University Press, Cambridge, MA, 1931–58, 5.520, 6.6, 1.128.

3. *Collected Papers* 2.82 (the "real love of truth"); 1.43ff. (the "scientific attitude"); 1.34 (the "craving to know how things really are"); 5.583 (the "Will to Learn").

4. *Collected Papers*, 1.57.

5. *Collected Papers*, 6.3.

6. *Collected Papers*, 1.34.

7. In Carolyn Eisele, ed., *The New Elements of Mathematics*, Mouton, The Hague, 1976, vol. 4, p. 977; Peirce is referring to Paul Carus.

8. *Collected Papers*, 1.135.

9. Joseph Brent, *Charles Sanders Peirce: A Life*, Indiana University Press, Bloomington and Indianapolis, 1991, p. 16.

10. M. Manilii, *Astronomicon I*, London, 1903, xliii; see Harry Frankfurt, "The Faintest Passion," *Proceedings and Addresses of the American Philosophical Association*, 66.3, 1992, pp. 5–16.

11. Roger Bacon, *Opus Majus* (c. 1266), trans. Robert Belle Burke, Russell and Russell, New York, 1962, p. 4.

12. When I heard it, this was attributed to Burton Dreben, but Israel Scheffler tells me that his recollection is that the original source was Talmudic scholar Saul Lieberman, and the original saying, "nonsense is nonsense, but the history of nonsense is science."

13. See essays 5 and 6, this volume.

14. *Collected Papers*, 8.142.

15. From the statement of purpose supplied by the editor, Steve Fuller: "The journal is committed to both examining and exhibiting the social structure of knowledge; thus, its policy is to publish 'collaborations' which are the collective product of several authors" (*Directory of American Philosophers*, 1994–95, p. 228).

16. Louise Rosenblatt and Sidney Ratner suggested *Principia Mathematica* as a possible candidate; but I think this is better described as combining Russell's philosophical work with Whitehead's mathematical work.

17. Sandra Harding, *The Science Question in Feminism*, Cornell University Press, Ithaca, NY, 1986, p. 251.

18. *Chronicle of Higher Education*, 27 April 1994, p. A15.

19 See my *Evidence and Inquiry: Towards Reconstruction in Epistemology*, Oxford, Blackwell, 1993, chapters 6, 7, and 8.

20. See "Science as Social?—Yes and No," essay 6 in this volume.

21. "Politics and the Morality of Scholarship," in *Morality and Scholarship,* ed. Max Black, Cornell University Press, Ithaca, NY, 1967, p. 73.

22. Alvin Goldman, "Epistemics: The Regulative Theory of Cognition," *Journal of Philosophy,* 75.10, 1978, 509–23, p. 523.

23. See also Daniel Bonevac, "Leviathan U," in Howard Dickman, ed., *The Imperiled Academy,* Transaction Press, New Brunswick, NJ, 1993, pp. 1–26.

24. Peirce, *Collected Papers,* 1.645.

25. Kenneth Arnold, "University Presses Could Still Become the Cultural Force for Change and Enlightenment They Were Meant to Be," *Chronicle of Higher Education,* 29 July 1987, cited in Charles Sykes, *Profscam,* Regnery Gateway, Washington, DC, 1988, p. 129.

26. Gary Gutting, "The Editor's Page," *American Philosophical Quarterly,* 31.1, 1994, p. 87: "Learned journals are ostensibly dedicated to presenting essential new discoveries to a community of scholars. This purpose alone, however, cannot explain the immense volume of contemporary journal publications. . . . None of us can hope to read more than a very small percentage. . . . The obvious implication is that most articles published in journals are not essential scholarly contributions. . . . One common, if seldom explicitly noted, reason [for publication] is to certify the academic competence of their authors."

27. My estimates are based on the *Directory of American Philosophers* and the *International Directory of Philosophy;* they can be only estimates, because the information there is incomplete, and, in particular, does not include data about journals that folded. But aren't there, after all, many more philosophers now, as well as many more journals, than in 1900 (a challenge pressed by Louis Pojman)? Indeed, there are. But the idea that there are, in the United States alone, 9,000 or so people all capable of genuinely significant philosophical work, strikes me as itself preposterous.

28. In a recent telephone conversation, an employee told me that Oxford University Press now prints some academic monographs in runs of only 200 copies.

29. In an article entitled "Seeking Profits, College Presses Publish Novels" (*Wall Street Journal,* 20 September 1994, pp. B1 and B8), Marj Charlier writes that for Mr. Luther Wilson, director of the University Press of Colorado, "even to mention profits indicates a shift in academic publishing," and continues, "traditionally, universities subsidized their presses so they could publish definitive—and probably money-losing—treatises. . . . But now, universities are reducing their subsidies, and budget-strapped libraries are cutting back on their academic purchases," and university presses are having to seek moneymaking projects. See also Robert S. Boynton, "Routledge Revolution," *Lingua Franca,* March/April 1995, 25–32, on the present condition of a once highly respected academic press.

30. My source is Bruce Wilshire, *The Moral Collapse of the University,* SUNY Press, Albany, NY, 1990, pp. 106–7.

31. I owe to Mark Migotti the following splendid quotations from Nietzsche,

Human, All Too Human (1878), trans. Marion Faber, University of Nebraska Press, Lincoln, NE, 1984, section 284, "In favour of the idle": "One sign that the valuation of the contemplative life has declined is that scholars now compete with men of action in a kind of precipitate pleasure, so that they seem to value this kind of pleasure more highly than that to which they are really entitled and which is in fact much more pleasurable"; and section 285, "Modern Restlessness": ". . . agitatedness is growing so great that higher culture can no longer allow its fruits to mature; it is as though the seasons were following upon one another too quickly. From lack of repose our civilization is growing into a new barbarism."

32. *Character and Opinion in the United States: With Reminiscences of William James and Josiah Royce and Academic Life in America,* Charles Scribner's Sons, New York, 1920; my source is Morton G. White, *Science and Sentiment in America,* Oxford University Press, Oxford, 1972, p. 244.

33. See also "As for that phrase 'studying in a literary spirit' . . . ," essay 3 in this volume; and my "Between the Scylla of Scientism and the Charybdis of Apriorism," in Lewis Hahn, ed., *The Philosophy of Sir Peter Strawson,* Open Court, La Salle, IL, 1998, 49–63, for an articulation and defense of a conception of philosophy which I there describe as "scientific but not scientistic."

34. *Collected Papers,* 5.17.

35. In "How the Critical Common-sensist Sees Things," *Histoire, épistémologie, langage,* 16.1, 1994, 9–34, I try to relate Peirce's approach to this question to J. J. Gibson's and R. L. Gregory's.

36. Quine—in whose work a plausible naturalism sits side by side with an implausible scientism—makes the first of these diversionary maneuvers; Alvin Goldman makes the second. See my *Evidence and Inquiry,* pp. 130–35 on the former problem shift, and pp. 152–57 on the latter.

37. A peculiar affinity manifested in this bizarre conference announcement: "VIRTUAL FUTURES 1995 is an interdisciplinary event that examines the role of cybernetic and specifically dissipative or non-linear models in the arts, sciences, and philosophy. The conference explores the relationship between postmodern philosophy and chaos theory, with topics ranging from: information technology, hypertext and multimedia applications, virtual reality and cyberspace, C_3, complexity theory, cyberfeminism, artificial life and intelligence, neural nets and nanotechnology. Literary themes such as apocalypse, narcotics, cyberpunk science fiction, and annihilation are all welcome. Philosophically, the conference emphasizes materialist schools of Continental philosophy and neurophilosophy." No, I am not making this up! It is taken verbatim from a poster for a conference organized by the Centre for Research in Philosophy and Literature at the University of Warwick in May 1995, sent to me by Jenny Teichman, who comments, "Aaargh."

38. Paul M. Churchland, "The Ontological Status of Observables" (1982), in *A Neurocomputational Perspective: The Nature of Mind and the Structure of Science,* Bradford Books, MIT Press, Cambridge, MA, 1989, pp. 150–51; Richard Rorty, *Con-*

sequences of Pragmatism, Harvester Press, Hassocks, Sussex, 1982, p. 165, and "Science as Solidarity," in John S. Nelson, Allan Megill, and Donald McCloskey, eds., *The Rhetoric of the Human Sciences,* University of Wisconsin Press, Madison, WI, 1987, p. 46; Patricia Smith Churchland, "Epistemology in the Age of Neuroscience," *Journal of Philosophy,* 75.10, 1987, p. 549; Sandra Harding, *Whose Science? Whose Knowledge?* Cornell University Press, Ithaca, NY, 1991, p. xi; Stephen P. Stich, *The Fragmentation of Reason,* Bradford books, MIT Press, Cambridge, MA, 1992, pp. 118ff.; Steve ("yours in discourse") Fuller, E-mail posting, 5.4.94.

39. *Collected Papers,* 1.57–59.

40. There are exceptions, such as Louise Antony, who tells us that "the real problem with the ruling-class world-view . . . is that it's false." ("Quine as Feminist: The Radical Import of Naturalized Epistemology," in *A Mind of One's Own,* ed. Louise Antony and Charlotte Witt, Westview, Boulder, CO, 1993, 185–226, p. 114.)

41. For example, Andrea Nye, *Words of Power,* Routledge, London, 1990; Val Plumwood, "The Politics of Reason: Towards a Feminist Logic," *Australasian Journal of Philosophy,* 71.4, 1993, 436–62.

42. The relevance of feminism to social philosophy is clear enough; but more recent, more imperialist, feminism is marked by an insistence on extending its relevance to all areas of philosophy, including the most central. This is manifestly the agenda in, for example, Sandra Harding and Merrill Hintikka's *Discovering Reality: Feminist Perspectives on Epistemology, Metaphysics, Methodology, and Philosophy of Science,* Reidel, Dordrecht, The Netherlands, 1983. See also my review of this book in *Philosophy,* 60.232, 1985, 265–70, and "Knowledge and Propaganda: Reflections of an Old Feminist," essay 7 in this volume.

43. The tendency to mutual admiration in recent academic feminist writing is noted by Margarita Levin in "Caring New World: Feminism and Science," *American Scholar,* 57, Winter 1988, 100–106.

44. Sandra Harding, "Who Knows? Identities and Feminist Epistemology," in Joan E. Hartman and Ellen Messer-Davidow, eds., *(En)gendering Knowledge,* University of Tennessee Press, Knoxville, 1991, p. 109.

45. See "The best man for the job may be a woman . . . and other alien thoughts on affirmative action in the academy," essay 10 in this volume.

46. Francis Bacon, *The New Organon* (1620), Book I, aphorism LXXXVIII.

47. C. I. Lewis, *The Ground and Nature of the Right,* Columbia University Press, New York, 1955, p. 34.

Acknowledgments

"Confessions of an Old-Fashioned Prig" was presented at a conference on Truth at Santa Clara University in February 1998 and, with "The best man for the job may be a woman . . . and other alien thoughts on affirmative action in the academy," was the subject of a marathon symposium conducted by Ronald Dworkin, Thomas Nagel, and Jürgen Habermas in the School of Law at New York University in December 1997. It is published here for the first time. (A very short precursor paper, "Concern for Truth: What it Means, Why it Matters," appeared in *The Flight from Science and Reason*, edited by Paul R. Gross et al., *Annals of the New York Academy of Sciences*, 775, 1996, and reissued by Johns Hopkins University Press, Baltimore, MD, 1997, 57–63.)

"'We Pragmatists . . .': Peirce and Rorty in Conversation" was performed as after-dinner entertainment at the conference of the Society for the Advancement of American Philosophy in Boston in 1995, with myself as the young C. S. Peirce, Bruce Wilshire as Richard Rorty, and Donna Wilshire as Susan Haack; and again at the University of Granada in 1997, this time in Spanish, and with me as myself. It is published here by permission of *Partisan Review*, where it appeared (LXIV.1, 91–107) in 1997.

"As for that phrase 'studying in a literary spirit' . . ." was published in *Proceedings and Addresses of the American Philosophical Association*, 70.2, 1996, 57–75, and appears here by permission of the American Philosophical Association. The Ninth Annual Patrick Romanell Lecture on Philosophical Naturalism, it was delivered at the Central Division Meetings of the American Philosophical Association in 1995; it has also been presented in colloquia at Dalhousie, Stockholm, and Turku, and at an International Seminar on Analytic Philosophy and Pragmatism at the Federal University of Minas Gerais in Belo Horizonte, Brazil.

"'Dry Truth and Real Knowledge': Epistemologies of Metaphor and Metaphors of Epistemology," which was presented at, among other places, the Department of English at McGill University, first appeared in *Aspects of Metaphor,* edited by Jaakko Hintikka (Kluwer, Dordrecht, the Netherlands, 1994), 1–22, ©1994 Kluwer Academic Publishers. It is reprinted here by permission.

"Puzzling Out Science" is based on my contribution to a panel on "What Do the Natural Sciences Know, and How Do They Know it?" and published, together with the papers of fellow-panelists Gerald Holton and Steven Weinberg, in *Academic Questions,* Spring 1995, 25–31. It is reprinted here by permission of Transaction Publishers. The present version includes some material from a very short piece entitled "Towards a Sober Sociology of Science," also in *The Flight from Science and Reason.*

"Science as Social?—Yes and No" was written for and published in *Feminism, Science and Philosophy of Science,* edited by Jack Nelson and Lynn Hankinson Nelson (Kluwer, Dordrecht, the Netherlands, 1996), 79–93, ©1996 Kluwer Academic Publishers, and appears here by permission. In its original version it was presented at numerous universities and colloquia, including a meeting of the Swiss Society for Logic and Philosophy of Science in Lausanne. The expanded version printed here was prepared for presentation at the Center for Philosophy of Science in Pittsburgh in 1996, and was also presented at the University of Santiago de Compostela and at a symposium on Science and Power at Universidad Complutense, Madrid, in 1997.

"Knowledge and Propaganda: Reflections of an Old Feminist" was first presented at the Eastern Division Meetings of the American Philosophical Association in 1992, and appears here by permission of *Partisan Review,* where it appeared (LX.4, 556–63) in 1993. A related paper, "Epistemological Reflections of an Old Feminist," some material from which is included in the essay published here, appeared in *Reason Papers,* 18, fall 1993, 31–43.

"Multiculturalism and Objectivity" was first presented at the Eastern Division Meetings of the American Philosophical Association in 1994, and appears here by permission of *Partisan Review,* where it was first published in 1995 (LXII.3, 397–405). In 1997 it was reprinted in *Ethical Issues for Canadians,* edited by Eldon Soffer (Broadview Press, Peterborough, Ontario). The somewhat longer essay that appears here includes some material from "Irrationalism and the Calm Sunlight of the Mind," my unpublished response to Thomas Nagel at the Trilling Seminar, Columbia University, 1995.

The table of varieties of relativism with which "Reflections on Relativism: From Momentous Tautology to Seductive Contradiction" opens was first sketched on the blackboard in response to a plaintive question from a student: "Dr. Haack, what is relativism?—I know Dr. X [a colleague] is against it, but I don't know what it *is*." This piece appeared in *Philosophical Perspectives, 10: Metaphysics*, edited by James E. Tomberlin (Blackwell, Oxford, 1996), and in the Supplement to *Noûs*, 1996, 298–314. It has been read in various philosophy departments and institutes, from NYU to Munich to Uppsala, and in January 1996 was presented at a conference on "Verdad, Lógica, Representación y Mundo" ("Truth, Logic, Representation and the World") at the University of Santiago de Compostela, Spain.

The much shorter paper which was the precursor of "The best man for the job may be a woman . . . and other alien thoughts on affirmative action in the academy" was written for a panel organized by the Committee on the Status of Women in the Profession, chaired by Martha Nussbaum, at the Eastern Division Meetings of the American Philosophical Association in 1996, and appeared in *Partisan Review* in the spring of 1998. The full-length essay that appears here for the first time was my Matchette Lecture, delivered at the Center for Ethics at Georgia State University in 1997 to an audience including affirmative-action officers from both the university and the city of Atlanta. The present version has been slightly expanded in the light of helpful discussion on that occasion, and at that marathon symposium at NYU Law School mentioned earlier.

"Preposterism and its Consequences" was written for and presented at a conference organized by the Center for Social Philosophy and Policy in Bowling Green, Ohio, in 1995; the organizers took it in good part. It was published in *Social Philosophy, and Policy,* 13.2, 1996, and in *Scientific Innovation, Philosophy, and Public Policy,* edited by Ellen Frankel Paul et al., (Cambridge University Press), 1996, 296–315, and appears here by permission of the Social Philosophy and Policy Foundation.

The quotation from Bacon which serves as the motto of this book is from *The New Organon* (1620), Book One, Aphorism LXXXVIII. The "Higher Dismissiveness," in the Preface, I owe to Anthony Gottlieb, "the still small voice that whispers 'bosh,'" in the Introduction, to W. K. Clifford. "The calm sunlight of the mind" is Hume's marvelous phrase for rational thought.

I have occasionally cut the beginning or the end of a quotation without ellipses, and replaced some upper-case by lower-case letters or vice versa without square brackets; but all ellipses and addenda within quotations are indicated. In preparing these essays for this publication, besides pruning some footnotes and unifying references (which, however, I have kept self-contained for each essay), I have edited out some repetitions. But I have from time to time deliberately allowed a sentence or paragraph in one paper to echo a sentence or paragraph in another, in hopes that this will illuminate how these essays fit together—not in a linear argument, but like intersecting crossword entries.

I would like to thank all those who, in many different ways, helped with this project: Susan Abrams, whose idea it was to put such a collection together; all the many people who made helpful comments on the various occasions when these papers were presented; an army of helpful correspondents, among whom I should mention especially Mark Migotti and H. S. Thayer, both of whom read and commented on all or almost all of these essays, in some instances on more than one draft; the late David Stove, from whose witty, candid, and bracing letters I learned a great deal, even—perhaps especially—when he and I disagreed; Jacques Barzun and, especially, Robert Heilbroner, from whose pleasure in my pleasure in words I have learned and grown; and Howard Burdick, as always, for too many reasons to list.

Index

Absolute, the, 62
acceptance (of scientific theories), *see* warrant, acceptance and
Addison, Joseph, 63
advocacy research, 8, 97, 103 n.21, 146, 201
  see also inquiry, politicized; sham reasoning
affirmative action in the academy, 4, 167–87
  and blacks, 180–86
  in college admissions, 183–4
  forms of, 168–9; preferential hiring, 5, 170–76, 180–81, 185; procedural fairness, 170, 178, 180; —minimal, 173–4
  and women, 170–79
agapism, 51
Alcoff, Linda M., 124, 132, 133 n.4, 135–6 n.29
ambiguity, 61, 70, 71, 76
  see also equivocation, fallacy of
analogy, 38, 84
  see also metaphor; simile
analytic/synthetic distinction, 39, 50, 51, 120 n.4
Andreski, Stanislav, 27, 30 n.58
Annis, David, 150
anti-representationalism, 20, 24–5, 35, 40–41, 64
  see also pragmatism; representation
anti-science, 5, 91–4, 199–201
  see also New Cynicism
Antony, Louise, 124, 133 n.3, 135 n.25

a priori method, 50, 57, 66 n.10
Aquinas, Thomas, 39
arguments, circular, 38–9
  see also mutual support
Aristotelian Insight, the, 21–23, 26, 162
Aristotle, 72, 83, 87 n.7, 175
Aronowitz, Stanley, 92, 102 n.12
Arrogance of Theory, the, 23
Austin, J. L., 21, 22, 57, 162

Baber, Harriet, 175–6, 186 n.8
Bacon, Francis, vi, 23, 29 n.40, 43, 58, 120 n.25, 131, 140, 204, 208 n.46
Bacon, Roger, 192, 205 n.11
Barzun, Jacques
  on foam-rubber words, 186 n.4
  on preposterism, 4, 188, 192, 205 n.1
Belenky, Mary Field, *et al.*, 122 n.32, 125, 133 n.12
belief, 8, 18
  genuine versus pseudo-, 8, 11
  over-and under-, 14, 108
  Stich on, 15
  and the will, 14–15
Berggren, Douglas, 81–2, 84, 88 n.24
Berkeley, George, 56, 163
Bernstein, Richard, 138, 139, 147 n.2
bilingualism, 139
bivalence, 39
Black, Max, 72, 87 n.8
Bleier, Ruth, 117–8, 121–2 n.27

Bonevac, Daniel, 138, 147 n.2
Bradley, F. H., 25, 62
bullshit, 9, 27 n.11
    see also fake reasoning; obscurity, af-
        fected
buried secrets, problem of, 22, 26, 163–4,
    166 n.31
Bushmen, 141, 155
Butler, Samuel, 8, 27 n.7

Carnap, Rudolf, 158
Chamfort, Sebastien Nicolas Roche 149, 164
    n.1
Churchland, Patricia Smith, 48, 57, 201, 208
    n.38
Churchland, Paul M., 20, 29 n.34, 48, 57,
    201, 207 n.38
Cicero, 72, 87 n.7
Clifford, W. K., 14, 28 n.20
cognitive differences between the sexes, 117,
    125
cognitive dissonance, 59, 67 n.14
coherence, 39
coherentism, 85, 143, 146, 166 n.21
Cole, Mike, 141, 147 n.5
Cole, Stephen, 93, 102 n.14
collegiality, 173
Collins, Harry, 91, 101 n.11
community of inquirers, 50, 53, 145
    see also inquiry, as social; science, as com-
        munal
comparison, statements of, 73, 75, 84
    see also metaphor; simile
conceptual pluralism, 159
conferences, 192, 198
confirmation, 111
contextualism, 143, 150
    see also relativism, epistemic
conversation, 19–21, 64
correspondence theory, see truth, corre-
        spondence theories of
counterculturalism, see multiculturalism
Crick, Francis, 12, 13, 19
Critical Common-sensism, 37, 57, 60, 156,
    165 n.12, 166 n.22
crossword analogy, 2, 85–6, 89 n.32, 95, 106,
    107, 114, 143–4, 145

culture
    non-Western, 145
    respect for others', 140
    senses of, 138
    Western 138, 139, 141, 144, 146–7
Cuvier, Baron Georges, 41–2

Darwin, Charles, 8
Davidson, Donald
    on adverbs, 169
    on coherentism, 166 n.21
    on foundationalism, 84–5, 89 n.29
    on metaphor, 72, 75, 76–7, 87, 87 n.6, 88
        n.18
    as pragmatist, 24, 25, 28 n.30, 63
    on truth, 19, 24
deduction, 38
deductivism, 92
Delbrück, Max, 12
Descartes, René, 51, 56, 64, 124
de Waal, Cornelis, 26, 30 n.56
Dewey, John, 23, 62, 120 n.14, 139, 147 n.3
dichotomies, false, 5, 18, 64
    see also This-or-Nothingism
Diderot, Denis, 90, 100 n.2
dilettantism, 48, 53, 65, 66 n.3
discourse
    civil versus philosophical, 78–9, 81
    persuasive versus instructive, 78, 81
discovery versus justification, 80–81
    see also conversation; inquiry, stages of
discrimination, 169, 171, 185
disinterestedness, ix, 1, 7, 9–10, 17, 18, 48,
    100, 190
    see also inquiry, genuine versus pseudo-;
        scientific attitude; Will to Learn
Dismal Dictum, the, 40, 57–8
diversity, 168–9, 185
DNA, 9, 12, 13, 19, 20
Donohue, Jerry, 12, 20
Du Bois, W. E. B., 140

Edison, Thomas, 190
Eliot, George, 138, 204
Emerson, Ralph Waldo, 63
emotions, 142

empiricism
  and feminism, 118–9, 122 n.29
  and pragmatism, 24, 40
Enlightenment, the, 41
epistemic privilege of the disadvantaged,
  116, 126
epistemology, 5, 83–7, 90, 123, 126, 142–7, 161
  cognitive science and, 195–6
  democratic, 92, 104, 113–4, 116
  ethics and, 14, 15
  politics and, 132, 135 n.29, 136 notes 30
    and 31
  Republican, 3, 124
  standards of: not internal to science, 94,
    104, 118; objective, 93, 94, 96, 100, 131,
    142, 144, 151; as paradigm-relative, 96
  standpoint, 116
  see also coherentism; contextualism; evi-
    dence; feminist epistemology; founda-
    tionalism; foundherentism; inquiry;
    justification, epistemic
equivocation, fallacy of, 70, 71
essentialism, 43, 44
evaluative terms, 17–18
evidence, ix, x, 1, 11, 12–13, 20, 97, 110, 112,
    113, 128, 130, 147
  comprehensiveness of, 113–4
  disillusion with, 4, 93, 99, 186
  non-linear, 145
  standards of, 91, 95, 100, 105–6, 107, 127,
    130, 131, 142, 143, 144, 147; not internal
    to science, 94, 105; social values as
    built into, 111
  see also crossword analogy; epistemol-
    ogy; foundherentism
existential import, in syllogistic reasoning,
    60
expert witnesses, 109
explanation, 52

facts, 19, 33, 202
  see also truth, correspondence theories of
fake reasoning, 9, 53, 57, 62, 65, 189–91, 202
  see also inquiry, genuine versus pseudo-;
    sham reasoning
fallibilism, 12, 95, 146, 147
feminism, ix, 104

old and new, x, 123–4, 128, 175, 178–9
  and science, 91, 104, 119
  see also feminist epistemology; feminist
    philosophy of science; logic, feminist
    critique of; science, sexism in theories
feminist epistemology, 3, 4, 5, 116, 119, 123–
    36, 132–3 n.2, 133 n.5, 142, 203
  lesbian, 126, 134 n.15
feminist philosophy, 92, 174–5, 186 n.6,
    203–4, 208 n.42
feminist philosophy of science, 3, 93, 104,
    115–9, 195–6, 203
  contrary to women's interests, 119, 122
    n.31
  feminist empiricism, 118–9, 122 n.29
Festinger, Leon, 59, 67 n.14
Feyerabend, Paul K., 91, 101 n.10, 102–3 n.19,
    150
fictional characters, 59
Field, Hartry, 150
foam-rubber words, 169, 173, 183, 185
Fogelin, Robert, 73, 75, 77, 87 n.9
Foucault, Michel, 175
foundationalism, 84–6, 89 n.27, 143, 146
  see also coherentism; epistemology; evi-
    dence; foundherentism
foundherentism, 85–6, 102 n.17, 143–4
  see also crossword analogy
Frankfurt, Harry, 9, 27 n.11
Franklin, Rosalind, 12
freedom of thought, 97, 113
Frege, Gottlob, 25
Fuller, Steve, 92, 102 n.12, 121 n.17, 201, 205
    n.15, 208 n.38

Gergen, Kenneth, 91, 101 n.11
Gilligan, Carol, 125, 134 n.12
Glashow, Sheldon, 90, 100 n.3
Goethe, Johann Wolfgang von, 56
Goldman, Alvin I., 57, 206 n.22, 207 n.36
Goodman, Nelson
  on induction, new riddle of, 91, 101 n.8
  on irrealism, 150, 153, 155, 156
Gosse, Philip, 8
Green, T. H., 85, 89 n.30
Grice, Paul, 75
Gross, Elizabeth, 132, 136 n.30

Handel, George Frederick, 138
Hanson, Norwood Russell, 91, 101 n.7
Harding, Sandra
    on feminist empiricism, 118–9, 122 n.29
    on feminist epistemology, 124, 133 n.5
    on feminist philosophy of science, 115,
        116, 118, 119, 121 notes 18, 20, and 24
    on feminist science, 196, 205 n.17
    on male feminists, 179, 203, 208 n.44
    on rape metaphors in Newton, 169
    on science and politics, 97, 103 n. 21
    on social versus natural science, 92, 102
        n.11
    on strong objectivity, 102 n.11, 116
    on truth, 132, 136 n.31, 201
Harvey, William, 43
Heal, Jane, 7, 17–18, 23, 27 n.5
Heidegger, Martin, 44, 62, 73
hiring, academic, 172–6, 177–8, 186 n.5
Hobbes, Thomas
    on metaphor, 70, 71, 72, 87 n.2
    on value of rationality, 13, 28 n.19, 79, 80,
        88 n.21
Holtby, Winifred, 123, 132 n.1
Housman, A. E., 191, 205 n.10
humanity, 4, 123, 132, 147
human nature, 12, 145
Hume, David, 63
Husserl, Edmund, 44, 62

imagination, 41, 56, 57, 63
    imaginative versus imaginary, 57, 142
incommensurability, 64, 91, 96, 150
    see also meaning-variance
independence of thought, 58
induction, 38, 52, 95, 201
    new riddle of, 91, 101 n.8
inductivism, 90
inquiry, ix, x, 7–30, 147
    as conversation, negotiation, 1, 4, 19–21
    disillusion with, 19–20, 63–4, 203
    environment of, 191–2
    genuine versus pseudo-, 1, 5, 8–10, 31–3,
        49, 53, 57, 60, 68 n.34, 131, 146, 189–92,
        201–2
    goal of, ix, 94, 97, 105, 189

    as inner dialogue, 82–3
    metaphor in, 79, 80–83
    obstacles to, 135 n.27, 192, 205 n.11
    philosophy as, 42, 49, 57, 59, 62, 63–5,
        189
    politicized, 1, 104, 119, 131–2, 141, 146, 201
    presentation stage of, 58, 81, 82, 85
    as social, 50, 54, 145, 146
    stages of, 82–3; see also discovery versus
        justification
    standards of, 113, 130, 142; not internal to
        science, 94, 105
    utility-driven, 26, 65
    value of, 13, 145
    versus writing, 59
    see also fake reasoning; sham reasoning;
        truth, concern for
intellectual honesty, see intellectual in-
    tegrity
intellectual integrity, 1, 7, 10–15, 17, 18, 23,
    26, 27, 31–2, 195
irony, 36, 37, 42, 65, 74
irrationalism, 5, 142, 202
irrealism, 150, 153, 155, 156, 163
"is," senses of, 70

James, William
    American Philosophical Association and,
        198–9, 206 n.30
    on conceptual pluralism, 159, 166 n.18
    on ethics and literature, 67 n.23
    on pragmatism, 23, 25, 29 n.41, 30 n.46,
        31 n., 55
    on truth, 16, 23–4, 25, 28 n.42, 29 n.41, 30
        notes 48 and 53
    on Will to Believe, 24, 25, 28 n.17, 29 n.43,
        30 n.46, 133
Jowett, Benjamin, 12, 28 n.17
justification, epistemic, 20–21, 32, 120 n.8,
    212 n.18, 143
    see also epistemology; evidence; found-
        herentism; warrant

Kant, Immanuel, 33, 39, 200
kinks in the brain, 43, 126
knowledge

power and, ix, 141, 142, 145
propaganda and, x, 127, 142
as success-word, 126
Kuhn, Thomas S., 103 n.22, 126, 143, 150
on observation as paradigm-dependent, 95–6, 102 n.18
on scientific revolutions, 45, 91, 95, 101 n.9, 103 n.22

laboratory phenomena, 93, 113
labor market, 177, 182
language mastery, 79–80
Latour, Bruno, 92, 101–2 n.11, 102 n.12, 116, 121 n.17
laws of nature, 51
Lefkowitz, Mary, 138, 139, 147 n.2
legal proceedings, 13
Le Guin, Ursula, 77, 88 n.17
Leśniewski, S., 158
Lewis, C. I., 7, 23, 27 n.2, 121 n.19, 208 n.47
Liar Paradox, Strengthened, 60
linguistic innovation, ix, 2, 4, 42, 56, 63, 80, 100, 160
see also conceptual pluralism; metaphor
Linnaeus, 56
literary journals, 45–6, 52, 53, 55
literature
ethics and, 67 n.23
not a kind of inquiry, 59
philosophy and, ix, x, 2, 5, 9, 39–41, 42, 44, 48–68 passim
truth in, 2, 59
Locke, John
on discourse, types of, 78, 81
on fortress of knowledge, 57
on metaphor, 2, 60, 69–72, 78, 79, 80, 81, 84, 85, 87 n.1
on obscurity, affected, 58, 66 n.13, 190
on wit versus judgment, 71
logic, 38, 40, 43, 60, 95, 109, 133–4 n.9, 200
feminist critique of, 125, 133–4 n.9, 203
of relations, 200
triadic, 39
see also bivalence; deductivism; inductivism
Logical Atomism, 21, 22, 159, 162

Longino, Helen, 116, 118–9, 121 n.23, 122 n.29, 135 n.20
Lorenzo's Oil, 12
Lubiano, Wahneema, 141, 147 n.5
Lurie, Alison, 59, 67 n.14

Marx, Karl, 175
meaning, 54, 155
growth of, 42, 56
instability of, 71
literal versus metaphorical, 77
-variance, 150, 160–61
see also ambiguity; analytic/synthetic distinction; foam-rubber words; metaphor; precision; vagueness
mereology, 158–9
merit, 172, 185, 186, 203
meritocracy, 114, 179, 180
metaphor, ix, x, 2, 5, 41–2, 56, 60, 63, 69–89
as abuse of language (Locke), 69–70
as ambiguity (Hobbes, Mill), 70, 71, 76
as elliptical simile (Aristotle, Cicero, Quintilian), 72–7
as emotive (Locke), 69, 71
as fecund falsity (Davidson), 72, 75, 76–7, 87
live versus dead, 75
as pragmatic interaction (Fogelin, Haack), 75–7
as semantic interaction (Black, Richards), 72
sexist, 117, 121 n.25, 169
as speaker's meaning (Searle), 72, 76, 82
metaphors, philosophical
affected obscurity as "holes of foxes" (Locke), 72, 80
cable of reasons (Reid, Peirce), 51, 56
chain of reasons (Descartes), 51, 56
fortress of knowledge (Locke, Peirce), 57
jigsaw puzzle (Polanyi), 85
kicking away the ladder (Sextus), 83–4
leviathan (Hobbes), 70
metaphor as the dreamwork of language (Davidson), 87
metaphors as ignes fatui (Hobbes), 70
mind as a lake (Peirce), 56

metaphors (*continued*)
  mind as empty cabinet, blank paper, wax
    tablet (Locke), 70, 84, 85
  maps and unity of truth (Haack), 160
  philosopher as underlaborer to science
    (Locke), 70, 79, 84
  rebuilding the ship (Neurath, Quine, Put-
    nam), 84
  sun, cave, divided line (Plato), 83
  truth as a woman (Nietzsche), 84
  web of belief (Neurath, Quine), 84, 85
  words as the money of fools (Hobbes),
    70
  see also crossword analogy
metaphysics, 35–7, 41–2, 51, 56, 70
  see also irrealism; nominalism; realism;
    reality; relativism
Michener, James, 59
Migotti, Mark, 59
Mill, J. S., 70, 71, 87 notes 4 and 5, 120 n.14,
  121 n.21
Milton, John, 60
mind-independence, 154, 157–9
multiculturalism, ix, 4, 137–48
  counterculturalism, 139, 141–7; epistemo-
    logical, 142–7
  senses of, 137
mutual support, 39, 51, 85, 143
  see also arguments, circular; crossword
    analogy

naturalism, 48, 57, 207 n.36
  see also science, philosophy and; sci-
    entism
natural kinds, 51
Nazi science, 131
Nelson, Lynn Hankinson, 92, 102 n.12,
  116, 121 n.23, 122 n.29, 135 notes 20
  and 22
nepotism, 178
Neurath, Otto, 84, 88–9 n.25
New Cynicism, 3, 5, 92–4, 97, 98–100, 105,
  109, 127–30
Newspeak, 65, 88 n.22, 92
Nietzsche, Friedrich, 84, 89 n.28
nominalism, 25, 34–5, 56
Nye, Andrea, 125, 133 n.9

objectivity, ix
  of epistemic standards, 93, 94, 96, 100,
    131, 142, 144, 151
  disillusion with, 32, 91, 200, 202
  of persons, 100
  strong, 102 n.11, 116
  of truth and falsity, 4, 7, 32, 64, 100
Object Relations theory, 125, 133 n.11
O'Brien, Conor Cruise, 196, 203, 206 n.21
obscurity, affected, 58, 66 n.13, 69, 72, 80,
  142, 190, 200
observation, 50
  as paradigm-dependent, 95–6
  as theory-dependent, 91, 101 n.7
  see also perception
Old Boy Network, 5, 178
Old Deferentialism, 3, 5, 90–91, 94, 95, 96,
  99, 105, 106, 109, 127, 129–30
Orwell, George, 65, 136 n.32
  see also Newspeak, thoughtcrime

partiality, 12
  see also disinterestedness
"passes for" fallacy, 93, 94, 102 n.15, 117–9,
  146, 202–3
Pauling, Linus, 12, 13
Pearson, Karl, 121 n.16
Peirce, C. S., 7–15 *passim*, 23–7 *passim*, 31–
  46, 48–62 *passim*, 140
  on analytic/synthetic distinction, 39, 50, 51
  on Bacon, Francis, 43
  on buried secrets, 22, 26, 163–4, 166 n.31
  conversation with Rorty, 31–47
  on Critical Common-sensism, 37, 57, 60,
    165 n.12, 166 n.22
  on Descartes' "vicious individualism,"
    124
  on fake reasoning, 53, 190
  on fallibilism, 12, 28 n.16
  on imagination, 41, 56, 57
  on inquiry: blocking the road of, 135
    n.27; genuine versus pseudo-, 8–10, 27
    n.9, 28 n.14, 31–2, 49, 53, 167, 189, 190,
    201–2, 208 n.39; utility-driven, 26, 65
  on intellectual integrity, 7, 23, 26, 27, 27
    notes 1 and 8–10, 31–2, 203
  on James, William, 55

on Kant, 39
on kinks in the brain, 43, 126
on the literary spirit, 9, 29 n.10, 40, 48,
    52–7
on logic, 38, 40, 43; of relations, 200, 207
    n.34; triadic, 39
on the "masculine intellect," 125, 133 n.6
on meaning, 42, 54, 56
on metaphor, 41–2, 56–7
on metaphysics, 35–7, 41–2
on nominalism, 34–5, 56
on perception, 51, 162, 166 n.23
on philosophy, 37, 44, 49, 65, 188–9, 205
    n.2; literature and, 9, 27 n.10, 39–41,
    48, 52–7, 61–2; science and, 37–8, 40–
    41, 44, 45, 48, 49–52, 57–9, 61–2; society
    and, 43
on the Pragmatic Maxim, 35–6
on pragmatism, 2, 23, 25, 27, 40, 44–6, 51,
    55; and pragmaticism, 46, 51, 55
on the real, 56, 158, 163–4, 166 notes 14, 25
    and 27
on realism, extreme scholastic, 25, 34–5,
    51–2, 55–6
on representation, 24, 35
on Schiller, F. C. S., 55, 60, 63
on science, 36–9, 45, 90, 97, 100, 100 n.1,
    103 n.26, 105, 109, 115, 120 n.2, 121 n.16,
    193, 205 n.14
on scientific attitude, the, 49–50, 52–3,
    189, 205 n.3
on semiotics, 24, 64
on sham reasoning, 8, 31–2, 53, 167, 201–2,
    208 n.39
on terminology, philosophical, 45–6,
    52–6, 58, 61
on theologians, 49, 53, 189
on Things in Themselves, 163, 166 n.30
on truth 22, 23, 24, 26, 27, 31–4, 45, 64–5,
    154, 162–5, 166 n.25
on tychism, 26, 51
on the Will to Learn, 45, 49, 189, 205 n.3
perception, 4, 38, 51, 102 n.18, 161–2,
    205 n.35
    see also observation; phaneroscopy
phaneroscopy, 50, 56
    see also observation; perception

phenomenology, see phaneroscopy
philosophical novels, dialogues, plays, 59,
    67 n.23
philosophy
    abilities needed in, 172, 173
    analytic, 48, 57, 66 n.12
    condition of, 37, 188–9, 193–7, 199–204
    disillusion with, 37, 42, 65
    easy and obvious versus accurate and ab-
        struse, 63
    edifying, 65
    graduate programs in, 177–8, 182
    history of, 46, 63
    as inquiry, 43, 52, 57, 59, 62, 63–5, 189
    laboratory versus seminary, 40, 49, 50
    politics and, 43, 62, 65
    as profession, 43, 60, 182
    public versus private, 62
    reasoning in, 38–9
    social, 62, 123
    value of, 37, 42, 52, 65
    see also literature, philosophy and; sci-
        ence, philosophy and
philosophy journals, 192, 197
Plato, 60, 61, 83, 84
poetry, 42, 56, 61, 62
Polanyi, Michael, 85, 103 n.23, 115, 120 n.7,
    135 n.24
polygamy, 139
Popper, Karl R., 96, 101 n.7, 115, 120 n.14
    see also deductivism; observation; verisi-
        militude
positivism, 39, 41, 44, 51, 160
Potter, Elizabeth, 124, 133 n.4
pragmaticism, 46, 51, 55
Pragmatic Maxim, 25, 35–6
    see also pragmaticism; pragmatism
pragmatism, ix, 1, 2, 8, 23–27, 38, 39, 40–41,
    44–6, 48, 51, 55, 60, 62–3
    as anti-representationalism, 24, 35, 64
    positivism and, 44, 51
    vulgar, 2, 25
    see also Dewey, John; James, William;
        Peirce, C. S.; pragmaticism; Rorty,
        Richard; Schiller, F. C. S.
precision, 54, 55
prediction, 52

preposterism, 4–5, 119, 188–208
prestige, 173
propaganda, x, 127, 132, 142
publishing, academic, 192, 197–8
Putnam, Hilary
    on the a priori method, 66 n.10
    on conceptual relativism, 4, 150, 153–6,
        164 n.2, 165 notes 8, 9, 11, 12, 15, and 16,
        166 notes 17 and 22
    on metaphysical realism, 18, 153, 156
    on science as fleet of ships, 84, 89 n.26
    on truth, 154, 159, 162

quantifiers, sentential, 21–2
Quine, W. V. O.
    as feminist, 135 n.25
    on the mathematical cyclist, 59
    on naturalism, 57, 207 n.36
    on ontological relativity, 150, 164 notes 2
        and 3, 165 n.6
    on relativism of truth, 152, 165 n.6
    on science as communal enterprise, 115
    on underdetermination, 91, 101 n.6, 110–
        11, 128–9, 135 n.21
    on web and ship metaphors, 84, 85, 89
        notes 27 and 31
Quintilian, 72, 87 n.7

racism, 146, 173, 182
Ramsey, Frank P., 21, 21–2, 162, 166 n.24
Rand, Ayn, 125, 133 n.7
rationality, 13, 32, 79, 80, 91, 200
    senses of, 142
    see also irrationalism
Ravitch, Diane, 138, 147 n.2
realism
    extreme scholastic, 25, 34–5, 51–2, 55–6
    innocent, 156–64
    metaphysical, 18, 153, 156
    senses of, 100
reality, 3, 56, 93, 113, 156–8, 163–4, 202
reductionism, 160
redundancy theory, see truth, redundancy
    theory of
Reid, Thomas, 56, 167, 186 n.1
relativism, x, 4, 149–66
    conceptual, 4, 150, 153–6

cultural, 153, 154, 163
epistemic, 19–21, 32, 143, 144, 150–52; see
    also contextualism
linguistic, 150
ontological, 150
self-defeating forms, 152–3
shallow versus deep, 150–51
versus tribalism, 144, 151–2, 163
of truth, 152, 153
variants distinguished, 149–53
representation, 20, 24, 35
    see also anti-representationalism; semi-
    otics
retroduction, 38
rhetoric, 1, 61, 65, 69, 91, 92, 94, 143
Richards, I. A., 61, 67 n.17, 72, 87 n.8
role models, 171–72, 181
Romanticism, 41
Rorty, Richard, 18–21, 31–47, 48–68 passim,
    especially 62–5
    on anti-representationalism, 20, 24–5, 35,
        40–41, 64
    on bivalence, 39
    conversation with Peirce, 31–47
    on epistemic relativism/tribalism, 19–21,
        32, 150–52, 165 notes 4 and 10
    on imagination, 41, 63
    on inquiry as conversation, negotiation,
        19–21
    on irony, 36, 37, 42, 65
    on linguistic innovation, 2, 42, 63
    on metaphor, 41, 63
    on metaphysics, 35–7
    on nominalism, 34
    on objectivity, 7, 32, 64
    on philosophy: disillusion with, 37, 42,
        65; history of, 46, 63; literature and, ix,
        2, 39–41, 42, 44, 62–5; politics and, 43,
        62, 65
    on pragmatism, 2, 23, 24–5, 26, 30 notes
        47, 49, and 51, 35, 38, 40–41, 44–6, 62,
        64
    on science, 32–3, 37–40, 48, 63–4, 201,
        207–8 n.38
    on truth, 2, 7, 18–21, 24, 25, 26, 27 n.4, 28
        notes 24–8, 31–4, 45, 64–5, 162, 166
        n.26, 201, 204, 207 n.38

Royce, Josiah, 34, 199, 207 n.32
Russell, Bertrand, x, 21, 23, 62

Santayana, George, 63, 199, 207 n.32
scare quotes, 92, 117, 126, 146, 155–6, 202
    see also "passes for" fallacy
Scheman, Naomi, 141–2, 147 n.5
Schiller, F. C. S., 55, 60, 62, 63, 133–4 n.9
science: ix, 3, 32, 90–103, 104–22
    authority in, 114, 115
    classification of sciences, 36–7, 50
    as communal, 3, 85, 97, 107, 108, 146; com-
        petitive, 98, 104, 107, 108, 115, 119, 145,
        146; cooperative, 58, 85, 97, 104, 107,
        108, 115, 119, 145
    environment of, 98, 108
    envy and resentment of, 200–202
    epistemically distinguished, not privi-
        leged, 94, 96, 105
    funding of, 98, 109, 193
    goal of, 112
    history of, 45
    as ideology, 199–201
    imagination in, 41, 56, 57, 63
    internal organization of, 98, 99, 108
    as literature, 63–4
    philosophy and, x, 5, 37–41, 44, 45, 48–52,
        57–9, 61–2, 63, 200–201
    physical versus human, social, 3, 92, 98,
        104, 109, 113, 114, 116, 127
    politics and, ix, 92, 97, 109, 110, 127
    prejudice in, 108, 109, 116, 127, 129, 130,
        146
    present condition of, 98, 109
    progress in, 90–91, 99–100, 106, 109; hin-
        drances to, 98–9, 108–9
    sexism in theories, 116–7, 118–9, 122 n.28,
        127, 130, 134–5 n.17, 146
    as socially constructed, 3, 32–3, 93, 104,
        112, 114, 116
    social values in, 3, 110–11, 116, 128–9
    sociology of, 3, 91, 98, 98–9, 130
    solidarity as mark of, 33, 64
scientific attitude, 49–50, 52–53, 189
    see also disinterestedness; intellectual in-
        tegrity; Will to Learn
scientific careers, 114, 119

scientific method, 33, 37, 38, 45, 50, 62,
    96–7, 102–3 n.19, 105
    not exclusively logical, 97, 106
    not exclusive to science, 96–7, 106
scientific revolutions, 45, 91, 95
scientism, 5, 37, 61, 61–2, 66 n.11, 199–201
    varieties of, 57–8, 200–201
Scotus, Duns, 56
Searle, John, 72, 75, 76–7, 82, 87 n.13
self-deception, 11, 196
    see also wishful thinking
self-esteem, 140, 183
semantic theory of truth, see truth, seman-
    tic theory of
semiotics, 24, 64
    see also representation
sexism, 171, 175, 178, 179
    in scientific theories, 116–7, 118–9, 127,
        130, 146
sexist stereotypes, 115, 119, 125, 127, 146
Sextus Empiricus, 83–4
Shakespeare, William, 60, 73–4, 138
sham reasoning, 8, 11, 12, 31–2, 49, 52, 53,
    131, 167, 189–91, 201–2
    see also fake reasoning; inquiry, genuine
        versus pseudo-simile, 72–3, 75, 84
    see also metaphor, as elliptical simile
skepticism, 164
sneer quotes, see "passes for" fallacy; scare
    quotes
Snow, C. P., 138
social constructivism, see reality; science
social sciences, see science, physical versus
    human, social
Soviet science, 108, 120 n.10, 131
Stich, Stephen P., 2, 15–7, 23, 24, 25, 27 n.3,
    28 notes 21 and 23, 201, 208 n.38
Stove, David, 147 n.6
subjectivism, 149
synechism, 51
Szasz, Thomas, 104, 120 n.1

Tarski, Alfred, 19, 21, 22, 25, 29 n.31, n.35,
    162, 165 n.7
terminology, philosophical, 45–6, 52–6,
    58, 61
theologians, 49, 53, 189

This-or-Nothingism, 4, 21, 25, 72, 167, 184, 185
  see also dichotomies, false
thought and language, relation of, 78–80, 88 n.20
  see also linguistic innovation
thoughtcrime, 132, 136 n.32
Titchener, Edward Bradford, 77
tolerance, 140
triadomany, 2, 37
tribalism, 144, 151–2, 163, 178–9
  see also relativism
tropes, 73
  see also metaphor; simile
trust, 103 n.20, 115, 121 n.22
truth ix, x, 7–30, 31–4
  abstract versus concrete, 24
  Austin on, 21, 22, 162
  bearers of, 157
  claims to, 146, 147; *see also* "passes for" fallacy
  concern for, 7–27, 31–2, *passim*, 98, 189, 202; *see also* inquiry, genuine versus pseudo-; intellectual integrity; scientific attitude; Will to Learn
  consensus and, 18, 19, 32, 64
  correspondence theories of, 19, 21, 22, 24, 25, 33, 154, 162
  Davidson on, 19, 24
  Descartes' criterion of, 124
  Dewey on, 23
  disillusion with, 4, 32, 93, 132, 147, 186, 203
  disquotation and, 19
  Harding on, 132, 201
  Heal on, 17
  James on, 16, 23–4, 25
  Logical Atomism and, 21, 162
  Peirce on, 22, 23, 24, 26, 27, 31–4, 45, 64–5, 154, 162–4
  pragmatist theory of, *see* truth, Dewey on; James on; Peirce on; Rorty on
  prosentential theory of, 21–2, 29 n.39, 162
  Putnam on, 154, 159, 162
  Ramsey on, 21–2, 162

  redundancy theory of, 22, 29 n.36
  relativism of, 152, 153
  Rorty on, 2, 7, 18–21, 24, 25, 26, 31–4, 45, 64–5, 162, 201, 204
  Russell on, 21
  semantic theory of, *see* truth, Tarski on
  Stich on, 15–16
  Tarski on, 19, 21, 22, 25, 162
  unity of, 159–60
  value of, 16–17, 21, 204
  Wittgenstein on, 21
T-schema, 19
Tversky, Amos, 75, 88 n.11
tychism, 26, 51

underdetermination, 91, 93, 101 n.6, 110–11, 116, 128–9, 135 n.21

vagueness, 54
value-ladenness, 128–9
  see also science, social values in
verisimilitude, 91
Vygotsky, Lev Semenovich, 88 n.20

Waal, *see* de Waal
warrant
  acceptance and, 92, 94, 97, 99, 108, 110–12, 127
  disillusion with, 93
  ignored, 112
  justification and, 120 n.8
  played down, 110
  political ersatz for, 113–4
  see also evidence
Watson, James D., 9, 12, 13, 19, 20
ways of knowing, 94, 102 n.16, 141
  see also women's point of view
Whorf, Benjamin Lee, 150, 165 n.5
Wilde, Oscar, 137, 147 n.1
Wilkins, Maurice, 12
Will to Believe, 24, 25, 133 n.6
Will to Learn, 45, 49, 189, 191
wishful thinking, 10, 11, 14
  see also intellectual integrity; self-deception

wit versus judgment, 71
Wittgenstein, Ludwig, 21
women's point of view, 123, 125, 127
   serving women's interests, 125, 127–30
   women's ways of knowing, x, 119, 125–6,
     127
Woolgar, Steve, 92, 101–2 n.11

writing
   versus inquiry, 59
   philosophical: ambiguity in, 61; versus literary, 9, 53, 54–5, 57, 58, 61; literary flourishes in Peirce's, 59
   see also literature, philosophy and; terminology, ethics of